# COMMENTATING
# GREATS
### From Alliss to Wolstenholme

# COMMENTATING
# GREATS
## From Alliss to Wolstenholme

Nicolas Sellens

**WEST RIDGE**

Published by West Ridge Books
16 West Ridge, Sittingbourne, Kent  ME10 1UJ, United Kingdom

First published in September 2005

A CIP catalogue record for this book is available from the British Library.

Typeset in AGaramond and GillSans

ISBN 0-9540733-1-2

Printed and bound by Butler and Tanner, Frome

# Contents

# Acknowledgements

Sincere thanks to Phil Kingsford, Frank Blighe, Fiona Keen,
James Blake and the BBC photo library
for their valuable assistance in the production of this book.

Many thanks also to Val Pickering for her permission to reproduce the
photograph of Ron appearing on page 191.

Original illustrations by Paul Dutnall. Jacket design by Stuart Bowen.

ALAN PARRY AND BRIAN MARWOOD IN TANDEM AT SOUTHEND UNITED (PICTURE: TONY WALTERS)

# The Commentator's Lot

There have been few more successful double-acts during the last 80 years than sport and broadcasting. Together, these two blooming cultural phenomena provided arguably the soundtrack of the twentieth century.

The task of translating the spectacle of sport into a universal format that simultaneously instructed the uninitiated, gratified the connoisseur and ensnared the uncommitted was entrusted to a quirky and unseen collection of quick-witted extroverts who were to become the first superstars of the spoken media age. They were the sports commentators.

As sport gradually developed into a global mass movement, so too grew the commentator's influence. By getting across a sense of atmosphere that would otherwise have been denied the viewer or listener, he (and it was almost exclusively *he*) showed himself able to spread an enjoyment and appreciation of sport far beyond the confines of the grandstand or terrace. And, unlike the champion whose star usually burns out in just a few short seasons, the commentator retained the capacity to inspire, sometimes over the course of decades.

The great commentators would learn to respect the position of power they enjoyed, as vitriol would often be dealt those who allowed the whim of ego or the lure of ratings to compromise the core obligations of honesty and accuracy. They would also recognise that they were playing to the most unforgiving of audiences. Even by the very act of opening their mouths, they would offend the minority who feel that sport should be sampled as nature intended. And while snobbery denounces commentators as being a barrier to pure appreciation, envy is there also, bemoaning their free ticket to the best seat in the house.

The radio commentators, who practise the art in its purest form, have always enjoyed the greater tolerance. For them, their television colleagues' eternal dilemma of "to speak or not to speak" does not apply. What is more, they work in the knowledge that their words are of indispensable worth to those denied the gift of sight. The act of a grateful blind man in posting the BBC commentary team at Wimbledon "a couple of pounds to buy some strawberries and cream" underscores perfectly the functional value of their role.

But those who decry the worth of the television commentators don't appreciated that their presence can be equally practical. In his book *Games & Sets: The Changing Face of Television Sport,* leading media boffin Professor Steven Barnett argues that their work represents the crucial final element of the trilogy of the visual, the aural and the contextual:

> "There are other peripheral sounds which require transmission to complement the visual, such as cheering crowds, the ball hitting the post, or the anguished cry of a beaten competitor. But none of these can compare with that element of television sport which places the viewer in a substantially more privileged position than the spectator: a voice over accompaniment to describe, explain, analyse and predict the event as well as to contribute an occasional dramatic embellishment which the game itself may lack."

The grey area of "dramatic embellishment" comes closest to drawing the art of commentary into disrepute. It is a matter of degree, but essentially the more a commentator hypes the mundane, the less impact will be made by moments of genuine drama. Good commentary, then, is about maintaining perspective, a point made by the former BBC Head of Sport, Jonathan Martin, who every year took pains to remind his team that the Titanic was a "tragedy" and the Ethiopian drought a "disaster".

The knowledge that millions of expectant ears hang on their every word makes commenting one of the most demanding jobs in broadcasting, although few sympathise with the commentator's plight. In their expectation of consistent perfection, viewers and listeners decline to take into account the vagaries of the weather, the reliability of equipment and the competence of technicians. What is more, even if a broadcast runs smoothly, there is the possibility that they will find bias in a commentator's words, throwing doubt on his impartiality merely because events were not unfolding as hoped. Scottish exponent Archie Macpherson offered a dour and almost tear inducing assessment of the emotional and psychological burdens of his profession:

> "It is about trying to balance one's ambitions and inadequacies against the rigorous expectations of one's superiors, amongst whom you have to count the public. It is about selfishness and making a constant mistress of the suitcase. It is about sharing in folly and conceit and the massaging of the ego."

The root of the pressure is that commentating is oral journalism but without the luxury of a backspace key. As we regularly read, the strains of unscripted, simultaneous translation can disrupt the linkage between brain and tongue to such a degree that a footballer is able to "hit a precise shot wide," "chance his arm with his left foot" or even "piss a fatness test". But when a commentator makes a mistake, he knows it will be regurgitated in perpetuity by the slobbering editors of books, websites, periodicals and other registers of human error.

The commentator, then, must above all understand the power of words: offence may be caused by even the most innocent of observations. Early on in his golf commentary career, Peter Alliss learned a lesson when he bemoaned the freezing temperatures he was enduring at a tournament in Hawaii. It only took a couple of quips on the need for a second sweater for a government official to accuse him of attempting to destroy the island's tourist industry. At the worst extremity, a commentator who allows himself to be heard uttering something deemed morally unacceptable, as Ron Atkinson did, signs his own professional death warrant.

But the commentator can also be made to look foolish for a whole variety of reasons not of his own making. At the 1972 Olympics, the BBC's man in the gymnasium wisely waited until the final buzzer of a monumental basketball final before announcing that "the United States keep their unbeaten record in the most amazing and fantastic basketball finish of all time in the Olympic games!" These definitive words obviously threw down a gauntlet to the fates, who decreed that the referee should add on another three seconds, during which time the Soviet Union scored a basket to snatch the gold medal by 51 points to 50.

Then there are practical problems such as unpronounceable names. Print journalists, who are able to shift that responsibility onto their readership, only need to ensure the spelling is correct. Commentators are not so fortunate, seeing challenges to their composure mounted over the years by Madagascan athletes named Randriamahazomanama and Razafindrakovahoaka and a Mongolian distance runner Tschuuluunbaatar Ariunsaikhan. Try saying those with a mouthful of marbles.

Rude-sounding names would probably be more disconcerting still, had the commentator not got the fall-back of deliberate mispronunciation. Even so, while commentators can fob off their audience by calling the German footballer Uwe Fuchs "Foooks", there is nowhere to hide when Danny Shittu runs out onto the pitch or a basketballer named Yurin goes on a dribble.

There are also local difficulties. An Australian cricket commentator, working in England on an Ashes test, opted to give the score in the antipodean fashion, wickets before runs. This panicked a listener into believing that Australia's innings had progressed to "441 for two" when he had actually been told "four for 142."

These minor matters of regional etiquette pale into insignificance, however, when compared to the stresses of being dependent on the dismal presentational standards set by many host broadcasters. In 1971, for instance, the BBC athletics team had to contend with a German producer who would only frame competitors from the neck up, thereby concealing their numbers. His equally annoying habit of skipping from event to event exasperated the normally sanguine Ron Pickering. "Who on earth is that!" he screeched when yet another unfamiliar face suddenly filled the screen. "It's Lynn," replied the BBC's statistician Stan Greenberg, meaning Lynn Davies, the long-jumper whom Pickering had coached to an Olympic gold medal seven years earlier.

Even after he has packed up his microphone and gone home after a seemingly successful afternoon's work, it is still possible for a commentator to find egg on his face. In the very first edition of *Match of the Day*, the editors reorganised the highlights in such a way that a Liverpool player found himself on the receiving end of his own throw. "Now Yeats…", said Kenneth Wolstenholme as the ball was launched towards the penalty area, "…Oh Yeats could have only been a whisker away from it!"

So what qualities define a great sports commentator? Aside from the twin indispensables of voice and vision, there is no optimum blend of attributes. All commentators can do is to assess the essential character of their sport and construct a style to complement it.

Over the years, then, different strains of commentator have developed, with the "best in class" earning themselves levels of celebrity well in excess of the average broadcaster. The five categories of commentator that have evolved could be listed thus:-

"The Machine"
"The Insider"
"The Hysteric"
"The Thinker"
"The Raconteur."

The early commentators were classic "machines". Their task was simply to be the eyes of the radio audience, to visualise the run of play and offer, where appropriate, an explanation of rules and other technical points of interest. With this need for order, logic and unflappability in mind, the BBC recruited clergymen and former military officers to be their first sportscasters.

Machines have continued to plough their rather predictable furrow in a variety of guises, most notably in horse racing. Here, merit can only be judged through clarity of expression and efficiency of identification. Invariably copiously prepared, machines can be identified by rare or clumsy use of humour and, in 56.2 percent of occasions in the last 72.3 years, an over-reliance on statistics.

Like the machine, the "insider" is not a natural broadcaster. Nevertheless, by virtue of their unique specialist knowledge, this category of commentator often succeeded in transmitting their own enthusiasm to their audience. A typical "insider" was snooker's Ted Lowe, a broadcaster whose great affection for a game he did much to popularise was translated into intimate, folksy commentaries. Tennis' Dan Maskell, too, had little obvious talent as an orator but his voice distilled perfectly that sense of tradition and cultivation unique to Wimbledon.

Closely related to the "insider" is the "hysteric". These combustible individuals are to be found in fast-moving sports, where high vocal impact is required to complement the robustness of the action, or developing sports, where hype is needed to generate audience interest. For the hysteric, content usually comes second to delivery, a consequence of this being that the mouth sometimes races a yard or two ahead of the brain. With their occasional but over-publicised goofs, classic hysterics such as David Coleman and Murray Walker were unwittingly responsible for popularising the cult of the commentator.

On another level, hysteria comes in useful as a device for self-promotion. Capital Radio's erstwhile football commentator Jonathan Pearce, for example, used the excuse of "getting carried away by the passion of the game" to holler highly amusing but rather inappropriate lines such as "That is the greatest world cup goal you'll see and Argentina are heading out of the world cup and good bloody riddance!" It has been noticeable that, since his transfer to the BBC, Pearce has adopted, in relative terms, the bearing and demeanour of a village parson.

The slower, more genteel environs of the cricket ground or the golf links are inhabited by the "raconteurs" and "thinkers". These being slower-moving sports, often punctuated by extended gaps in play, a completely different approach is required. Typically, raconteurs will be able to draw on personal experiences and a databank of anecdotes to nurse their audiences, often with whimsical humour, through lulls in the action. These natural communicators, who operate without a script, will typically stray beyond the playing arena for their inspiration, commentating just as enthusiastically on spectators and the comings and goings of wildlife and public transport as on the play itself.

Thinkers share many of the characteristics of the raconteur, but are more cerebral and intense. Their realm is the psychological dynamic of sport. Their touch is likely to be less light, their use of humour less regular, their tone slightly more dark.

Within their particular categories, the great commentators have revealed themselves by their resilience, perspective and composure. They have all been able to add to the occasion, imparting knowledge unobtrusively and unpatronisingly and, in the process, have made a difficult job look easy. Henry Blofeld gave possibly the simplest and best summation of the requirements of the job when he said, "The greatest accolade anyone can pay to a commentator is 'You made me feel as though I was there'."

# A short history of commentating

Live sports coverage, like most other modern entertainment phenomena, was born in the USA. The date was 11 April 1921, the station was KDKA of Pittsburgh, the event was a ten-round bout of boxing between lightweights Johnny Dundee and Johnny Ray. Before the year was out, America's first commercial broadcaster broke further ground with Davis Cup tennis and baseball from New York.

Although the BBC was to go on to set the quality benchmark in the presentation of sport for the benefit of the armchair fan, it hardly exploded out of the blocks. By the time it received its public-service charter in January 1927 and was able to send reporters out to sporting events, NBC was broadcasting American football's Rose Bowl coast-to-coast across the US for the first time. The BBC was also beaten to the punch by a local Australian station, which offered ball-by-ball cricket commentary from the Sydney Cricket Ground in December 1925, and by 2RN, the forerunner of Radio Eireann, which transmitted live coverage of the All-Ireland hurling semi-final between Kilkenny and Galway in August 1926.

Until the award of the charter, sportscasting in Britain had taken the form of clipped reportages squeezed into the half-time turnaround or other breaks in play. The first live running commentary was made on 15 January 1927 when Captain H B T (Teddy) Wakelam described the England versus Wales rugby international from Twickenham. The following Saturday he performed radio's first football commentary, Arsenal's 1-1 draw with Sheffield United at Highbury Stadium.

Wakelam had been chosen as the BBC's first commentator by the trail-blazing producer Lance Sieveking. Sieveking was a talented individual whose ingenious solutions translated live sporting action into a format the radio listener could understand. For football and rugby matches, he developed a clever gimmick whereby listeners were able to follow the location of the play by matching numbers read out over the commentary to a special grid that had been printed in the *Radio Times*. Devotees of snakes and ladders may take issue, but it is generally accepted that the phrase "back to square one" originates from this system.

Commentating-by-numbers was an imaginative yet practical idea that proved to be popular with listeners. But, uninfused with the spirit of adventure, the commentators would normally stick rigidly to the system, often with amusing consequences. Prior to one rugby match,

**"Lobby" Lotbinière**

for instance, a commentator was roundly mocked for observing that "the goat of the Welch Regiment is in square two." Eventually, though, audiences grew frustrated by the frequent vocal collisions between the main commentator and the numbers announcer. It took the arrival in 1935 of the architect of the modern style of commentating, the extravagantly named Seymour Joli de Lotbinière, to draw up a clear set of guidelines.

As the new head of outside broadcasts (OBs), "Lobby" established the "pyramid method" by which commentators were instructed to layer information in a descending order of importance. After having set the scene with the teams, the venue, the weather and other essentials, the procedure then permitted the commentator, as the broadcast progressed, to embellish his narrative with "associative material" such as facts, figures and opinion.

Lotbinière's system is still relevant today, as is his recommendation that commentators should be first and foremost skilled communicators whose primary role is to describe the passage of play. Though the commentator would be well versed in the sport he was describing, well-known sportsmen (Olympic athlete Harold Abrahams was an early "number two") would be in close attendance to offer analysis and expert summaries.

When compiling the first unofficial commentating manual for the new breed, Lotbinière drew up a rudimentary four point code:

- Build up suspense interest, but only in moderation;
- When offering instruction, do so casually and not in too schoolmasterly a manner;
- However badly unsighted, never say, "I can't see";
- Never take sides - be completely impartial.

In the 1930s, the lip-microphone was used for the first time. More than just a practical tool, this British invention would quickly evolve into the commentator's trademark accessory. Although their faces were seldom seen, it did not take long for commentators to become recognisable "personalities". When George Allison, a football specialist, appeared on a train platform, a porter approached him with the question, "Are you the gentleman what radiates?" Disappointingly, and despite the appropriate association with hot air, the idea of "your match radiator" failed to catch on.

Before the war, the mantra of BBC Director General Sir John Reith was all-pervasive. His brand of starch-collared Puritanism obliged broadcasters to grin and bear draconian self-regulation. The first

commandment was "thou shalt not advertise" and woe would betide he who uttered a brand name or "proprietary article". One classic moment of infraction occurred on 14 May 1927, when the BBC went to Leyton to broadcast its first cricket match. While the two sides, Essex and New Zealand, took a break, the commentator, Canon F H (Gilly) Gillingham, found himself with twenty minutes to fill. He did admirably for the first ten, but then, as his inspiration turned to perspiration and then desperation, he proceeded to work his way around the ground's perimeter, painstakingly reading out all the advertisements.

R C Lyle, the BBC's first horse racing commentator, went one better. At the Derby, his observation that "the horses are now passing the advertisement hoarding for Booth's Dry Gin" affronted not only Reith's cardinal edict but also his teetotalism. Reith's mood hardly improved when Booth's rival Gordon's telephoned him to inquire how they could also take advantage of such generous free publicity.

As the BBC wrestled with moral issues, that outpost of cricketing fundamentalism, Australia, adopted a more hard-headed approach to the technicalities of broadcasting sport. In the days before satellites bounced their sounds and images across rooftops in every corner of the globe, Australian cricket fanatics were unable to tune in "live" to the overseas exploits of their batting demi-god, Don Bradman. The Australian Broadcasting Corporation met the challenge with an ingenious compromise that became known as "synthetic commentary".

Synthesising commentary was the act of recreating the atmosphere of a test match in an artificial environment. When the Ashes were being contested 8,000 miles away in England, ABC technicians patched together a facsimile of "live" action with the aid of a telex machine and recorded crowd effects. As runs were scored, the eminent Australian commentator Alan McGilvray would mimic the sound of bat on ball with the tap of his pencil before expanding, with no little creative licence, the bare bones of the telex-tape messages that were being fed to him. Such first generation technology may not have fooled anyone save the most wizened custodian of a Northern Territory sheep station, but these shamelessly contrived broadcasts attracted an enthusiastic following and foretold the talent for innovation which would come to characterise later generations of Australian broadcasters.

Although the radio coverage of sport continued during the war, albeit under strict censorship, the hostilities interrupted the BBC's experimental television service. On 21 June 1937, flickering images of the opening match of Wimbledon fortnight had been broadcast to

2,000 sets in the south-east of England. Thanks to the persistence of Gerald Cock, television's first OB executive, the Football Association, which was extremely wary of the potential of television to decimate attendance figures, agreed to allow the cameras into Wembley stadium. The first match to be televised was England versus Scotland on 9 April 1938, with the first FA Cup final following three weeks later. By the time war came, the BBC had also televised motor-racing from Crystal Palace, the University Boat Race and test cricket.

While the war suspended the development of television for seven years, it managed to throw up a number of "can-do" individuals who were to shape the development of sports coverage in Britain. The most prominent pioneer was an ebullient ex-squadron leader by the name of Peter Dimmock. When the television service restarted in 1946, Dimmock and his team set about discrediting the "stuffy old load of so-and-sos" who had been defaming the new medium.

The BBC's head of OBs at the age of only 33, the dynamic Dimmock sought to galvanise the organisation's television output and close the technological gap that had been opened by the Americans. That he succeeded in dragging British television into the brave new world was a testament to his considerable inspiration and improvisation. Typical of his seat-of-the-pants style was the introduction of the BBC's first autocue, which he cobbled together using an old laundry mangle, two sheets of glass, some paper and a felt-tip pen.

Aside from tackling the huge technical challenges posed by television outside broadcasts, Dimmock and his team had to battle against considerable scepticism on the part of sports administrators. The first post-war battleground was boxing. The promoters' fear that footage of their bouts would be "rediffused" to cinema audiences led to a tense stand-off between the BBC and the BBBC (British Boxing Board of Control) before the Postmaster General intervened with the issue of special licences. Within five years, however, attitudes to the presence of cameras relaxed as attendances at televised events bloomed.

Lobby Lotbinière's promise of bringing licence payers "flashes from every type of sport played in the British Isles" was on the verge of becoming a reality as the conversion to television became wholesale. In 1954 Peter Dimmock, who now had access to the cream of the sporting calendar and was paying virtually nothing for the privilege, launched the mid-week *Sportsview* programme. From 1954 to 1964 *Sportsview* set the style for the BBC's highly popular sports magazines. It would also introduce a new breed of commentator that not only

*"Don't mention the left wing. There must be no misunderstanding about this broadcast."*

The *Sunday Chronicle* spots an early political dilemma.

seized their chance but stamped their identity on their chosen sports, in some cases for almost half a century.

After the success of the Coronation coverage in 1953, the British people quickly fell under the spell of the new programming, becoming hooked on a diet of serials, dramas and, of course, sport. Although the arrival of ITV in 1955 brought the BBC its first taste of competition, its monopoly in television sports coverage remained virtually intact.

The first wave of post-war television sports commentators were either existing radio performers or plucky journalists who had been hurriedly co-opted on the basis of their rudimentary technical knowledge and ability to communicate. There was only one general principle that had to be obeyed: "Never speak unless you can add to the picture."

The fact that pictures complemented sound now placed television commentators under extreme pressure. In the old days, radio broadcasters took comfort in being able to "busk" if poor visibility or other extraneous factors suddenly intervened. If he mis-identified a player or gave an incorrect score, who would know? With pictures came accountability.

Television commentators, like politicians, had to accept the fact that you can't please all the people all the time. It quickly became evident that it was nigh impossible to strike a consistent balance between information and explanation. The commentator would regularly find himself patronising one segment of his audience whilst simultaneously baffling another.

Brian Johnston, the cricket commentator who, unconventionally, specialised in television before moving to radio, summed up the requirements of the craft:

> "The real art of television commentary is to know when and when not to speak, and to make sure when you do, your remark is short, concise and matches the picture…It is this need for neat, precise comment that makes television so much more difficult than radio. A gaffe, a joke which falls flat, or an inaccurate statement stands out like a sore thumb on television."

The television commentator's chances of keeping things pertinent are further eroded by the constant bombardment of instructions and technical verbiage fed through to him by the producer via his ear-piece. This so-called "dirty talk-back" can hopelessly befuddle unseasoned broadcasters. When a producer asked Raymond Robertson-Glasgow to give the score, the former cricketer replied testily, "For those who *weren't* listening when I gave the score just now, it *is*…".

## Idwal who?

The winner of *Sportsnight with Coleman*'s "Find a Commentator" competition was Welshman Idwal Robling (*seated*). Having earned his place in the 1970 World Cup squad, Robling disappeared into the relative obscurity of Welsh regional football coverage. Of the other hopefuls, only Ed Stewart failed to make a career in sports broadcasting.

As television broadcasting gained in credibility, sports commentating became recognised as a genuine skill. There is a variety of definitions as to what makes a good commentator. Brian Johnston believed that an out-going personality was vital, although the success of introverted characters such as racing's Peter O'Sullevan suggested that knowledge combined with faultless technique were the true secrets of career longevity.

Different sports had different requirements. Motor racing demands measures of intensity that are totally inappropriate to the deathly hush of the snooker arena. Therefore a style and manner that vocalised the "persona" of a specific sport was more important than its basic aural qualities.

The sixties saw the emergence of two highly talented yet robust individuals who would drive a new hard-nosed professionalism into BBC sports presentation. Bryan Cowgill on television and Angus Mackay on radio imposed a high quality threshold on the corporation's output. One of their principal achievements was the establishment of a team of commentators whose names were to become synonymous with the sports they covered.

As the decade progressed, the BBC's access to the crown jewels of British sport (which had been guaranteed by an act of parliament) gave it a seemingly unassailable dominance over commercial television.

## The Usual Suspects

From left to right, BBC-TV's
1978 World Cup line-up:
Alan Weeks, Barry Davies,
Jimmy Hill, John Motson,
David Coleman, Frank
Bough, Archie Macpherson
and Tony Gubba.

ITV's regional structure and subservience to the commercial break combined to leave the field clear for established BBC names like Peter O'Sullevan, David Coleman and Bill McLaren to stamp their identity over Britain's favourite sporting events.

England's hosting of the 1966 World Cup was pivotal in the development of sports coverage on British television. The tournament not only caused a second surge of set ownership in the UK, but it also helped illustrate for the first time, through Kenneth Wolstenholme's immortal preamble to Geoff Hurst's hat-trick in the final, the sports commentator's gift of being able to capture a nation's imagination with just a few ordinary words. "In theory, we are working with the same vocabulary that was available to Keats and Orwell," wrote ITV's Clive Tyldesley, "but the best we have come up with is 'some people are on the pitch…'."

On a technical level, the World Cup also introduced the action replay machine. It proved to be a revolutionary new gizmo as far as commentators were concerned. Before its introduction, commentators were required to commit large passages of play to memory for regurgitation in the event of their leading to a notable incident. Now, unfettered from their responsibility to mechanically transmit the run of play, they felt able to venture into analysis. Jimmy Hill, as the head of sport at London Weekend Television, made tough talking debate his principal weapon in the football ratings war and helped shake up television's traditionally sober approach to sports broadcasting.

With the arrival of colour in 1969, the BBC entered its most celebrated era of sports coverage. The ability of BBC2 to absorb hours of live and uninterrupted cricket, golf and tennis encouraged the likes of Henry Longhurst, Dan Maskell and Richie Benaud to forge the classically unruffled BBC commentary style.

As the essential shop window to seventies sport, the BBC relaxed in its untouchability. By the eighties, however, ITV signalled its intent to break the monopoly by purchasing the rights to domestic athletics in 1984, the Football League in 1988 and Five Nations rugby union in 1990. Athletics without Coleman? Football without Motson? Rugby without McLaren? Their replacement made many viewers realise just how integral to their enjoyment these comforting, familiar voices had become.

When the BBC was dominant, the role of the commentator was a crystallisation of the corporation's original mandate: to inform, educate and entertain. The arrival of commercial and satellite television meant that salesmanship too became an integral part of the job description. The fight for revenue, whether in the form of advertising sales or viewer subscriptions, saw the commentator dispatched to the front line.

Scientific studies had left broadcasters in no doubt as to the positive effect of commentary on the viewer's enjoyment of an event. In 1977, a US study on a televised ice hockey match found that viewers reacted more positively to a mundane passage of play that was accompanied by an enthusiastic commentary than to an exciting passage of play that was accompanied by a down-beat commentary. "It appears that, to a high degree, the sportscaster is a critical contributor to the spectator's appreciation of televised sports," concluded the report.

The potential for the noble art to slip into the mire of questionable ethics was illustrated by a further study which revealed how easy it was for commentators to manipulate viewers' enjoyment. By artificially creating an air of hostility between two tennis players, for instance, they were able to generate a higher level of viewer interest. In the clamour for ratings, the commentator was to come under increasing pressure to sacrifice his integrity for the sake of the spectacle.

The shift in the balance of power from the broadcasters to the various governing bodies forced some observers to question the commentators' objectivity. The delicate relationship between description and embellishment was indeed being skewed by the necessity of massaging a sport's popularity. In the eyes of some elements of the press, many commentators were losing the necessary critical perspective. Frank Keating, writing in *The Guardian*, pointedly bemoaned the readiness of football commentators to toady to the FA, citing John Motson's limp response to the torrent of racist jeers and abuse being aimed by England fans at a dreadlocked Dutch player at Wembley: "And Gullit getting good-natured barracking from the crowd."

By the turn of the millennium, the emasculation of sports commentators was being compounded by a slew of presentational innovations. Giving the score was, according to Lobby Lotbinière, the commentator's *raison d'être*, but now even this responsibility had been removed by the use of a simple and ever present device in the top left corner of the screen. Referees and even cricket stumps became wired for sound and digital viewers became able to switch camera angles and even commentary feeds at the touch of a button.

The hundreds of television and radio hours that are now dedicated to coverage of sporting events of no particular quality has further diluted the commentator's art. Even by the early seventies critics such as *The Observer*'s Clive James were warning that hackneyed phraseology and lazy enunciation were eroding the standards. As commercial radio stations won the right to share the crown jewels of British sport, the words of commentating *enfant terrible* Jonathan Pearce at a World Cup qualifier in 1999 crashed home the final nails into the coffin of the noble tradition of Reith, Lotbinière and Sieveking: "Welcome to Bologna on Capital Gold for England versus San Marino with Tennent's Pilsner, brewed with Czechoslovakian yeast for that extra Pilsner taste, and England are one down."

It was time to take stock of a never-to-be-repeated age…

# THE
# COMMENTATORS

24

# Peter Alliss

The broadcasting gods have undoubtedly indulged enthusiasts of televised golf. It seemed improbable that there would ever be another commentator worthy enough to be mentioned in the same breath as the venerable Henry Longhurst, yet his apprentice Peter Alliss now appears to be chiselling himself an equally exalted plinth in the commentary hall of fame.

Alliss was born on 28 February 1931 in the grounds of the chic Wannsee golf club, just outside Berlin.[1] His father, Percy, a well-known Ryder Cup player and resident professional, had moved to Germany in 1926 to spread the golfing gospel among the many well-to-do Germans who were keen to mimic the style and manners of the "English country gentleman". But, as war clouds gathered and the club's membership prepared to swap their mashies for Mausers, the Allisses opted to decamp back to Blighty, settling finally at Ferndown Golf Club, a pretty, tree-lined course set in the pine and heather of rustic Dorset.

His world steeped in this most ancient of games, there was only one logical path for the academically unspectacular Alliss to follow. His natural, rhythmical swing soon became harnessed to a powerful physique and, as he matured, a golfer of championship potential started to emerge. On leaving school he became assistant pro' at Ferndown and, at the age of 16, went to Hoylake to play in his first Open Championship.

By the time he was 22, rumours of a boy wonder had percolated through to the Ryder Cup committee and, in 1953, Alliss was selected to represent Great Britain & Ireland for the ritual biennial drubbing at the hands of the United States. Events at Wentworth that year would taint what was otherwise a most accomplished professional career. With his team seemingly edging towards a rare victory, Alliss's nervous stab from only a few feet on the eighteenth green opened the door for his opponent, Jim Turnesa, to snatch the pivotal match and turn the tables in favour of the Americans. The Wentworth *debâcle* - which became known unfairly as "the Ryder Cup that Alliss lost" - left a deep divot-mark in the young man's psyche and compounded a festering complex about short putts.

Had his nerve been less brittle from six feet - a distance from which he once five-putted at the US Masters - Alliss could have possibly joined

> It's only a silly old stick and ball game, but it tears your heart out sometimes.

[1] He was a thumping 14lb, 11oz baby. It was a long-standing European record.

PETER DAZELEY

## Achilles Heel

Alliss' frailties on the green
curtailed a glittering
tournament career.

the elite. That said, when he retired from professional golf in 1974 with a career record of 23 tournament wins and eight Ryder Cup appearances, including a victory over Arnold Palmer in his pomp, Alliss would graduate to his second career behind the microphone as one of the most authoritative voices in the sport.

Alliss got his first taste of broadcasting at the 1961 Open Championship. Having overheard him spinning yarns on a flight back from Ireland, BBC producer Ray Lakeland invited Alliss to scale the commentary tower to offer a player's perspective of Royal Birkdale. Alliss's affinity for English prose, gleaned from his long hours of solitary confinement next to the family wireless-set at Ferndown, had endowed him with such an easy way with words that the corporation promptly payrolled him at £60 a tournament.

Emboldened by the fundamentals of timing, intonation and enunciation that he had acquired making the *Shell Wonderful World of Golf* films for television, Alliss gradually unseated Bill Cox from the

BBC-TV commentary box. There, he forged a memorable partnership with Henry Longhurst, a man whom he would hold in the highest affection and regard. Surprisingly, Alliss doesn't credit his great friend as being his principal commentating mentor. "That was really a fellow by the name of Jack Hargreaves, who did this show on Southern TV called *Out of Town*," he insists. "He'd sit in a garden shed, with a battered hat and an old pipe and just ramble."

Alliss's commentary style, like his golf-swing, is languid and uncomplicated. He leaves the technical minutiae of stance, grip and wrist break to his colleagues with teaching credentials, such as his long-time sparring partner Alex Hay. His remit, he contends, is to "point out to the viewers the difficulty or ease of the shot, the magic, the genius, of the player." Forelock firmly in hand, he goes on to suggest that the basic art of television commentary is "in appreciating the power of the camera and therefore of knowing when to stay quiet and say nothing." For a self-confessed prattler, this seems a little rich, as a typical accompaniment to the meandering progress of a twenty yard putt testifies: "Now then...up she comes...oooh, look at this - I tell you what, it's not going in the hole is it? By jingo it is you know. Well I never...would you believe it?"

When Alliss talks about his commentary career, he does so with a contradictory mixture of humility and hubris. His gratitude for being given what he describes as a "second way of life" is immense. Yet, at the same time he doesn't appear to lack appreciation of his own abilities. "I have never found my job overly difficult," he brags in his first autobiography, "...when it comes to casual chat, ad-libbing and talking off the cuff, I appear totally at ease."

Some may say his attitude is only a lob-wedge short of arrogance but the truth is that Alliss is indeed the raconteur *par excellence*. Taking the view that golf commentary should be conversational, he effortlessly weaves golden threads of personal reminiscences into the patchwork of drives, pitches and putts that comprise the standard telecast. He also appears to have appointed himself honorary secretary of the amateur golfing community, happily interrupting the action to report miscellany such as the fact that so-and-so at Moor Allerton is still playing to a handicap of seven at the age of 93 or that they have just put new rakes in the bunkers at Troon.

Another of Alliss's broadcasting tenets is to "interpret their [the players'] mental attitudes and processes in their approach to the sport and its situations." His reaction to Jean van de Velde's seventy-second hole antics at the 1999 Open Championship at Carnoustie left several

27

journalists questioning whether it was, in fact, the commentator's marbles that had gone astray. The Frenchman's suicidal safari into the gorse, by way of the waters of the Barry Burn, seemed to reawaken Alliss's own demons.

"Totally ridiculous. What are you doing? What on earth are you doing?" he wailed as Van de Velde, trousers rolled up, paddled around like a bewildered freemason. "Someone kindly go and stop him. Give him a large brandy and mop him down."

Strangely oblivious to the unfolding drama and the record viewing figures, Alliss garrulously heaped more indignation on the play-off contenders by accusing them, amongst other things, of playing "absolute junk". The press berated him for his "pompousness" and "wilful, open contempt for the viewer".

Alliss readily admits that he's not always the cuddly uncle in a vee-neck sweater, as some of those who have played with him in pro-am tournaments would probably concur. "People think of me as being quiet and calm," he conceded, "but I can be very moody, and there is a mean streak there, oh a mean streak."

He reserves particular disdain for transgressors of golfing etiquette. He is simply appalled by bad manners. The cameras once caught the otherwise saintly Tiger Woods depositing a sphere of spittle of similar hue and dimensions to an old Dunlop 65 onto the apron of a Wentworth green. "Ah, I see the age of Ivor Novello is alive and well", sighed the commentator wearily.

Alliss's unimpeachable standards of moderation were tested further by Ken Brown and Mark James' failure to wear the team uniform on their departure for a Ryder Cup match in America. While it is all blood under the bridge as far as Brown (now his mild-mannered co-commentator) and James are concerned, rancour simmered on between Alliss and Nick Faldo, who took to heart the stream of quips on the sullenness, boorishness and lack of humour of the new generation of players. Aloof yet often ready to criticise, Alliss has rarely been top of the locker-room popularity leaderboard.

But with the viewing public, Alliss is king. He is cherished because he is the undisputed master of whimsy. His famed one-liners reach beyond the hard-core of golf junkiedom and draw in those who are understandably disinclined towards this uniquely pedestrian sport. Many women, for example, find the gentleness of his voice extremely sexy, while his droll humour has won devotees from all quarters.

He inherited his wit from his father, whose wry, sardonic approach to dealing with golf's snootier set cast the young Alliss on his life-long

> ‘ 5-5-5-4-7. It's like the dialling code for Tierra del Fuego. ’

mission to seek out and deflate overblown egos. At the 2001 Open, the camera caught the inscrutable David Duval removing his trade-mark sunglasses. "Ooooh look," he piped up mischievously, "it's daylight!" He also cut the headstrong young Spaniard Sergio Garcia down to size by likening him to an Irish Setter: "Beautiful in many ways, but a bit wilful. The sort of dog that runs in from the garden and jumps up with muddy paws on a lady in a white dress, then knocks the Waterford crystal off the table, and goes and has a pee in the corner. And then somebody will say, 'ah but isn't it a lovely dog?'"

The other capital weapon in the Alliss armoury is the gently mocking aside. Ulster golfer David Feherty, himself now a successful "announcer" on American television, recalled Alliss's banter with a BBC cameraman who had lost the flight of the ball. "I believe that one is

GETTY IMAGES

**Alliss through the hooking grass**

In a rare spot of bother, as his minders look on.

29

probably over on the left side...no, I mean the *golfer's* left," he puffed as the hapless lensman panned ineptly. "Okay, to your right…dear God, by the time he gets there Gauguin could have painted it!"

What tickles many viewers is Alliss' ability to look beyond the drama unfolding on the players' side of the ropes and develop oddities from the broader tableau. Rarely does a spectator's questionable piece of headgear or the progress of an errant rabbit escape adornment with some trinket of impertinence. Celebrity golf enthusiasts are especially ripe fodder. During an Open Championship at St Andrews, a huge crow took off down the Firth of Tay, fooling the commentator into thinking he had spotted an old friend, "and there goes Christopher Lee on his way back home." Neither can comely young actresses expect immunity. When a mis-hit approach shot made surprisingly strong progress towards the pin, Alliss dug out a beauty, "Oh that's perfect. A little fat, but almost perfect...bit like Kate Winslet..."

Sometimes the local colour interferes directly with play and Alliss is in his element. There was a highly amusing and indeed unique occasion when Severiano Ballesteros, addressing his ball in front of a large bunker, had his concentration broken by the scratching of a ginger tom who was preparing his latrine in the sand behind him. "Now then pussy-cat," cautioned the commentator, "that's not a very nice thing to do!" The director indulged him by framing the crouching, flat-eared, quiver-tailed moggy in gory close-up. "Orf! Gawd blimey O'Reilly," huffed Alliss as the cat evacuated its bowels onto its fantasy litter tray, "I needed that!"

It's a wonder that American television, with its remorseless roster of drive-putt-leaderboard-commercial, ever took to Alliss' avuncular, anecdotal style of broadcasting. He is, nevertheless, one of the most popular commentators on the US networks, having titillated ABC viewers as the quintessential quaint Britisher since the mid-sixties.

While in America, he is spared the lash-up of the ramshackle "studio-on-stilts" and instead recounts his tales from a luxuriously appointed personal caravan. Golf is, after all, a sport where a commentator's nose is not required to smell the liniment and Alliss reasons that a comfortable boudoir with a pair of monitors - one for live pictures and the other for graphics - are all that is required to perform the function. He makes a fair point when he insists, "you don't have to be Sherlock Holmes to check if the wind is against at the first hole." What is more, when you have wandering radio-mikes like Clive Clark and latterly Julian Tutt patrolling the course offering yardages from every rabbit scrape, why forego the home-comforts?

'The sensible commentator is the one who will take the picture as the foundation and try to put a bit of his own baroque on top of it.'

30

In the late seventies a three-way play-off developed between the BBC, ABC and ITV for the exclusive services of the new voice of golf. In the end, thanks to the acumen of his manager, Mark McCormack, Alliss secured lucrative contracts with both the BBC and ABC, plus two television series, *Around with Alliss* and *Pro Celebrity Golf*.

The incongruous images of check-trousered Kojaks, Columbos and Val Doonicans uprooting clods of prime Scottish linksland introduced the game to a new generation of viewers who, seduced by its hypnotic charm, proceeded to clad themselves in Pringle and offload billions into the coffers of Wilson, Titleist, Callaway, *et al.* Having written over twenty books on the game and designed a number of premier courses, including The Belfry, Alliss must stand at least partially indicted for this mushrooming phenomenon and the resultant cult of golf widowhood.

So does Alliss merit a nomination for the greatest sports commentator? True commentary greatness owes much to delivery and Harry Carpenter, Alliss' BBC link-man for many years, noted with admiration that he sat on the phrase "Elementary my dear Watson" through four days in the 1977 Open until Tom Watson's decisive second shot to the eighteenth at Turnberry finally overcame Jack Nicklaus' challenge in the "Duel in the Sun". Another celebrated moment occurred during the play-off for the 1987 Masters when the unassuming and unheralded Larry Mize holed an outrageous 140 foot chip to deny Greg Norman. "Ho, ho, ho," hooted Alliss, "and they say the meek shall inherit the earth!"

With his sumptuous knowledge, immaculate timing and rapier wit, Alliss has indeed got all the shots, yet his acclaim is far from universal. His pontifications inevitably alienate some, while his ambiguous positioning *vis-à-vis* the "Establishment" is mistrusted by others. He may be a communicator extraordinaire, but his habit of conveying appreciation with the type of drooling noises that should be confined to the vicinity of an occupied carry-cot irritates many. He has also had his card marked on several occasions by the liberal press, who would have you believe he is little more than a cantankerous old reactionary with a tiresome fixation for the "good old days".

Yet Peter Alliss is a born entertainer and his commentaries reach beyond the golf fan to beguile those who would normally be indifferent to a sport that Mark Twain pertinently termed "a good walk spoiled". Asked to make his appraisal, one viewer commented simply, "It's a game and he makes it fun." The greatest? Well, he's not a million miles away.

# Rex Alston

"Play has ended here at Southampton, but they play until seven o'clock at Edgbaston, so over there now for some more balls from Rex Alston." An unfortunate handover, but no uncharitable inference should be taken as "Balston", as Brian Johnston called him, was one of the BBC's most respected all-round commentators. "The possessor of a pleasant, courteous, laid-back microphone style that has now sadly gone out of fashion," recalled *The Times*.

After seventeen years as a teacher at Bedford School, Alston joined the BBC as a billeting officer in 1942, but was quickly co-opted by the corporation's OB producers on the strength of his sprightly voice and good all-round knowledge of sport. In his youth, he had been a gifted and multi-talented sportsman, having won an athletics blue at Cambridge (where he came a creditable second in the sprints to Harold Abrahams), captained Bedfordshire in minor counties cricket and played rugby for Rosslyn Park. In the immediate post-war years he became head commentator on all his specialist areas and the first overseas correspondent to report on cricket. It was with tennis, though – a sport about which he happily conceded he knew almost nothing – that he would be most closely associated.

Alston admitted to being "the prim schoolmaster" in the commentary box. But while he was aware of the need to maintain discipline among his junior colleagues, he was also able to earn their regard with his friendly and nurturing manner. The young rugby union commentator Bill McLaren, under whose wing he nestled, remembered him as "one of the most wonderful, caring men I ever met."

While Alston was quick to administer the ruler to the knuckle of any violator of the Corinthian code on the field of play, he was never less than scrupulously fair and precise. Yet his high moral stance was not always roundly appreciated. When reporting on a test match in Port of Spain in 1960, he was alleged to have caused a disturbance when he referred to a section of the crowd as behaving like "animals". Those spectators who had been listening on their transistor radios responded by pelting the commentary box with bottles. Alston always denied ever making the accusation.

When commentating, Alston would often hold his head in his hands and look straight out in front of him. The dangers of this habit were highlighted during a test match when he asked for a view from his

## "Balston"

"Lindwall has now finished his over, goes to the umpire and takes his sweater and strides off."

"Louise Brough cannot serve at the moment as she has not got any balls."

"Your next commentator, Old John Arlott from Trafford."

"The band playing, the tents with their club flags, the famous lime tree, people picnicking round the ground, whilst on the field hundreds of little boys are playing with their balls."

summariser. With no response forthcoming, Alston swivelled round to spy a note on the desk saying "Gone to spend a penny. Back in a moment."

Alston left the BBC staff in 1961, but continued to contribute as a freelancer. In 1985, he had the dubious distinction of being able to read his own obituary, which was printed by error in *The Times*. His eulogy had been intended to be filed in the "pending" tray with other living celebrities of certain age but somehow found its way onto the presses. Having been admitted to Westminster Hospital the previous evening with food poisoning, Alston was presented with grim news the next morning by the nurses on his ward. With typical good humour, he merely expressed his gratitude at the warmth of its tone.

Rex Alston did eventually keep his *Times* appointment. He died on 8 September 1994, just seven short of his century.

# Eamonn Andrews

Eamonn Andrews, the epitome of easy-going Irish charm, was a popular and influential all-round broadcaster who, at his peak, was the highest paid personality on British television. Although best known as the genial host of fluffy light entertainment programmes, Andrews was to carve his reputation through sport. He was the BBC's best-known boxing commentator of the fifties and long-time presenter of the Light Programme's Saturday five o'clock round-up *Sports Report*.

The son of a Dublin carpenter, Andrews made the unlikely transition from prize-winning choir-boy to champion boxer in the All-Ireland juvenile middleweight division. Having discovered a talent for creative writing and, with his insurance company employers complaining that he was turning up for work with black eyes and fat lips, he eventually decided his future lay on the safer side of the ropes and impudently touted his services to Radio Eireann, Ireland's newly established broadcaster. Omitting the fact that he was still only sixteen, Andrews applied with the words: "I am an expert on boxing, I have studied elocution. Please give me an audition."

His success at a trial set him on course to dominate the Irish airwaves. As well as commentating on boxing, rugby, football, fencing and even hare coursing, he would present his own show and even act in plays, one of which he wrote himself. His standing and influence would be such that in 1960 he was invited by Ireland's prime minister to chair the committee responsible for setting up Irish television.

Andrews may have been the most adaptable of broadcasters but he simply could not fathom horse racing. Having been offered a commentating audition, he became so bewildered by the variations of colours on display that he decided to cheat and identify each horse solely by its number. But as the race got underway, a gusting wind lifted up the number flaps, making recognition quite impossible. Andrews' attempts at concealing his error with a busk were brought to an unceremonious halt by a nearby punter who lowered his binoculars to sneer, "The horse you say is leading fell two fences back. The horse you say is second is now second last. And the horse you say is third is last!" The experience taught Andrews a valuable broadcasting lesson. "Take a job outside your powers," he wrote, "and you will probably spend the rest of your life in fear that you'll be found out." The candidate they hired that day was Michael O'Hehir.

## Halleluja!

Whilst he may have earned a Papal knighthood, Andrews' business interests included owning night clubs.

British audiences first heard Andrews' soft Irish burr in 1949 when he accompanied the touring Joe Loss band as chairman of a "Double or Nothing" quiz. Desperate to establish himself with the BBC, he got his big break when the well-known commentator and presenter Stewart MacPherson decided to return to his native Canada, leaving the host's chair vacant on the radio show *Ignorance is Bliss*. During the next fourteen years with the BBC he chaired television's most popular panel game *What's My Line?* and took custody of the famous red book in *This Is Your Life*, a show that was resurrected by ITV after he left the corporation in 1964.

On radio, he lent his sympathetic tones to an eclectic range of programmes including *A Book at Bedtime* and *Housewives' Choice*. On the box, his friendly persona was perfect for children's television and he kept many a little cherub quiet with tea-time regulars such as *Crackerjack* and *Playbox*. He was named Television Personality of the Year four times.

Andrews made his debut as a boxing commentator in Britain in October 1950 when he was drafted in to Wembley to offer his local knowledge for an amateur match between England and Ireland. Omens for an extended career in front of the cameras were, however, bleak when he conducted his first post-fight interview without his clip-on bow-tie, which had liberated itself on a rope as he climbed into the ring.

## Sports Report

The *Sports Report* team in 1960. Eamonn Andrews (*seated on right*) is joined by (*left to right*) Jacob de Vries, Bill Hicks, Angus McKay, Gerald Sinstadt, W Barrington Dalby and Cliff Morgan.

He was making a better impression on radio, where he performed the first live commentary from America. Andrews' coverage of Don Cockle's courageous attempt at wresting the world heavyweight title from Rocky Marciano in his own back yard was a surprise hit both for his BBC bosses and the national grid which, at three o'clock in the morning, groaned under the unprecedented requirements of several hundred thousand kettles.

The sheer unpredictability of boxing delivered him several edgy moments. He remembers climbing into the ring at Madison Square Garden in a desperate attempt to pad out a broadcast after, against all the odds, Ingemar Johansson knocked out Floyd Patterson in the first round of a world title bout. Having prized a couple of words from film star John Wayne, he cornered the celebrated boxing journalist A J Liebling. "What do *you* think about that fight, Mr Liebling?" asked Andrews in the expectation of a gushing resumé. "Shocking surprise," replied his interviewee, handing back the microphone.

It all went wrong at the rematch, too. On returning to his seat following a most moving human interest interview with the defeated and semi-conscious Johansson, Andrews found to his disbelief that he had been faded out even before he had even reached the Swede's corner.

Back home there were further forgettable moments as Andrews underestimated the memory of the average Irish fight fan. He had travelled to Belfast with W Barrington Dalby to commentate on a British and Commonwealth title bout between the East End's Sammy McCarthy, whom he had interviewed briefly on *Sports Report* two months previously, and local fighter Billy Kelly. "You're a right ___ing Irishman!" said one of his old colleagues from his amateur days. "You wished Sammy McCarthy good luck!" Andrews was pelted by programmes as he sat in his commentary position and later had to take cover under the ring after the fight as the police arrived to remove a half sozzled Welsh boxer, Jimmy Wild, who had climbed through the ropes to proclaim he could have "beaten either of them with one hand."

But despite the fraught moments that are part and parcel of covering such a combustible sport, Andrews earned the regard of the boxing community with the technical appreciation he brought to his commentaries. Harry Carpenter, his inter-round summariser in the early days, remembers him as having a particularly astute eye. He was just about the only pundit, for instance, to correctly predict that the then Cassius Clay would "whup the ass" of the fearsome Sonny Liston.

Boxing aside, Andrews' overall sporting knowledge was relatively thin, but he nevertheless established himself as one of the most indominatable of link-men. He was a producer's dream, being able to both filter talk-back in his earpiece with incredible efficiency and tease unexpected candour from interviewees whom he had placed cleverly at their ease.

After falling out with his bosses at the BBC following their decision to "rest" *This Is Your Life*, Andrews took the skills he honed during a dozen years on *Sports Report* to ITV where, in 1964, he became the first presenter of *World of Sport*.

In 1968, Andrews moved his focus from sport to current affairs, presenting the week-night *Today* programme for ten years. *The Eamonn Andrews Show*, which went out on Sunday nights, became the blue-print for the modern chat-show.

Andrews was born on 19 December 1922. He died on 5 November 1987, his place in the hereafter doubtlessly assured by the Papal knighthood he had received in 1964 for his charitable works. Warm, witty and utterly dedicated, both to his family and to his work, he was quite probably Ireland's favourite son.

Next to his hospital bed, covered in notes in his favourite green ink, they found a script for a forthcoming *This Is Your Life* tribute to sports producer Cliff Morgan. Eamonn Andrews, the ultimate professional, was still giving his all right until the very last.

# John Arlott

In whatever sphere he found himself, whether as a poet, journalist or broadcaster, John Arlott performed *in excelsis*. He will be remembered most fondly, though, as the most celebrated of all cricket commentators. Asking for little more than an open microphone and a glass or two of Beaujolais, this "most felicitous of phrasemakers and memorable of aphorists" adorned English summers with vividly painted aural pictures of shirts billowing in the breeze and stumps leaning drunkenly in the evening sun. "You could smell the grass when he was talking," suggested one of his producers.

Couched in his distinctive "warm bees buzzing Hampshire rumble", Arlott's descriptive brilliance had root in an acclaimed talent for poetry. Having been too rebellious and scornful of authority to succeed at school, he took an interest in literature during his service in the police force in the second world war. On his secondment to the local libraries to file war reports for the Special Branch, he became mesmerised by the treasures they contained. He began to move in literary circles and his own work rapidly acquired a reputation. Arlott's novelty value as the poetry-writing constable led to him being asked to represent the police force in the BBC's VE Day broadcast.

During his wartime service Arlott made his first and only appearance in a first-class cricket match. Being on friendly terms with the Hampshire players, "PC Harlot", as one newspaper reported, was drafted into the outfield during a county game against Worcester.

Cricket, with its long history and infinity of statistics, was an ideal font of trivia for a young man with a voracious appetite for accumulating facts. At school he had avidly compiled the complete county championship record of Glamorgan but it was when he went to The Oval to see England regain the Ashes from Australia that his enthusiasm was properly fired. A game that had previously lain inert as columns of figures in an exercise book had suddenly been brought to life by the elan of Hobbs and Larwood.

Although his afternoon patrolling the boundary at Worcester hardly qualified him as a "former first-class cricketer", Arlott's occasional broadcasts on the game earned him an invitation to describe the 1946 Indian tour of England for the BBC's Overseas Service. His blossoming repute as a poet had brought him increasing radio exposure and, in 1945, he had been appointed to succeed George Orwell as the producer

## DAVID GOWER'S DEBUT, EDGBASTON, 1978

"And now instead of Roope, Gower is coming in. Gower of Leicestershire, Kentish born, the young left-hander who's England's cricketer of the moment. This splendid, stylish stroke-maker, superb timer of the ball and this couldn't have been better stage-managed that he should come in at this moment. And now Wasim Bari's decided to put the pressure on him...and Liaquat come in, bowls to Gower, and Gower turns and he hits if for four behind square leg. Oh what a princely entry!

He's a good player this boy - perhaps the only class player in the side - and he's hit his first ball in test cricket for four. And if that doesn't make him feel better, he's a very odd young man as well as a brilliant one."

of literary programming for the overseas listeners. The opportunity to report on his sporting passion therefore came as an unexpected bonus.

Arlott's commentaries were so well received in India that the BBC set aside its usual disdain for regional voices and invited him to perform to the domestic audience. Despite Arlott's literary achievements, attitudes amongst the corporation's Oxbridge *cosa nostra* remained dismissive of the lorry-fitter's son from carrot-crunching country. On hearing Arlott's rustic tones, his colleague Robert Hudson sneered, "My God, no-one with an accent like that will ever get anywhere." Lobby Lotbinière was only slightly more charitable. "A vulgar voice, but an interesting mind," he famously estimated. But the most ironic comment came from Arlott himself on hearing a recording of his voice for the first time: "That's my script but they've brought in a country chap to read it!"

Arlott's natural descriptive talent was reinforced by the keen observational skills he had acquired on the beat. He became one of the first students of body language and, by noting every nervous tick, he brought thoughtful analysis to the mental tribulations of the county pro' as he tackled "the loneliest game of them all".

One of his most pertinent pieces of psychological diagnosis came at The Oval in 1948 when the great Don Bradman was bowled second ball for nought in his final test innings: "Now I wonder if you see a ball very clearly on your last test in England, on a ground where you've played out some of your best cricket of your life, and when the opposing team have just stood round you and given you three cheers, and the crowd has clapped you all the way to the wicket...I wonder if you really see the ball at all?"

Yet Arlott's early enthusiasm in offering his own interpretation of the fears and motivations of those in the middle drew criticism from his seniors. His imagination was so colourful that, once into his stride, he would invent drama where there was none. Flat, grassless pitches suddenly bloomed into labyrinths of lush capriciousness when Arlott came to the microphone and lead commentator Rex Alston felt obliged to rein in the tyro's "misconstructions".

In the late forties, Arlott's "sharply etched aural refractions", as his biographer David Rayvern Allen described them, were nevertheless turning him into a household name. His audience fell under the spell of the imagery he would conjure, letting out a communal purr when he talked about a bowler running to the crease like "Groucho Marx chasing a pretty waitress."

Arlott had a luxurious ability to give expression to the dynamics of the game. He would describe a googly as heading for the wicket "like a pecking gull", a bowler's right arm "cutting away like a canoeist's paddle" or a technically deficient batsman prodding away "like an old lady poking her umbrella at a wasps' nest". Puns, too, flowed from his lips. Among the most notable was his reference to "Mann's inhumanity to Mann" as the batting of George Mann of Middlesex struggled to address the bowling of "Tufty" Mann of South Africa.

Arlott's work was also punctuated by bouts of impish humour, as illustrated by his weary appraisal of yet another unfathomable Ashes conundrum:

> "What I really want to know, Bill, is if England bowl their overs at the same rate as Australia did, and Brearley and Boycott survive the opening spell, and the number of no-balls is limited to ten in the innings, and assuming my car does 33.8 miles to the gallon and my home is 67.3 miles from the ground, what time does my wife have to put the casserole in?"

He also had the commentary box in stitches when a naked interloper - or "freaker" as Arlott famously termed him - hurdled the stumps at Lord's in 1975. "And a freaker, we've got a freaker down the wicket now. Not very shapely, and it's masculine...And I would think it's seen the last of its cricket for the day. The police are mustered, so are the cameramen, and Greg Chappell. And now he's had his load. He's being embraced by a blond policeman, and this may be his last public appearance, but what a splendid one. And so warm..."

Arlott may have gained huge popularity with his audience, but he appeared less concerned about cultivating the affection of his commentary box peers. An extremely private individual, he maintained a detachment from his colleagues, preferring to keep his working relationships on a strictly professional footing. He collaborated well, however, with Jim Swanton, whose superlative close of play summaries dovetailed perfectly with Arlott's peerless live action narration. He chose not to involve himself in the frippery of the later Brian Johnston years and would often show sensitivity if the target of the humour.

Like many great natural talents, Arlott was a mercurial performer. It was impossible for him to be on his most imperious form for every delivery of every over, although his ability to suddenly put in a virtuoso display when an important visitor was standing at his shoulder hinted at a tainted professionalism. Should the cricket be dull and the audience be uninteresting, Arlott was as capable as any of going through the motions.

> 'I talk about what I see. A lot of commentators tend to talk about what they are thinking rather than what they are watching.'

"Botham runs in like a shire
horse, cresting the breeze."

"The umpire signals a bye with
the air of a weary stork."

"Butcher drops his head, both
hands behind his back, and
looks sheepishly down the
wicket like a small boy
stealing jam."

"...the stroke of a man
knocking a thistle-top off with
his walking stick."

"Umpire Alley, the solitary
dissident."

"That ball went through
Boycott's defence like a
bullet through a hole in a
Henry Moore."

"Taking a foreign body, as the
St John's Ambulance refer to
it, out of his eyes."

"Now he [Dickie Bird] goes
back to holding the front of
his coat up, like a pinafore,
squats slightly, and..."

"He [David Gower] passes
Boycott, who's got his helmet
underneath his arm, like a
Knight at Arms, 'alone and
palely loitering'."

That Arlott occasionally slipped into cruise control was to be expected considering the staggering number of commitments he had accumulated. Aside from his duties with the BBC's staff training unit, to which he had transferred from the Overseas Service, he somehow found time to compile poetry anthologies, compose verses for the BBC hymnal, chair *Twenty Questions*, commentate on football and fill the columns of various newspapers with articles on a bewildering range of subjects. It was calculated that, at its peak, the Arlott prose machine would churn out around 5,000 words a day and the burden of his commitments eventually became so great that it forced the break-up of his twenty-year marriage to Dawn.

Incredibly, Arlott believed he could also shoe-horn into his schedule a career as a full-time parliamentarian. Although something of a male chauvinist, he had inherited a strong social conscience from his mother and grandfather and was a life-long supporter of the Liberal Party. In the fifties he made two gallant, if unsuccessful, attempts at contesting the seat of Epping. He was particularly outspoken on the subject of apartheid and the offence he caused over the South African government's "Nazi" tendencies caused him to be handed the crippling punishment of a three-year ban from the panel of *Any Questions*.

At the turn of the sixties, Arlott succumbed to a creeping melancholia. He should have been on the plane as *The Guardian*'s football correspondent for Manchester United's visit to Red Star Belgrade in the 1958 European Cup and when a colleague, not he, perished in the disaster at Munich airport, he was consumed by guilt. Four years later he suffered a trauma from which he would never properly recover when his eldest son, James, died when he fell asleep at the wheel of his sports car. There would be further tragedy in 1976 when his second wife Valerie died of a brain haemorrhage.

Arlott's well-documented nose for wine stemmed not from any need to escape his despondency but from a genuine passion for the grape. His connoisseur's palate had been activated during a stop-off in Sicily on the return from an England tour of South Africa in the late forties. It was a habit that resulted in the removal of an estimated 2,000 corks a year at his Alresford home. Indeed, when he left for his retirement in the Channel Islands, an auction of just part of his cellar raised £30,000. Arlott's system became so attuned to a tipple that when he was hospitalised after a bad fall, his physician ordered that he be drip-fed with alcohol.

As Arlott reached his sixties, his Bacchanalian excesses began to take their inevitable toll. An expanding girth and a bronchial condition brought on by his years of smoking caused his ascension to the commentary position to mimic the death throes of a vintage accordion. Forced to wear spectacles with special yellow lenses to assist his failing eyesight and with sweat saturating his brow at almost every exertion, he resolved to step down before his decline became discernible.

In *Test Match Special* terms, Arlott was a mere stripling of 66 when he made his final broadcast at Lord's in September 1980. It was an event that aroused intense media interest. How would this master communicator mark his departure from the stage? What sumptuous line would he bequeath as his commentating epitaph? In the end he slipped away without any fuss, bidding not a thank you or a farewell, merely a regulation hand-over to the next incumbent, "After a word from Trevor Bailey it will be Christopher Martin-Jenkins."

"I thought you would have reflected for a moment and said something more romantic than that," remarked his friend and colleague Tony Lewis. "What's more romantic than a clean break?" replied the ever-shy Arlott, doubtlessly fearing a breach of the emotional floodgates.

Leslie Thomas John Arlott was born on 25 February 1914. He died at his home on Alderney on 14 December 1991. At the time of his death, his entry in *Who's Who* made no mention of the word "cricket". It was as if, in his heart, he wanted to be remembered as a poet.

Arlott was the most human of human beings: cantankerous, difficult and private on one side, humorous, warm and generous on the other. But whatever his contradictions, no one could question the overwhelming gifts that made him a national treasure.

Journalist Brian Glanville, quoted in one of David Rayvern Allen's several entertaining tomes on the life and work of Arlott, believed that it was the perfect combination of "manner with matter" that made him the most rounded practitioner in his field:

"There have been, and are, commentators with splendid voices but no feeling for words and little for the game on which they commentate. There are others who know their subject inside out, may well have excelled as players, but come over the air as dull as dogs, with unattractive voices and no style. Arlott, it seems to me, has all three positive attributes."

John Arlott was a broadcaster who built a unique rapport with his audience, receiving affection in equal measure to the enjoyment he gave. Yet at the same time there was no one more modest, as Tony Lewis observed at his memorial service: "…he would prefer to be recalled today and always as the loving father of his children and husband of his wife and a true friend of cricketers and craftsmen the world over."

# Ron Atkinson

The executives of television sport used to say that silence was golden. But that was then. From 1980 to 2004, the only golden objects to be found on any ITV football commentary gantry were those adorning the fingers, wrists and hairy chest of Scouse motormouth, Ron Atkinson. Touted as "The King of Bling", Atkinson created a persona as overblown as his sartorial tastes and in doing so assumed the mantle of Malcolm Allison as television's favourite and, ultimately, most controversial wide-boy of punditry.

The distinctive street-philosophy peddled by "Big Ron" during his eight-club managerial odyssey was perfect for the punchy presentational style that ITV had made its "unique selling proposition". "We had a very constructive discussion at half time," he once told reporters after an Aston Villa game in 1993, "then decided to give it the full bollocks."

In the commentary box, Atkinson was equally expansive with his observations, frequently baffling the viewer with his unorthodox logic. Consider this, for example: "Now Manchester United are 2-1 down on aggregate, they are in a better position than when they started the game at 1-1." An extrapolation into infinity of the relationship between footballing psychology and the away goals rule gives only a hint as to what he's talking about. Yet even this pales next to the one about the flat back four: "You can see the ball go past them, or the man, but you'll never see both the man and ball go past at the same time. So if the ball goes past, the man won't, or if the man goes past they'll take the ball."

"Ronglish", the cataloguing of which became something of a cottage industry, proved to be to the English language what the Sioux nation was to the Seventh Cavalry; it involved galloping roughshod over syntax in order to perform a merciless scalping of a cluster of petrified nouns and phrases. "To be fair", as Ron would habitually adjudicate, his flair for the metaphor was always unconventionally pleasing. What better way is there of describing a forward's glancing nod across the face of the goal than a "little eyebrow at the near post"?

The most illustrious of his contributions to the alternative dictionary of football was "early doors", a phrase of such unfathomable derivation it could only have been lifted from the archives of *The Old Grey Whistle Test*. Other Atkinson neologisms included the verb "to predate", as in "Van Nistelrooy is predating around the opposition box", and the compound-adjective "well-get-at-able", which neatly pigeon-holes

"I would not say that he [David Ginola] is one of the best left wingers in the Premiership, but there are none better."

**"Their strength is their strength."**

"He's not only a good player, but he's spiteful in the nicest sense of the word."

**"That was Pele's strength - holding people off with his arm."**

"There's a little triangle - five left-footed players."

**"How are they defensively, attacking-wise?"**

"You don't want to be giving away free kicks in the penalty area."

**"Liverpool are outnumbered numerically in midfield."**

"He is without doubt the greatest sweeper in the world, I'd say, at a guess."

**"Well, Clive, it's all about the two Ms - movement and positioning."**

LWT/REX FEATURES

defenders of questionable technique and/or temperament.

Students of Ronglish will point to "spotter's badge" and "wide-awake club" as being amongst its creator's best work. A "spotter's badge" is awarded to a midfielder whose vision allows him to pick out a striker's dangerous forward run, while a "wide-awake club" member is a defender who is alive to such ambition. Disappointingly, Ron never explained which one these two scenarios – the footballing equivalent of the irresistible force and the immovable object – would prevail when set in direct opposition.

The beauty of Ronglish is that it is able to function using only a handful of core elements. The word "situation", for instance, is a well-used and handy expedient that allows Ron to bypass uncharted semantic territory in moments of high dudgeon ("That's really given the situation for the goal" being a typical example). The economy of style was particularly well illustrated in his review of Ryan Giggs' twinkle-toed evasion of several Arsenal defenders on the way to scoring his 1999 FA Cup semi-final replay wonder goal: "An unbelievable angle! That has

"When Scholes gets it [tackling] wrong, they come in so late that they arrive yesterday."

"Well that's really knocked the sails out of the wind for Inter."

"Ryan Giggs is running long up the backside."

"The Spaniards have been reduced to aiming aimless balls into the box."

"You know when I say that things happen in matches? Well, it just happened there."

"Beckenbauer has really gambled his eggs."

"It's actually better for managers to start out at smaller clubs like Shrewsbury or Carlisle than to be handed a top job on a silver bed of roses."

"If you score against the Italians, you deserve a goal."

"He'll take some pleasure from that, Brian Carey. He and Steve Bull have been having it off all afternoon."

"There's a lot of balls dropping off people."

to be one of the great FA Cup goals of all time! One…two…see ya! Bib-bib, BANG!"

Brian Moore, ever loyal, believed his long-time side-kick to be the "master of co-commentary", a broadcaster blessed with "good use of words, great feeling for the swaying motions and emotions of the game and an agile football brain that is as quick as anyone's to spot the small changes within a game that often turn out to be crucial ones." Some would argue that Ron's clumsiness of expression masked the genuine incisiveness of his observations, but there is little denying that their strong rapport, which bloomed into a unique conversational style, made them the most entertaining football commentary double-act of the eighties and nineties.

In Atkinson's defence, he never gave ITV less than full value for money, embroidering the main commentator's narrative with an opinion at regular fifty-second intervals. The ability to manufacture over a hundred intelligent-sounding nuggets over the course of 90 minutes is a talent few summarisers possess. Drivel, after all, is intrinsic to the art. In the very first commentary at Twickenham in 1927, one of the first contributions made by Teddy Wakelam's summariser was, "Do they always play with an oval ball?" At least Atkinson was always true to his motto of "trying to give the viewer something they wouldn't have got themselves."

Unhappily, Big Ron's "route one" approach to summarising proved to be his downfall. His propensity to speak first and think later first caused a stir in the 1990 World Cup when he referred to Massing, of the Cameroon, as "having no brain". Most main commentators dissolve into paroxysms of panic when the bongo drums of political incorrectness start to thump and "wide-awake club" associate member Brian Moore rode swiftly to the rescue: "What I think you mean, Ron, is that Massing at times hasn't got a *footballing* brain."

Ron didn't take the hint and, during half-time, made what Moore described as a "flippant remark about those who had been watching at home in Cameroon."[1] Unbeknown to the commentary team, the ITV feed was still going out live to Bermuda and Ron's indiscretion was splashed all over the newspapers the following day.

One of the golden rules of commentary is to always assume the microphone is live. Yet Big Ron refused to heed the lesson and gained an unwelcome reputation for excruciating *faux pas*. "He actually looks like a little twat, that Totti. Are there any sandwiches? I'm starving," he supposedly remarked as AS Roma and Arsenal trudged off at half-time

[1]Reportedly, "I'll only get in trouble if his mother is watching the game sitting in a tree."

46

in the Champions League. The fact that he was born in Liverpool didn't stop him making a disparaging, though admittedly droll, quip about former Anfield idol Steve McManaman lifting the European Cup with Real Madrid: "You won't see that again now that the Scouser's got it!"

Atkinson's career as a pundit disintegrated in April 2004 when, after a Champions League semi-final, he referred to Chelsea's Marcel Desailly as being "what some schools would call a 'f__ing lazy thick nigger'." The comments slipped out live to the Middle East via an open mic and the ensuing furore prompted a profusely apologetic Atkinson to resign immediately from his lucrative job with ITV and his weekly column with *The Guardian*.

Despite the inflammatory nature of what he said, many black footballers reflected the affection in which Atkinson was held within the game by suggesting his comments were stupid rather than racist. While at West Bromwich Albion in the late seventies he had, after all, done more than any manager to integrate black players into the First Division. "They could be yellow or purple and have two heads, as long as they can play," he would insist.

Despite a fulsome act of contrition for the mother of all "rickitts", the press couldn't resist a sneer. "He'll get by," scoffed Kevin Myers in *The Sunday Telegraph*, "rattling his ingots on the forecourt of some used-car lot or on stage in the North of England club circuit, carefully patting that strange array of quiffs across his scalp and baring teeth that appear to have been acquired from the Commonwealth War Graves Commission." But the gaunt, haunted look he still carried months after the aberration betrayed the toll of one of the most spectacular falls from grace in the history of broadcasting.

The press may have cared little but, as "the Gaffer" took his leave, the majority of football viewers mourned the departure of one of television sport's last great characters. It may have been fashionable to deride his broadcasting skills, but he never fell into the classic trap of just repeating what the commentator was saying. In the words of Big Ron's great hero, Frank Sinatra, "the record shows, he took the blows, but did it his way."

# Richie Benaud

Only time will tell if Richie Benaud eventually eclipses John Arlott to be the most revered of all cricket commentators. A master of timing and the supremely judged *bon mot*, this cricketing oracle has proved himself to be an immaculate broadcaster with no obvious weakness.

Richard Benaud was born in Penrith, New South Wales on 6 October 1930. His ancestry, as the name suggests, is cosmopolitan. His mother's relatives had emigrated from Essex in the mid-1800s, roughly the same time that Captain Jean Benaud, a sea-farer from Bordeaux, became an Australian citizen. The pioneering family endured its share of hardship as the Depression years took their toll but Benaud, like many other impoverished young Australians, found refuge on the cricket field.

Although he trained as an accountant, Benaud's ripening talent with bat and ball, which had been nurtured by his father Lou, caught the attention of the State selectors. He made his Sheffield Shield "dayboo" in 1949 and was selected for Australia three seasons later. He went on to captain his country 28 times, never losing a series, and would stand ultimately at the side of Ian Chappell and Mike Brearley as one of the shrewdest tacticians ever to lead a test team. Benaud's playing record was almost as impressive. His aggressive batting and wily leg-spin bowling made him the first player to do the "double" of 2,000 runs and 200 wickets at test level.

Benaud was eminently qualified to take up his seat in the BBC commentary box on his relatively early retirement from the game in 1964. Not only had he been there, seen it and spun it, but he had spent several years writing about "wrong uns" of a more sinister variety as a police reporter for the *Sydney Sun*. In 1956, he had the foresight to enrol himself on a training course with BBC television and in doing so became the first player to acquire a proper understanding of the media and its requirements. This developing technical appreciation, allied to the most astute of cricketing brains, enabled Benaud to make a seamless transition from pitch to commentary box.

Although the slightly curious, waspish tones of "Benaud-speak" may have appeared unorthodox to British viewers not yet attuned to the strained vowels of the neighbours of Ramsey Street (he says "two" as if imitating an ASDIC pulse hunting a submarine), it has been since adopted as the *lingua-franca* of cricket. "Everyone talks Benaud,"

> '
> Don't even bother looking for that, never mind chasing it. It's gone straight into the confectionery stall and out again.
> '

## THE RICHIE BENAUD
## TEST CAREER

| | |
|---|---|
| Tests | 63 |
| As captain | 28 |
| Runs | 2,201 |
| Centuries | 3 |
| Highest score | 122 |
| Batting average | 24.46 |
| Overs | 2,727.2 |
| Maidens | 805 |
| Wickets | 248 |
| Bowling average | 27.03 |
| Best bowling | 11/105 |
| Catches: | 65 |

explained Jim White in *The Guardian* in his appreciation of this much-imitated phenomenon. "It involves taking a word, working it slowly around the little hollow formed between thrust-forward bottom lip and the front teeth, and simultaneously raising one eyebrow in knowing commentary."

Establishment eyebrows were also raised when the 33-year-old Australian upstart was invited to join the venerable BBC. But it became obvious from his first broadcasts - the dramatic 1963 series between England and the West Indies - that he was a natural summariser. "He is just so observant. Nothing gets past him at all," remarked his BBC producer Alan Griffiths. "He has seen everything over how many years as a player and commentator and he has forgotten absolutely nothing."

Despite his early exposure to the ebullience of Brian Johnston, Benaud established a very considered, methodical style. He also resolved to be his own man: "There is no point in trying to be someone else as a commentator, it will almost certainly sound false," he advises. "The most important thing is to have your brain in gear before you open your mouth." He regards patronising the viewer as a cardinal crime and therefore drew up a blacklist of horror phrases such as "of course" and "as you can see on the screen".

The measured, heedful approach that he used to such success on the cricket field followed him into the commentary box. Drawing on the successful captain's art of processing several streams of thought simultaneously, Benaud would tend to isolate himself from his colleagues as he juggled his many and varied commitments. "He is capable, on any given day's play," explained his co-commentator David Gower, "of watching the cricket, betting on three hundred horses, writing an autobiography and at the same time he won't miss a ball."

Benaud's celebrated cool was illustrated perfectly when, at Headingley in 1981, his countrymen contrived to lose an Ashes test from a seemingly impregnable position. He was a model of even-handedness as Ian Botham and Graham Dilley went bananas with the bat and then Bob Willis sent back eight baggy-capped batsmen for 43 runs to wrest for England "one of the most fantastic victories ever known in test history". However, by the mid-eighties his exasperation became almost palpable as Australia's cricketing fortunes adopted the same telemetric relationship as "anvil" and "mineshaft". "I don't believe it, he's done it again!" he would lament as the "happy hooker" Andrew Hilditch suckered himself into swatting yet another short ball down the throat of deep backward square-leg, so helping condemn his compatriots to another Ashes reverse.

Yet his frustration may well have had less to do with partisanship than with "stupid" cricket. This particular Benaud *bête noir* is essentially a most un-Australian mode of play that involves players either falling for obvious psychological ruses, like Hilditch, or simply playing too soft. The latter strain is viewed with far more derision, especially the scenario of a batsman politely tossing the ball back to a fielder after finishing a defensive stroke. It's a crime that rarely escapes the standard reprimand of "why *do* they do that?"

Conversely, good cricket makes Benaud purr and the elegance of a Sachin Tendulkar drive, the disguise of a Shane Warne googly or the reactive brilliance of a Ricky Ponting slip-catch are always communicated with a combination of unbridled pleasure and entertaining imagery. "Ho ho! My that was hit," he cackled as the jug-lugged Aussie batting phenomenon Adam Gilchrist smashed another English half-volley to the boundary, "he just laid back his ears and whacked it!"

A Benaud commentary employs the subtle variation of a demon spinner and is largely a cliché-free zone. The closest he gets to repetitious phrasing is "What a catch, what *A* catch" as a howitzer shell is plucked out of the air by a flailing hand at cover point. There is also his "shot of the day" routine as a good length ball scorches its way to the extra cover boundary, usually just after tea, and the regulation "goddim!" when the sticky mits of the slip cordon send another unfortunate victim back to the pavilion.

He is also the driest of humorists and his wry observations are always delivered with immaculate timing. Sublime understatement is his most trusted device and he's cleverly trivialised many an on-field *contretemps* with a neatly crafted piece of tongue-in-cheek. During one Ashes encounter, Merv Hughes, an Australian seamer with an attitude to match his prodigious facial thatch, fielded off his own bowling a defensive stroke from England's Mike Atherton and launched it petulantly back in the opener's direction. Reviewing the replay, Benaud offered his usual oblique slant on such incidents: "There are various ways to return the ball to a wicket-keeper at the end of the over, which the bowler *should* do, and this is one of them."

Benaud made one of his most droll quips as England were easing themselves towards an eight wicket victory over South Africa at Trent Bridge. Atherton, seemingly the catalyst for the Australian's finest work, was looking to reach his century before the decisive runs were scored. Benaud's co-commentator at the time was Geoffrey Boycott, one of cricket's most notoriously "self-focused" batsmen. Boycott advocated

CHARLES KNIGHT/REX FEATURES

## Human after all?

"The spectators are jumping around like Dervishes at a teddy bears' picnic."

"The replay, which the umpire doesn't have the benefit of, shows that he was either an inch in or an inch out."

"Laird has been brought in to stand in the corner of the circle."

"The only possible result is a draw. The alternative is a win for England."

"That slow motion replay doesn't show how fast the ball was travelling."

"There were congratulations and high-sixes all round."

"He's usually a good puller, but that time he couldn't get it up."

that Atherton monopolise the strike but added hastily that it was something he would never do himself and that he "had read it in a book". After a short pause Benaud ventured the killer punchline: "Autobiography?"

Benaud pleases the viewer with his humour but positively stuns him with his intuition. His ability to interpret the developing match situation and unravel the minds and motivations of the main protagonists is formidable, almost spooky. He appears, for instance, to enjoy an almost telepathic relationship with Shane Warne, the greatest leg-spinner ever to cock a wrist. After five probing Warney leg-breaks, Benaud would occasionally tap into the vibe to predict a piece of sneaky variation: "now Warne might just be thinking about giving him the flipper". More often than not the aforementioned scuttler (Benaud's favourite delivery) is dispatched, regularly leaving the bemused victim trapped plum LBW. "Just like that!" he chirps, oozing quiet glee laced with a dash of self-appreciation.

Nobody reads a game better than Benaud. He has a cricketing brain that's always half an over ahead of the rest. As soon as bat meets ball, he is on the case, weighing up the situation. "They'll get three for that," he states as holy writ as the little red cherry zips through the infield.

That's not to say he gets it spot on every time. In one of his first seasons as a commentator he was at the microphone when Fred Trueman took his three hundredth test wicket. "I can state quite safely and surely," he assured BBC viewers, "that this is a feat that never again will be matched...certainly not in my lifetime and probably not anyone else's." Shane Warne and Muttiah Muralitharan clearly have other ideas: both are closing in on 600.

Benaud has been major player in the modernisation of cricket. In April 1977, he bumped into the tycoon Kerry Packer at a golf club and a conversation ensued on the general exploitation of players by the ultra-conservative Australian cricket "administrators" (there is invariably a twang of contempt in his voice whenever he utters their name). The players' relatively meagre pay and lack of input into the game in Australia were issues so close to Benaud's heart that he needed little persuasion to become a key member of the team that was to launch the breakaway World Series Cricket.

The new format made its debut in front of 50,000 people at the Sydney Cricket Ground nineteen months later and the game of cricket was never to be the same again. The gaudy new world of pyjamas, floodlights, white balls and black sightscreens also heralded a sea-change in the way cricket was televised. The new techniques and innovations pioneered by the Channel Nine team set the standards that other broadcasters have followed and helped broaden the mass appeal of cricket so successfully that a billion people watched the final of the World Cup in 1996.

Benaud's contribution to the movement was not welcomed by his more traditionally minded commentary box colleagues. Radio's Brian Johnston suggested that, in order to preserve the warmth of their friendship, the topic of World Series Cricket should never be raised.

It is a tribute to Richie Benaud that when the personalities that populate cricket are ultimately assessed by some higher panel, his remarkable achievements as a cricketer will still pale next to his reputation as the doyen of the latter-day commentators. It was a measure of his undiminishing appeal that Channel Four, who had promised a clear-out of commentary box relics when it won the test and county broadcast rights from the BBC in 1999, should have turned to a white haired 69-year-old to lead their coverage.

A super piece of thinking, that, I thought.

# Henry Blofeld

Henry Calthorpe Blofeld is a cricket commentator who resides, some would contend, in a universe that is parallel to conventional sports-talkers. His is a semi-surreal world where the every day comings and goings of buses, helicopters, pigeons and seagulls appear to share top-billing with the main protagonists. "My job is to entertain and I do it to the best of my ability. I try to see the bigger picture," he pleads in apology for his flights of fancy. "Cricket, after all, is only a small aspect of human endeavour, and not a terribly important one at that."

His healthy sense of perspective and remorseless *joie de vivre* derive in part from two near-death experiences. While at school at Eton, Blofeld suffered appalling head injuries when he collided with a Women's Institute bus while out cycling. Public transport has been something of an obsession ever since. Later in life, he fell into a coma after suffering acute kidney and liver failure. "Hello darling," he chirped with characteristic nonchalance to his wife when he came round after four days, "I gather I almost snuffed it."

Blofeld's appetite for life has been reflected in his unwillingness to board the tedious gravy train as recommended by his well-to-do family. His disdain for conformity prompted his premature departure firstly from King's College, Cambridge and then from his rich uncle's City bank on the grounds that it was "boring".

Blofeld's lust for adventure could have been sated by a career as a first-class cricketer (he played minor counties cricket for Norfolk and once scored a fine 138 at Lord's for Cambridge against the MCC). In the end, he decided his talents were better suited to journalism and, from 1962, he crafted cricketing communiqués on behalf of a number of quality broadsheets.

Whilst covering England's 1963/64 tour of India for *The Guardian*, Blofeld almost won himself an international cap. On the eve of the second test in Bombay, half the tourists were down with a regional variant of Delhi belly and Blofeld would have played had vice-captain Mickey Stewart not dragged himself out of his sick-bed at the eleventh hour.

Blofeld's broadcasting career began in 1965, when he successfully auditioned as a television commentator on county cricket for Rediffusion, the ITV company that served London during the week. It didn't take long for his famously roving eye to get him into trouble.

**We *do* expect
you to talk!**

Ian Fleming, a school-
friend of Blofeld's father,
borrowed the family name
when inventing
Ernst Stavro Blofeld, the
would-be nemesis of
James Bond.

Having invited the cameras to frame a bare-chested gentleman reclining on a balcony overlooking The Oval, he discovered to his consternation that on closer inspection it was in fact a woman showing off her deep fine leg and a little bit more besides.

In 1969 Blofeld was invited to have a trial for BBC Radio, but he had to wait until 1972 to describe his first county cricket and one-day internationals. Two years later he gained admittance to *Test Match Special* company and was christened "Blowers". At *TMS*, he embarked on a steep learning curve, being admonished by Jim Swanton for having the temerity to mention his own "puny" cricket career and, even worse, for stealing Swanton's slot as close-of-play play summariser.

A far juicier spat was to sizzle between Blowers and the famously testy Australian commentator, Alan McGilvray. Blowers claims he was sent to Coventry for eighteen months merely for suggesting that two scores of 70 by Englishman Derek Randall in the bi-centenary test of 1977 were more deserving of a man-of-the-match award than the seven wickets taken by Australian Rodney Hogg. Four years later, with the bridges barely rebuilt, they fell out again when Blofeld noted on air that the

"final nail" was going in the coffin for the Australians during the Old Trafford Ashes test. "You'll be all right, Henry, when you learn to grow up," hissed McGilvray as Blofeld tried to squeeze past him though the commentary box door. Blowers' reply of "I wish I had the same high hopes for you" led to diplomatic relations being severed for a further year and a half.

In profiling the bumptious new-boy, Christopher Martin-Jenkins illustrated how "Blofeld's rich voice, unquenchable enthusiasm and quick eye for anything from a leg-break to the colour of the pattern on the red skirt in Row H, Section C, have made him as instantly recognisable as his deliberately cultivated catch-phrase, 'My dear old thing.'"

Blofeld's effervescent wit, expansive vocabulary, willingness to speak his mind and general erudition succeeded in offsetting some of the more dour, narrow-minded elements of the *TMS* troupe. What is more, when on top form, his observations are on a par with John Arlott's. When, for instance, the prolific South African batsman Graeme Smith plundered from England yet another century, Blowers noted that some of his team-mates on the balcony seemed to be stifling a yawn. "They don't begin to take notice until he's approaching his second one," he quipped.

With the heavyweight presence of Arlott and Brian Johnston dominating the airwaves, Blowers remained something of a supporting act. But with the death of Johnston in 1994, he returned from a three-year self-imposed exile at Sky Television to establish himself as the lead "personality" at *TMS*.

Over the years he has proved himself to be no less an eccentric than Johnston. His fascination for the mundane paraphernalia that comes with a day's cricket has become every bit as essential to the programme as his senior colleague's penchant for cake and practical jokes. Blofeld's obsession with London buses is not merely confined to assiduously reading out their numbers. Johnston suggested the fascination went yet deeper, when at The Oval in 1982 he recalled his colleague schmoozing, "Here comes a *good-looking* bus."

Although he thinks he sounds like "pompous prat", Blofeld is blessed with one of the most characteristic of broadcasting voices. Cultivated in the pristine air of his family's Norfolk country estate, the Blofeld baritone is redolent of the "priceless relic of the English aristocracy" as described by an admiring fellow scribe. He is also one of radio's great talkers, able to launch himself into frenetic monologues about whatever takes his fancy. Brian Johnston remembered the wet afternoon when he wound himself up into a minor rant on his cherished subject of Kerry Packer. Oblivious to the fact his colleagues, who were also stifling yawns, had quietly filed out of the commentary box, he found himself staring in panic at a note his producer Peter Baxter had placed under his nose: "Keep going till 6.30 pm."

Henry Blofeld is a prolific writer, with over a dozen titles to his name, mostly on cricket. In between commentating commitments, he regales after-dinner audiences with mischievous anecdotes gleaned from his broadcasting career. He also finds time to be wine correspondent for *The Oldie* magazine.

# Geoffrey Boycott

No summariser shoots from the lip more voraciously than English cricket's answer to Margaret Thatcher, Geoffrey Boycott. From Bradford to Brisbane, the man styled by some as the "Greatest Living Yorkshireman" is revered for keeping his talking as straight as his legendary batting stroke.

Boycott boasts the perfect curriculum vitae for employment in match summary; a prolific playing record, an instantly recognisable voice, a shrewd mind, a distinctive way with words and a bluntness of manner that corresponds perfectly with the geography of his birth.

Yet Boycott's undoubted commentary-box flair has always been sharply at odds with his reputation as one of the most obdurate of opening batsmen. "If Geoffrey had played cricket in the way he talked," sniped his county colleague Fred Trueman, "he would have had people queuing up to get into the ground instead of queuing up to leave."

Boycott's candour is only part of the appeal, however. His skill at reading the nuances of the game has earned him the respect of his producers and commentary colleagues alike. Jack Bannister even rates his technical nous ahead of that of the likes of Richie Benaud and Raymond Illingworth. "If you take all the people I have worked with, Boycott is a mile ahead of any of them," eulogised his Talk Sport colleague, "his great strength is that he can see batting problems and faults more quickly, more incisively and to a greater depth than anyone else."

The almost peerless knowledge and experience comes via the osmosis of 24 years in the first-class game. As Chris Broad put it in *...and welcome to the highlights,* "He knows how to bat on a bad wicket, a flat wicket, a turning wicket and an uncovered wicket against fast bowling, slow bowling, good bowling and bad bowling."

Boycott's unshakeable confidence in his opinions means that he feels able not only to comment on something that has just happened, but also on something that is *going* to happen. He is never afraid to put his head on the block because he knows he'll be coming up grinning, albeit lop-sidedly, every time.

Realising he was not endowed with the natural talent of a Sobers or a Bradman, Boycott strove to reach the pinnacle of his sport through application and steely dedication. Throughout his career, he kept a dossier on the strengths and weakness of his fellow professionals that proved to be the foundation of his repute as both a coach and a commentator. Boycott, a master of observation, could not only assess a player's technical competence; he was also brilliant at reading body language.

Boycott's earnest professionalism also shaped his steady development into a highly proficient broadcaster. Keen to prolong his involvement in the game after he retired, he employed his gift for technical analysis to dissect (and studiously ignore) the commentary styles of Benaud and Jim Laker. At first, the BBC had been wary of inviting the outspoken, obstreperous Yorkshireman into the commentary box, but the success of his absorbing autobiography meant that he could be gagged no longer.

He was criticised for being far too negative in his early days, but it wasn't long before the BBC had to concede the extra dimension Boycott brought to their coverage. "He gave us a bit of grit, ensuring our commentaries weren't so bland as they were in the past," remarked his director for television, Alan Griffiths. With Boycott around, there was invariably a harsher edge to the banter. "Come on," he would chide the more timorous David Gower once the microphone was off, "get off the fookin' fence". His sharp exchanges with Ian Chappell on Australia's Channel Nine were regularly more absorbing than the cricket itself.

Boycott's talents as one of sport's most efficient, yet unconventional communicators are underpinned by an uncanny ability to sum up an aspect of play perfectly in one or two pithy words. The John Bunyan-esque "corridor of uncertainty" phrase he invented to describe a bowling line that teases the batsman into playing outside the off-stump became a regular favourite, as did his "just add two wickets to the score and then see how comfortable you feel" reminder to batsmen who allow themselves to drift into the comfort zone. Boycott is also pleasingly adept at pigeon-holing players. Dermot Reeve's brand of bumptious enthusiasm, for instance, earned him the epithet of "jack-in-the-box creeketer", while Carl Hooper was dismissed as a "lollipop bowler" due to his habit of serving up slow, succulent long-hops.

While the accusation of lobbing down confectionery left the laconic West Indian unfazed, Boycott's tagging of Dominic Cork as a "show-pony" hit such a nerve that the England all-rounder challenged the commentator to a television show-down. But Boycott wasn't bothered. He would criticise anybody on air if he believed he was right – even those he was coaching. "I coach them. They play badly. I say so," he declared in what could be construed as crushing indictment of his own prowess as a batting guru.

While involved with the England test side, however, his dual role as coach and commentator led to a conflict of interest that upset several

> Look, it's a good job. Better than my father had. He had to work down the coal mines six days a week wondering if the bloody roof was going to fall on his head.

> ❛ As the ball gets softer, it loses its hardness. ❜

members of the team. "One instance that upset us," moaned Allan Lamb, "was when he had been coaching the players and then outlined on television the best way for the Aussies to get Jack Russell out."

Although he appears to be unaware of it, Boycott has a good, if somewhat quaint, sense of humour. While he gets viewers cackling with his chirpy regurgitation of dressing-room put-downs such as "my granny could have caught that in her pinny" or "my moom could have hit that with a toothbrush", he sometimes appears flummoxed by the more erudite comedy style of certain fellow commentators. Once, when Boycott was talking about "snakes in the pitch" at Headingley, David

Gower ventured, "are you talking cobras?" After twenty seconds of deliberating whether to play the remark or leave it, Boycott could only offer a rather limp, "Is that cobras, or cobblers?"

The hectoring voice, that has become louder and more self-confident with the passing years, is a crucial part of the package. Its uneven modulation, especially when talking about himself ("When *I* was a player/if that were *me*), gives a clue as to the Narcissism that is seized upon by his detractors, but overall it represents the ideal vehicle with which to peddle forthright views.

The skewed vowels of his broad Yorkshire accent have won Boycott a large following all over the world, but particularly across the sub-continent. Accustomed to the bland monotone of home broadcasters such as Ravi "he's hit the ball very hard" Shastri, Indian cricket fans came to prize Boycott's brusque and unpartisan castigation of "roobish creekit". Lines such as "if that's out, I'm a Pakistani" made him the star turn of Indian television coverage.

In 1998, the whiff of scandal threatened to end Boycott's commentary career. His conviction in France for assaulting his lady-friend - by all accounts the most outrageous umpiring decision to which he had ever fallen victim - caused a media sensation which led to his being dropped by the BBC.

Those who knew Boycott well believed he was incapable of committing such a cowardly act, but there is little doubt that he has always had an ambiguous attitude towards women. "Nice tits," he has been reported to say if a generously upholstered woman entered the commentary box. Yet, in the peculiar manner of a non-chauvinist sexist, he generally champions the rights of women and even supported their admittance into the pavilion at Lord's.

The diagnosis of throat cancer in 2002 undoubtedly played some part in leading him to finally settle down. After enduring a course of chemotherapy, Boycott recovered sufficiently to be able to marry Rachel Swinglehurst, the mother of his daughter. His recuperation was accompanied by rehabilitation. He was invited to join the Channel Four commentary team for an entertaining cameo at the end of the 2003 season and, having been welcomed back like a prodigal son by the viewers, was signed up properly for the whole of 2004.

The novelist Pearl S Buck once wrote, "The truth is always exciting. Speak it, then. Life is dull without it." A more fitting motto for the great Yorkshireman's second career there could hardly be.

'I have no history of violence. I can knock down every point she has made.'

# Peter Bromley

Purveyor of the perfectly paced, multi-geared crescendo, Peter Bromley, BBC radio's horse racing commentator for 41 years, had one of the most exhilarating voices in sports broadcasting. Rarely mellifluous, but always resonant, it brought the sport alive for millions.

Bromley's skill was not in the words he used, but the way he used them. Anyone who heard his frantic description of a gutsy grey battling back to victory in the 1989 Cheltenham Gold Cup, for instance, could not have been anything other than thrilled by his oratory:

> "Yahoo and Desert Orchid are together. Desert Orchid back in contention – it's only going to be courage from here on in. Listen to the roar of the crowd. They're absolutely level! Charter Party in third place and up the hill, Desert Orchid, they're level! DESERT ORCHID won't give in! DESERT ORCHID is fighting back! DESERT ORCHID gets in front! It's a desperate finish! The noise is tremendous! Des-ert Orchid wins it, Yahoo is second, Charter Party is third. The hats go up in the air!"

From 1960, when he took over from Raymond Glendenning, to his retirement in 2001, Bromley commentated on 202 classics, missing just two[1]. Television's Peter O'Sullevan may have commentated on more Grand Nationals, but BBC Radio's guaranteed access to every major meeting meant that the virtually omnipresent Bromley – with his vast World Service audience – was regarded by many as the true voice of racing.

Bromley was born on 29 April 1929 in Heswall in The Wirral. The son of a dentist, he first took an interest in racing during his school days at Cheltenham College, when he cycled over to meetings at the nearby home of the National Hunt.

The military bearing that characterised his orderly, no-nonsense commentary style was acquired at Sandhurst, where he trained as a cavalry officer. A fine horseman and an excellent shot, Bromley proved himself proficient at two of the five disciplines of the modern pentathlon and probably would have been selected for the 1952 Olympic team had he been a stronger swimmer.

Having been stationed in the equestrian town of Catterick, Bromley had mixed with several leading figures in racing. He was invited to

'Game Spirit…a lovely horse that was owned by Her Majesty the Queen Mother, who dropped dead here after a long and distinguished career.'

[1] Both St Legers, one due to a holiday, the other after injuring himself falling down some stairs.

**Tommy cruiser off ze starboard bow!**

At Aintree in 1987 with binoculars first used by the Germans in World War II.

become assistant to the Hampshire trainer Frank Pullen when his regiment moved south and he even fostered ambitions to ride regularly as an amateur until a fractured skull, sustained when his mount fell on him, cut short his days in the saddle.

His intitial efforts to get into racing journalism were unsuccessful, although the sharpness of vision that won him shooting's Bisley Cup in 1951 helped him get a job with the British Racecourse Amplifying and Recording Company. As Britain's first on-course commentator, Bromley spent five years on the public address, during which he spoke the immortal line, "Atom Bomb has fallen." He freelanced briefly with television on both BBC and ITV, but decided to switch to radio, thankfully ignoring a woefully misplaced plea by Peter Dimmock, "Why go to radio? O'Sullevan can't go on forever!"

Having fortuitously spared himself 38 years of heel-kicking, Bromley made his first broadcast at Newmarket on 13 May 1959. Shortly afterwards, he was awarded a licence to editorialise as the BBC's first "sports correspondent", although any personal satisfaction he may have had from his rapid career development was brought into tragic context in the same year by the death in a car accident of his first wife, Mary.

## Phenomenal Stayer

Peter Bromley
commentated on over
10,000 races, including
42 Grand Nationals.

Bromley's vibrant commentaries somehow bottled the colour, spectacle and excitement of horse racing. "You have to imagine you are talking to someone in a dark room," he commented. But it was more than that: he had the ability to inspire as well as illustrate. "I've got a tape at home with me winning the two hundredth Derby on Troy and to me hearing his voice was just fantastic," squeaked Willie Carson in warm reminiscence.

The passion of the man – which was occasionally reflected in terse rebukes to underperforming producers and technicians – often had the power to move. When Bob Champion and Aldaniti came back against all the odds to win the 1981 Grand National, an emotionally drained Bromley was in tears.

Radio racing commentators, unlike their television colleagues, have the luxury of not being held accountable by the cameras. Bromley, however, never succumbed to the temptation of busking his way through a race. Despite the fact that no listener could ever dispute his ordering of the mid-field, his preparation remained assiduous. It took weeks for him to build up for a big race. "You can't know too much about horses," he said. "Happiness is a hotel in sight of your commentary box and a room where you can concentrate." Like O'Sullevan, he would take the race card and painstakingly colour-in each jockey's silks as an *aide-mémoire*. He presented the completed masterpiece to the winning rider after each Derby and Grand National.

No amount of preparation can ever cover all eventualities, however, especially when it came to the National. "Lucius, the winner in 1978, was every commentator's nightmare," he recalled. "He lost his cap. By the time they came back over the Melling Road, he had been called a faller, so I had to put him back on his feet."

Aside from The Foxhunter Chase, where most of the runners were unknowns, Bromley was daunted most by the 30-runner Stewards' Cup at Goodwood. The field would start out of sight of the grandstand and would emerge over a crest, strung out across the course as if charging the Russian guns at Balaclava. Bromley described it as "quite the most unnerving 72 seconds of a commentator's year." Yet he was not infallible. His worst moment came in 1993 when poor visibility led him to mis-call the winner of the Cesarewitch.

Bromley commentaries were never to be compromised by the emotional entanglements of horse ownership, but his enjoyment of a wager sometimes added unnecessary spice to the final half-furlong. Nobody would have guessed, however, that Shahrastani's controversial eclipse of Dancing Brave in the 1996 Derby had lost the commentator a tidy sum. "That horse cost me a holiday in Barbados," he huffed to a colleague afterwards.

Galileo's triumph in the 2001 Derby was the last of Bromley's 10,000-plus race commentaries. Sadly, his retirement to Suffolk to shoot game and train gun dogs was cut short when he lost his fifteen-year battle against pancreatic cancer. When he died on 4 June 2003, aged 74, the tributes were fulsome for a respected and well-liked broadcaster who, according to Peter Salmon, the BBC's Director of Sport, had "set the gold standard for horse racing on British radio".

"He described in an unmistakable way a powerful, colourful sport and in doing so converted many people to racing," said Cornelius Lysaght, his successor to the post of racing correspondent. Few could doubt that "radio's favourite foghorn", as another colleague described him, defined Saturday afternoon listening.

## SHERGAR ROMPS TO VICTORY IN THE 1981 DERBY

"Shergar's going for the guns. He's gone five, six, seven, eight lengths clear. Shotgun's under pressure. Two furlongs out. The Derby is a procession! Shergar is ten lengths clear. Scintillating Air gets into second place. Church Parade and Shotgun, Glint of Gold comes next. There's only one horse in it! You'll need a telescope to see the rest! Shergar wins The Derby!"

# Bryon Butler

Bryon Butler was one of the BBC's most enduring radio football commentators. His deep, textured voice worked pleasingly in tandem with the lighter tones of Peter Jones, with whom he forged a distinctive partnership during the heyday of *Sport on Two*. He was certainly no less a wordsmith than the masterful Welshman - as the BBC's football correspondent from 1968 to 1991 he related hundreds of beautifully crafted critiques on the well-being of the national game.

Butler's commentaries were notably measured and composed. When Diego Maradona carved his way through the English defence to score his momentous second goal in the 1986 World Cup quarter-final, Butler's trembling, almost evangelical accompaniment celebrated the genius with which English footballers have never been truly anointed: "Maradona turns like a little eel and comes away from trouble. Little squat man, comes inside Butcher, leaves him for dead, outside Fenwick, leaves him for dead, and puts the ball away! And that is why Maradona's the greatest player in the world!"

Yet, like all commentators, Butler was vulnerable to the occasional lapse in concentration. When describing an FA Cup tie at Selhurst Park, he looked up from his notes to see the ball in the back of the net. "It's there, it's there," he confirmed, "...and such was the quality of that goal, the Crystal Palace fans are on their feet applauding. It's Crystal Palace 1, Swansea City 3!" His touching faith in the generosity of latter day football supporters in clapping opponents' goals was perhaps a decade or three out of date. The Eagles fans were, in fact, celebrating their own team's equaliser: it was Palace 2, Swansea 2. Butler was big enough, however, to own up to his error.

He wasn't quite so ingenuous when England went to Tbilisi for a World Cup warm up in 1986 and found he was too far away from the pitch to read the Adidas numbers on the Soviet players' shirts. On the basis of what the listeners didn't know, wouldn't hurt them, he chose - in a benign variant of Russian roulette - to randomly select players' names from a list he had taped to the glass screen in front of him.

Ewart Bryon Butler was born on 5 June, 1934. He was brought up in the West Country, where he attended Taunton School. After National Service, he wrote for several regional newspapers before joining the *News Chronicle* in 1959 and then *The Daily Telegraph* in 1962. A highly respected journalist, he penned several official histories

## BUTLER'S BLUNDERS

"It's Ipswich 0 Liverpool 2, and if that's the way the score stays then you've got to fancy Liverpool to win."

'The fair, long hair of Adrian Heath has been thrown into the action."

"Butcher goes forward as Ipswich throw their last trump card into the fire."

## THE HAND OF GOD

"Maradona on the ball. Always a danger. Lays it outside him, finds Valdano, he can't turn. Maradona's there, rises above Shilton...and is that going to be allowed? The ball flicked through by Valdano, he turned it inside and ... [sees replay on monitor]... hand ball! No question about that! That was the only reason Maradona was able to rise above the incensed Peter Shilton. He got his left hand to the ball, he stretched, he turned it past Shilton. Shilton could not believe it and the ball, with a little sigh of an apology, just bounces into the open English net. The score: England 0, Argentina 1!"

BBC

of English football - ironically his second favourite sport behind cricket - as well as co-writing the autobiographies of personalities such as Billy Wright and Ron Greenwood. He attended seven World Cups and missed only one FA Cup final from the mid-fifties to the end of the century. He died on 26 April 2001.

# Harry Carpenter

Few commentators have been held in as high public affection as Harry Carpenter. His beady eyes, rounded face and friendly smile combined to create a reassuring presentational persona to which viewers found it easy to relate. Under Carpenter's steady hand, thousands of hours of live and recorded BBC sports programming were beamed into British homes. Those famously clipped tones brought with them one over-riding message: sit back and enjoy.

His face will always be associated with blue riband entries in Britain's sporting calendar: Wimbledon, the Open and the Boat Race. But Carpenter's voice will always be remembered as that which gave boxing its signature for over 40 years.

Carpenter gleaned his interest in the fight game from his father (Harry senior) who, as a fish wholesaler at London's Billingsgate market, mixed with a veritable shoal of expert pugilists on a daily basis. A regular customer was Jack Solomons, the leading fight promoter of the day, who would later teach the aspiring commentator all he needed to know about the noble art.

The family seat - a semi-detached house in Shirley, near Croydon - was hardly anchored in prime boxing territory, but its proximity to the one of the first television transmitters allowed the Carpenters to be among the privileged few to be able to pick up the BBC's first post-war broadcasts.

While he may have been fascinated by the new service, Harry junior attempted to take a more conventional route into broadcasting by touting his services to BBC radio. A speculative letter led to an interview, followed by an instant audition. To the candidate's dismay, the projector sampled not boxing but a first division football match. His spluttering attempts at describing the "scurrying ants" that flickered before him left him in little doubt that he would never pass muster as a commentator of any description.

A few months later, BBC-TV's head of OBs, Peter Dimmock, telephoned Carpenter to invite him to commentate on a night of amateur boxing. His regular commentator had gone abroad and he was left short of options. On 15 January 1949, having gamely grabbed his chance, Carpenter made his way to the Madison Square Garden of north London, the Rotax factory canteen at Willesden, and described 50 minutes of live prime-time boxing for the benefit of about 50,000 Saturday night viewers.

While he had no practical experience of broadcasting whatsoever, Carpenter did at least have a grounding in sports journalism. On leaving the navy after the war, he had helped put together the *Speedway Gazette* before finding sub-editor jobs on the *Sunday Graphic* and then the *People*. It was not until after his television debut, when he moved to the *Sporting Record*, that he penned his first proper boxing article.

In 1954 he joined the *Daily Mail* as its boxing writer, later becoming the paper's sports columnist. The BBC continued to offer him television work and, as Eamonn Andrews' inter-round summariser, Carpenter brought a new, journalistic edge to the sport's television coverage. In some sports, boxing included, amateurs were often referred to by their initials, not their Christian names. Carpenter's inquisitive mind started to delve beneath such quaint formality and he began to paint boxers as rounded, three-dimensional characters. It was an approach that drew satirical comment from *Punch* magazine, where a cartoon appeared depicting a husband and wife watching boxing on the television. As a fighter lay pole-axed, the wife observed, "That's not a very nice thing to do to a 24-year-old unemployed plumber with three children who plays guitar for a hobby."

At ringside, Carpenter wore a uniform of dark suit and dark tie to mask any of splashes of blood. Stylistically, he generally commentated within himself, preferring to jab with short, clipped sentences rather than wade in with outrageous metaphorical hay-makers. He was also careful to avoid fight-game parlance, rarely referring to boxers "getting on their bike" or "show-boating".

Apart from the occasion in the mid-sixties when he was given police protection after receiving threatening accusations of bias against an Irish boxer, Carpenter attracted little controversy. He was the paragon of calm, objective impartiality but, being human, he could not always keep himself immune from the "emotionality" that has always been part and parcel of boxing. His most well-known transgression of the neutrality act was the infamous bout in 1971 when Joe Bugner acrimoniously relieved Henry Cooper, the nation's favourite heavyweight, of his British, European and Empire titles. Cooper knew he had won, the crowd knew he had won and Carpenter knew he had won, yet when the referee, Harry Gibbs, inexplicably raised the Hungarian émigré's arm, pandemonium erupted. Carpenter dropped his guard, lost his cool and openly questioned the decision: "I find that amazing," he shrieked, "how can you take away a man's three titles like that?" And the rancour never died. The British public has never forgiven Bugner and Bugner has never forgiven Carpenter.

## CARPENTER'S CLANGERS

"He looks up at him through his blood smeared lips."

"And there he is sitting in exactly the same place on the other side of the ring."

"He certainly handed out more than he gave."

"He's got a cut on his left eye – it's just below his eyebrow."

"We haven't seen any more rain since it stopped raining."

"They said that it would last two rounds. They were half wrong – it lasted four."

"And, somewhat surprisingly, Cambridge have won the toss."

"It's quite clear that Virginia Wade is thriving on the pressure now that the pressure on her to do well is off."

British amateur boxing flourished in the 1950s and when Carpenter commentated on his first Olympics in 1956, the British boxing team won an unprecedented five medals, including two golds. This achievement was eclipsed, however, by the night in November 1961 when Great Britain whitewashed the Americans 10-0 in a match at Wembley. The drama and excitement of it all was, however, starting to take its toll on Harry. When in the early hours of the morning he swapped ring-side for the Wembley General bed-side of half a dozen dazed Americans, his need to pop stress-busting tablets convinced him that his mushrooming commitments were becoming detrimental to his health.

In 1962, Carpenter rationalised his work-load by leaving the *Daily Mail* and joining the BBC full-time. Having been given a more restful brief, the commentator found himself Stateside with a roving commission to get under the skin of the principal contenders in the compelling heavyweight scene. Carpenter was ideally suited to the role. His unthreatening demeanour helped him charm his way past the various entourages, after which he would use his journalistic wiles to tease a disclosure or two from some of sport's most surly individuals. Muhammad Ali needed somewhat less stimulus to reveal his motivation. Carpenter first met Ali, then using his "slave name" Cassius Clay, when he interviewed him at the top of the Empire State Building. Entitling the interview "The Greatest meets the Highest" Carpenter played up cunningly to the future champion's ego and they went on to develop a close rapport.

The individuality of their relationship was illustrated no better than when Carpenter went to Miami to interview Ali prior to his second fight with Sonny Liston. Ali came back to his house with a croquet set and asked his interrogator to explain the rudiments of the game. There were no hoops that Harry was not prepared to go through to get his story and the odd couple adjourned with their mallets to a grassy island in the middle of an adjacent highway to do battle.

Twenty-five years later, when the commentator was the subject of *This Is Your Life*, Ali was amongst those who paid tribute. When Ali was voted BBC Sports Personality of the twentieth century, Carpenter was the first to offer his congratulations. "He is not only the most remarkable sports personality I have ever met," eulogised Carpenter, "he is the most remarkable *man* I have ever met."

His affection for Ali was evident from the tone of his commentaries and when in 1974 the former champion came back from a hiding on the ropes to stop the fearsome George Foreman, Carpenter almost went berserk. His description of one of sport's most astonishing reversals of fortunes became one of the most memorable pieces of commentary ever:

> "Suddenly Ali looks very tired indeed. In fact, at times now, he looks as though he can barely lift his arms up...Oh he's got him with a right hand! He's got him! Oh you can't believe it! And I don't think Foreman's going to get up! He's trying to beat the count. And he's out! Oh my God, he's won the title back at 32!"

A different but no less remarkable relationship was forged with Frank Bruno, an endearing British heavyweight who may have stung like a bee but unfortunately danced like a refrigerator. The public and Carpenter convinced themselves that the muscle-bound contender had the raw power to blast his way to the world title and his brutal progress past a succession of shuffle-footed journeymen was greeted with increasingly deluded enthusiasm. After each contest, Carpenter's microphone captured what became one of the most celebrated, if vacuous, soundbites of eighties sport: "Know wha'a-mean, Harry?" Before long, they were doing television commercials for HP sauce together and sparring in front of the Queen at the Royal Variety Performance.

It was ironic that Carpenter's fame should have been so amplified by his ability to trade vapid post-fight small-talk with big Frank. In truth he had a loathing of the media's obsession with the "nannies" (nanny goat - quote). "How many times have I climbed through the ropes at the end of a fight and thrust a microphone under the winner's nose?" he beefed. "And how many times has it produced anything worth hearing?"

The BBC's claim on Bruno was not exclusive. When the time came to put the villainous Joe Bugner in his place, ITV trumped the corporation for the rights. After the fight, it was Jim Rosenthal's turn to engineer some repartee with the victorious Bruno. He had barely opened his mouth before Frank cracked him and ITV one flush on the chin. "Where's Harry?" inquired the big man, gloriously indifferent to the sensibilities of the evening's paymasters. "I was sitting at home watching on the box," recalls Carpenter. "I nearly fell out of my seat!" How eighteen million viewers chuckled.

Before he retired, Carpenter was desperate to describe a British heavyweight in a world championship belt but when the matchmakers paired Bruno with the nemesis of the division, the almost satanically destructive Mike Tyson, the commentator, like the British public, must have secretly feared for their favourite's well-being. Yet the big man acquitted himself courageously and when he rocked Tyson with a sledge-hammer right, a punch that the champion later described as the

"And it's stopped! It's
stopped in the third round!
And Hagler's on his knees
acclaiming victory! He said he
was the rightful champion,
and he's won it in three
rounds...AND PEOPLE ARE
THROWING BEER CANS
AND ONE'S LANDED ON
ME! Beer cans are being
hurled all over the ring!
There's a fight started over
Hagler. Somebody's attacking
him and there's chaos,
absolute chaos! I'm
smothered in beer! So are all
my colleagues around me!
And people are trying to
attack Hagler - police are
trying to move into the ring
to protect Hagler. I've been
struck on the head by a
bottle, and this is the worst
scene we've ever had at
Wembley - in any boxing ring
in this country! It's absolute
chaos! The crowd are mad
with this. And clearly they're
accusing Hagler of using his
head against Minter, causing
him to lose the world title
and the rage has broken out
all around Wembley and the
scenes are a shame and a
disgrace to British boxing!"

hardest he had ever taken, the prospect of a monumental upset briefly glimmered. "And he's hurt Tyson...get in there Frank!" urged Carpenter, disregarding the cardinal rule of editorial distance to his eternal professional shame. "I can only plead," he wrote in mitigation, "that up there was my mate Bruno hurting Tyson, my mate Bruno threatening to fulfil the one remaining ambition of mine." Alas poor Frank bit the canvas in the fifth.

With Larry Holmes and Tyson ruling the roost in the heavyweight division, eighties boxing was dominated by a quartet of ferocious middleweights, the like of which had never been seen before. In 1980, Marvin Hagler, a shaven-headed destroyer sporting a diabolical goatee, announced another era of American domination with a crushing defeat of Britain's Alan Minter. Amid disgraceful scenes at Wembley, Carpenter found himself caught in crossfire of bottles that had been launched by unsavoury elements of the home fighter's support. One caught Harry a glancing blow while he was commentating, earning its owner two months' detention at Her Majesty's pleasure.

Carpenter was more than merely the voice of boxing. In 1954 the BBC sent him to the dogs and his commentaries on greyhound racing helped to fuel an instant surge in popularity of the sport. He also reported on football, athletics and the University Boat Race.

Carpenter had a long association with the annual varsity race, an event that in 1977 inspired him to let slip one of the most famous sporting *doubles entendres* ever to sully the airwaves: "Ah, isn't that nice? The wife of the Cambridge president is kissing the cox of the Oxford crew." Despite its outward gentility, rowing had always been prone to titillate the dirty-minded. At the Henley Royal Regatta, an uncredited broadcaster unwittingly combined filth and blasphemy with memorable brillo: "It's a very close race. Lady Margaret and Jesus are rowing neck and neck. Perhaps Lady Margaret is just ahead...but no, Jesus is now definitely making water on Lady Margaret!"

The BBC recognised Carpenter's imperturbability and started to offer him regular sports presentation roles. As the live anchor, he was unshiftable. He made the first of his occasional appearances in the *Grandstand* chair in 1962 and would later present over 300 editions of *Sportsnight* from 1975 to 1985. Away from the studio, Carpenter would handle OBs with similar aplomb. In 1965 he was asked to take over golf presentation from Cliff Michelmore and immediately relished the change of pace. "What I enjoyed," he wrote in a review of his 25 years of introducing major tournaments, "was the quiet dignity of the game, the essential slowness of it, the immaculate turnout of the competitors and the controlled excitement of the spectators."

Carpenter would link in and out of the live action, and would therefore share the discomfort of the commentary box with the likes of Henry Longhurst, Peter Alliss and Bill Cox. The elements were an unrelenting foe and during the World Matchplay Championship at Wentworth in 1965 the wind was to play a particularly bizarre trick. When Arnold Palmer approached the 15th green, which was adjacent to the BBC commentary position, Carpenter passed his colleague Cox a note. A swirling gust then took the piece of paper and deposited it on the green. The defending champion strode over to it, picked it up and read Carpenter's curt observation: "Palmer has three-putted the last three greens." It proved to be useful motivation. Having placed it in his pocket, the American then settled over his ball and sank the twenty footer.

The elements were guaranteed never to interfere with Carpenter's Wimbledon presentations. A few years after he had stepped into David Coleman's shoes for the 1967 Championships, he was installed in a

Churchillian bunker, deep under the show courts. From his underground den, "the Mole", as he was nicknamed, would draw together the strands of the day's play and conduct "fantasy" interviews with the stars of a sport that had enthralled him since his childhood. As an eleven-year-old he had listened on his aunt's wireless to Dorothy Round beating the Pole Jadwiga Jedrzejowska in the 1937 ladies' singles final. In an uncanny parallel, she would be his studio guest 40 years to the very day of her victory.

On his retirement from the BBC in 1994, Carpenter, like several other outgoing commentary stalwarts, bemoaned the state of his specialist sport. The unpalatable fact was that, until Audley Harrison and Lennox Lewis signed up in 2002, the corporation had nothing left to show. Carpenter blamed American television and its unquenchable thirst for the "big" fight. When penning his autobiography in 1992 he lamented the debased currency of boxing: "there are no fewer than 64 alleged world champions spread over seventeen weights. Fifty years ago there were eight champions at eight weights and we knew and respected them."

As a broadcaster, Carpenter had more than made his mark. In 1957, when covering the European Amateur Boxing Championships from Prague, he had commentated on the first sports event to be transmitted from behind the Iron Curtain. Five years later, having flown to Chicago to cover the Floyd Patterson - Sonny Liston fight, he made the first satellite TV sports broadcast from America to Britain.

The professionalism with which he adapted himself to such a broad palette of sports earned the admiration of broadcasters, sportspeople and viewers. In 1989, he was honoured by the American Sportscasters' Association.

Carpenter's name became a codeword for BBC Sport: when the champions were asked to have a few words with "Harry", all instinctively obeyed. He may not have had physical stature, but he had presence. As Muhammad Ali concurred, "He's not as dumb as he looks!" The final word is best left to Tim Gudgin, the racing and football results announcer, who, when co-opted to link into some boxing following a technical failure, informed his viewers that "the carpenter is Harry Commentator."

# David Coleman

The voice of David Coleman, arguably the most recognisable and prolific of all British broadcasters, is synonymous with televised sport. Born on 26 April 1926, less than a week after the present Queen, Coleman was a television blue-blood who earned world renown as the master in his field.

While appearances for Stockport County reserves suggested he could have made a career as a professional footballer, the young Coleman's real talent lay in middle distance running. In 1949, he became the first non-international athlete to win the Manchester Mile. When a nagging hamstring forced him to hang up his spikes, Coleman turned to journalism, a craft he had learned on the army newspaper *Union Jack* during his national service in the Royal Signals. An ambitious, energetic and forceful individual, he made fleet-footed progress through the newsrooms of his native north-west, becoming editor of the *Cheshire County Press* at the tender age of 22.

In the pioneering days when speculative telephone calls to broadcasting organisations were occasionally rewarded with a 50-year commentating franchise, Coleman rang the BBC asking if he could cover athletics for them. It proved to be a well-timed inquiry as the corporation saw in him the blend of practical, professional and telegenic qualities that would support its drive to modernise and popularise its sports coverage through the fifties. They 'phoned back, leaving a message with his mother, requesting that he proceed to Bradford to cover a race featuring Roger Bannister.

"The funny thing is," he recalls, "BBC Radio gave me the job without even hearing me speak. I could have had a stutter or anything. I didn't ring back, just in case they didn't like the sound of me." He need not have worried. As a presenter, link-man and commentator, Coleman, with his light regional accent, was to bring accessibility and indeed informality to the BBC's then-stuffy presentational style.

The flagship of the BBC's new mass-market strategy was to be the Saturday afternoon sports magazine *Sportsview*. Coleman, who had joined the staff formally in May 1954, was selected by the head of OBs, Peter Dimmock, to be its first presenter.

The immaculately groomed Coleman was to make himself unassailable as the voice and face of television sport. By the sixties, he was not only anchoring sixty editions of *Grandstand* a year, but popping

## BBC tv GRANDSTAND

**Err...and we believe**

Coleman anchored 60 editions of the BBC's sporting flagship a year. For the programme he wore a suit specially tailored to accommodate pounds of technical paraphernalia.

up mid-week on his own *Sportsnight with Coleman* programme. With the BBC obviously starting to run with the "cult of personality" concept, Coleman's face was to become as familiar as the potter's wheel.

The BBC also started to use Coleman as a commentator on occasions of national or international importance. As well as being on hand for events as disparate as royal weddings and cosmonaut splash-downs, he was the corporation's man-on-the-spot when The Beatles arrived back at Heathrow following their 1964 American tour. "Christ," gasped Paul McCartney, "*Grandstand*! We must have arrived!"

*Ersatz* Richard Dimbleby he may have been, but it is with television athletics commentating that Coleman truly won his spurs with the viewing public. He built his reputation on his coverage of the Olympics, an event that holds special personal resonance. "I'd have given the lot away to run in one", he sighs. "I've been obsessed with the Olympics since listening to the 1936 Games in Berlin on a fading battery set in our front room in Cheshire."

Yet over the course of over a dozen Olympiads, Coleman's contribution to the movement was far greater than would have been achieved by a solitary appearance in a heat of the 1,500 metres. Since the war, Britain's successes at the Games have been little more than spasmodic, but whenever an athlete did strike a track and field gold, it was inevitable that Coleman's emotional accompaniment would be there, capturing the moment for nation's sporting scrapbook.

Coleman spoke perhaps his most memorable Olympic words when Ann Packer stormed round the final bend in the final of the 800 metres in Tokyo in 1964:

"And Ann Packer is moving up on the outside. She's got a lot of running to get there but she's doing it. Here she goes on the outside! A tremendous sprint but she's had to come the long way round. She really had to come a long way round, and she's moving into second place! And here she comes on the outside, a tremendous run and she's going to do it! Ann Packer's going to take the gold medal. It's Ann Packer, Great Britain! Oooh, what a consolation! Ann Packer wins, Dupureur second, Chamberlain third, and she's done it! Oh fantastic run! Magnificent, magnificent, magnificent! And we think it's a new world record!"

"It certainly was a world record, too," chuckled anchorman Cliff Michelmore back in the studio, "anyone would have thought David Coleman had broken it, wouldn't they!"

In the rarefied atmosphere of Mexico in 1968, Coleman needed to be close to his peak. In a heat of the 100 metres, a Greek by the name of Papagiorgiopoulos and a Madagascan called Ravelomanatsoa were running in adjacent lanes.

"By the time I'd named them both, they'd crossed the finishing line," he recalls. "I used to go to bed at night praying Ravelomanatsoa would get knocked out, but he went right through to the final. By which time, I have to admit, he'd become 'the tiny Madagascan in lane eight.'"

Even if a 100 metres race does not feature a runner with a name resembling a brace of unsolved *Countdown* conundra laid back-to-back, it still represents ten seconds of unsurpassable commentating intensity. Yet at the Olympics, the 100 metres is not just a sprint, it's a marathon. Eight first round heats with 64 competitors, the majority of them unknowns, make 90 minutes of high mental attrition for the man at the microphone.

The start is particularly onerous. Eight runners in perfect line abreast for the first twenty metres. What is there to be said? Experts like Coleman, however, always had a trick up their sleeve. At the sound of the starter's gun, his ploy was to buy his brain a split-second of processing time with a stock phrase such as "the Olympic final is underway" or "this time they've all got away well". His BBC colleague, Alan Parry, took heed of this lesson when he went he went to cover athletics for ITV. It proved to be a most useful device, except for the time he informed the viewers that all the runners were all away cleanly, only to look back in embarrassment to see an oblivious Linford Christie still glued to his blocks.

"He just can't believe what's not happening to him."

"He's even smaller in real life than he is on the track."

"This is a truly international field, no Britons involved."

"He's 31 this year - last year he was 30."

"He won the bronze medal in the 1976 Olympics so he's used to being out in front."

"We estimate, and this isn't an estimation, that Greta Waitz is 80 seconds behind."

"This could be a repeat of what will happen in the European games next week."

"It's a battle with himself and with the ticking fingers of the clock."

"One of the great unknown champions because very little is known about him."

"The runner is 87 years old – he'll remember this day for a long time."

"A fascinating duel between three men."

"There you can see her parents – her father died some time ago."

"It's gold or nothing…and it's nothing. He comes away with the silver medal."

"The test match begins in 10 minutes, that's our time of course."

Although he could read a race superbly, Coleman's commentating strength was his ability to ratchet up tension as the athletes took their marks. With hushed, reverent tones he milked the drama in copious long-hand, altering the timbre of his voice only on the appearance in shot of a British vest: "The Olympic final of the men's 100 metres. Silvio Leonard, Cuba, lane one; Alexander Aksinin, Soviet Union, lane two; Vladimir Muravyov, also Soviet Union, lane three; Marian Woronin, Poland, lane four; Petar Petrov, Bulgaria, lane five; Herman Panzo, France, lane six; Osvaldo Lara, Cuba, lane seven; ALLAN WELLS, Great Britain, lane eight…" It did things to the hairs on the back of the neck.

Coleman's other great talent was his adaptability. He showed himself to be the master of styles that could embroider the garish pageant of the opening ceremony, unravel the tactical intrigues of the 5,000 metres and bring alive the plodding toil of the 50km walk. It was, though, at the Munich Olympics of 1972 that the true brilliance of Coleman was revealed. When terrorists stormed the Olympic village and took hostage a group of Israeli athletes, he anchored the coverage of the tense 34 hour stand-off with sublime professionalism, somehow managing to eke out the slivers of information being fed into his earpiece by his producer Bryan Cowgill.

"It was unreal, because there were events going on elsewhere and as every deadline set by the terrorists passed, we would have to leave the track and return to scenes from the village," he told *The Daily Telegraph*. It was an emotionally chastening experience that forced him to pull out of several athletics meetings in the aftermath. The scars have yet to heal: "It's sad when you look back over the Olympics – to Owens, Zatopek, Daley Thompson - that your outstanding memory of the Games is not of sporting achievement but the murder of eleven athletes and coaches."

As monochrome gave way to colour in 1969, Coleman was in the process of unseating another broadcasting institution, Kenneth Wolstenholme, from his post as BBC-TV's senior television football commentator. While Wolstenholme's name will be forever synonymous with 1966 and all that, the signature of Coleman was writ large over Mexico 1970, the seminal World Cup finals.

He was at one end of a crackling Guadalajara telephone line as England played out the match of the tournament against the champions-elect, Brazil. His silence spoke volumes as Jairzinho wheeled away in celebration after blasting the South Americans into the lead. But it was a save, not a goal, for which the game would be most readily remembered: "Carlos Alberto…that's dangerous…Jairzinho…oh he left

Cooper standing... PELE! ...WHAT a save! Gordon Banks...*picked* that out of the net!" Coleman, who was the corporation's best football commentator according to veteran *Match of the Day* producer Alec Weeks, would remain pre-eminent until John Motson completed his apprenticeship in time for the 1979 FA Cup final.

The drama and unpredictability of English football in the seventies, ideally complemented Coleman's uncompromising delivery. It was noticeable that the more earth-shattering the goal, the fewer words he spoke. "One nil!" was his stock-in-trade, although this word-count was twice as large as some of his most memorable exclamations. Who could forget the 1973 Cup final and "PORTERFIELD!"?

Coleman was always keen on the dramatic pause to underscore efforts of rare panache. It gave extra impact to the definitive editorial that normally followed: "...and *that* is what skilful, attacking football is *all* about!" He also used it to great effect when communicating moments of national footballing calamity. When Gerd Muller volleyed home West Germany's winning third goal in the World Cup quarter final in Leon in 1970, Coleman uttered not a word for 15 seconds.

As the decade developed, Coleman concentrated on commentating as Frank Bough gradually took over the *Grandstand* hot seat. When Coleman did appear, he always added value, especially with his double-act with the results teleprinter. His encyclopaedic knowledge of the current form of all football league clubs on both sides of the border was,

BBC

**Compère beyond compare**
With Peter Alliss and Arnold Palmer in 1968.

to use his own vernacular, "quite remarkable". Almost every result coming through was garnished with a titbit of trivia and there was hardly a household in the country that wasn't aware that Burnley had gone 16 away games without a draw or that Crewe hadn't been awarded a penalty at Halifax for 38 years. Bough knew he was trailing in the wake of a virtuoso, remarking that Coleman had "made his considerable reputation from being able to take talkback in his ear, change his mind in a trice, get his facts right, sight-read all the results on the teleprinter, but also interpret them and amplify them in the most amazing way."

He was also the most uncompromising of professionals. As captain of the ship, Coleman the perfectionist was often explosively intolerant of any colleague, whether producer, cameraman or technician, who failed to match his own impeccably high standards. He was even more sensitive to the competition, promising to "blow the bastards out of the water" when ITV dared to rival *Grandstand* with their own Saturday afternoon effort, *World of Sport*.

His thinly disguised contempt for commercial television was naturally not appreciated by some of the individuals concerned. Brian Moore, whose modest fair-mindedness was the antithesis of Coleman's Olympian bravado, took particular exception to his rival's bolshy competitiveness. "I once went to watch a game in Cardiff where he was broadcasting," recorded Moore in his autobiography, "'You looking for an audience?' he said with that mixture of smile and sneer."

Coleman's status as TV sport's headline act inevitably drew him close to the claws of satirists and the regular "Colemanballs" column in the magazine *Private Eye* did little to enhance his reputation. For Coleman's good name to be intimately associated with other commentators' clangers, although a back-handed compliment, is unwarranted and he is known to be intensely irritated that he is regularly attributed the goofs of colleagues. He denies having said virtually all of them. Coleman was, for instance, "credited" with the famous "and there goes Juantorena down the back straight, opening his legs and showing his class" howler that was actually perpetrated by Ron Pickering.

The raw deal suffered by Coleman in relation to his "blunders" was highlighted by Will Buckley of *The Guardian*, who spotted that the gaffe-coefficient of the Colemanball "if that had gone in it would have been a goal" would have been neutralised had its spotter included the words that immediately preceded it: "the linesman's flag stayed down, so…" An inexact science indeed.

The occasional *double entendre* or piece of chewed-up prose was

"Goals pay the rent, and Keegan does his share!"

"One nil, and Corrigan didn't even see it!"

"Gemmill, good play by Gemmill… and again. 3-1! A brilliant individual goal by this hard little professional has put Scotland in dreamland!"

"What a goal! You don't blame goalkeepers, you congratulate the scorer!"

"Moore, beaten for once, but back again!"

"McCalliog to Stokes, who's on-side. One nil!"

"Best is up front...and there he is, with the defence split. Can he do it? He surely must!...What a goal to score and who could score it but George Best? With the skill, the timing, the confidence to take it on and on and on until the net was bare!"

harmless, even endearing, but when Coleman allowed his Achilles' heel, over-excitability, to get the better of him, the results could be more destructive. A case in point was when he barked home the placings at the end of the Olympic 400 metres hurdles in 1968: "David Hemery's first, Hennige West Germany second and who cares who's third!" To his undoubted embarrassment, the bronze medal position was occupied by John Sherwood...of Great Britain.

Having tired of football commentary by 1984, Coleman divided his time between athletics and hosting the BBC's long-running *A Question of Sport* programme. It was a welcome change of pace for the broadcasting veteran as his vocal elasticity was fading. Murray Walker and Bill McLaren were septuagenarians who had succeeded in nursing their voices through five decades' hard labour at the microphone. Coleman was less fortunate. As the march of time started to take its inevitable toll on that celebrated searing rasp, the press began to sense vulnerability in the BBC's great warhorse. Following the 100 metres at the Athens Olympics, Giles Smith picked him off cuttingly in *The Daily Telegraph*: "'Nine eight eight is unbelievable,' he shouted - or rather was revealed to have shouted after a sophisticated, FBI-endorsed voice-decoder had been run over the tapes which, until that moment seemed only to contain the words 'nigh aid aid iz unburgle'."

In December 2000, after a 48 year broadcasting career that spanned nineteen summer and winter Olympic Games, eight Commonwealth Games, a host of World Cups and innumerable other major sporting events, Coleman retired as probably the most acclaimed television sports commentator. He led the BBC's sports coverage at a time when it indisputably led the world and rightly collected the plaudits.

He was an integral member of the BBC-TV team that won the International Olympic Committee's Golden Rings Award for the best television broadcaster at both the Barcelona and Sydney Olympics. For the Barcelona award, one member of the international jury panel commented on the simplicity of the decision, "David Coleman is recognised as the absolute master the world over. The British television audience is in the company of greatness." Awarded an OBE in 1992, he was honoured in 2000 by IOC President Juan Antonio Samaranch for services to the Olympic movement.

Following his Mexico City triumph, David Hemery summed up the magic of a Coleman commentary: "His voice actually engenders some of the adrenalin that people identify with, and he can create such a spirit of excitement that it helps people to live the moment."

Viewers of television sport will not see his like again.

# Barry Davies

The *cognoscenti* would argue that the wit, articulacy, versatility and indeed durability of Barry Davies qualify him as the best all-round sports broadcaster ever to pull on a sheepskin coat for the BBC. Well-crafted, perfectly measured and lightly drizzled with laconic humour, his laid-back accompaniments have set new standards of urbane sophistication. He is the essential "thinking-fan's commentator".

Davies was probably the most naturally humorous of all the television football commentators. "These two centre backs are in armchairs," quipped his summariser Mark Lawrenson as England outmanoeuvred a lumbering Albanian defence. "Well let's hope they're on casters!" flashed back Davies by return. Puns are his preferred currency and he notes that one of his great regrets was not being in the commentary box to holler "By George!" when Charlie of the same name slotted Arsenal's winning goal in the 1971 FA Cup final.

In between the clever plays-on-words, Davies punctuated his commentaries with gasps, whoops and screeches of the seasoned terrace-dweller. It was a contradictory style that appeared to be caught in a limbo between erudition and populism. One minute he was sagely contextualising football as merely a mirror of life's joys and disappointments, the next he had both feet over the touchline yelling blue-murder over a questionable offside or a team's "lack of width".

The Mr Hyde half of Davies' microphone persona has led to some highly unorthodox observations, a few of which have entered commentating lore. When a third goal for Great Britain finally sealed a hockey gold against the old enemy in the 1988 Olympics his remark "And where were the Germans? But frankly, who cares?" may have been mischievously irreverent, but it nevertheless struck a resounding chord with that generation of Englishmen who had been brought up on the notion of Teutonic sporting invincibility.

The *Match of the Day* archives are also raided regularly for the occasion when a young Davies lost his composure totally following the infamous Jeff Astle goal that robbed Leeds United of the Championship in 1972. "And Leeds will go mad! And they've every right to go mad!" he shrieked as an irate middle-aged gentlemen in a fetching pastel yellow shirt was evicted from the pitch by approximately 43 members of the Yorkshire constabulary. BBC Sport's Rob Bonnet paid tribute to Davies, estimating that he "beats most of the rest because he clearly

> ' Mabbutt has gone forward, with Stewart to the right, Lineker and Howells to the left. Is Gascoigne going to have a crack? Oh he is you know! Oooh I say! That has to be one of the finest free-kicks this stadium has ever seen! '

believes there's a world out there beyond the stadium." Not always so: Armageddon was playing itself out at Elland Road that day.

His flick-of-a-switch excitability was most memorably reflected in the "Interesting....VERY INTERESTING!!" line he used to describe Francis Lee's rasping goal for Derby County against Manchester City in December 1974. Davies' voice cracked into a yodel when he invited the viewer hysterically to "look at his face, just LOOK at his face" as the camera framed Lee's chubby features, contorted in a grimace of quasi-orgasmic rapture.

"Interesting...VERY INTERESTING" is typical of Davies' habit of hanging onto a word or phrase in the hope that something "interesting" happens by the time his lungs finally empty of breath. A standard Gary Lineker effort, whereby the striker would burst through on goal, trip on the edge of the box, stumble towards the penalty spot, knee the ball over the line from two feet and then throw himself into the back of the net would draw the typical accompaniment "Linekaaaaaaaaaa, SCORES!" A variation on this theme is the familiar "tries to curl it...AND DOES" device.

Davies can be co-credited with David Coleman with the introduction of the extended pause into football commentary. When Coventry City's Ernie Hunt famously volleyed Willie Carr's donkey-kick into the Everton net, he left fourteen seconds between "Oh, what a goal!" and "Well they don't come much better than that! Right out of the book and on the first line too!" He was also notably stumm when Gareth Southgate missed his penalty in the semi-final of Euro '96. "I said: 'Oh, no.' Then I didn't say anything for ages," he recalled. "What was the point? There was nothing I could say. The whole country was speechless. In various forms, and with probably a few adjectives, 'Oh, no' is what everyone sitting at home was saying."

This habit of letting the drama of sport speak for itself has not always been roundly appreciated by his producers. "If I've had 50p for the number of times over the years when a producer's said, 'Have we lost Barry?', I'd be rich," he quips. But the importance of silence is critical, according to Davies, who is scornful of those who irritate by talking lots but saying little. "Sometimes you don't need to say anything," he insists, "If you get that right, it adds so much to your broadcast. Sometimes I think I'm a dying breed in that respect."

From that, it could well be deduced that Davies - the prime exponent of the "open" style of commentating - is less than enamoured with the more insistent, work-a-day style of many of his peers. He certainly doesn't believe in the copious preparation so relied upon by his principal BBC rival, John Motson. Davies prefers to live on his wits, a pragmatism that was brought into focus by the 1985 Heysel disaster. "That evening taught me that you have to be prepared to bring whatever you see into the living rooms of the viewers," he recalls. "You can't arrive at a match with a five point plan."

It was no doubt grating to Davies that he never really emerged from the shadow of Motson, the BBC's senior television football commentator since 1979. It may be that he became a victim of his own flexibility as his ability to commentate with authority on hockey, badminton, gymnastics, Wimbledon tennis and even the Royal Tournament fooled producers into believing he was less of a specialist, more of a Jack of all trades. Another possible explanation is that the people's game needed a voice to which the average fan was able to relate. Motson's chirpy enthusiasm and schoolboy fascination for statistics was seen as more the average terrace-tumbler's cup of Bovril than the lumpier broth served up by his university-educated rival. Motty was safer, too. He was far less liable to damage football's brand by lambasting poor play in the way Davies was wont to do.

'I've had a very good rapport with most players and managers, but because I tell the truth as I see it I've sometimes been slightly on the edge.'

But times changed, and the relative success of England's World Cup campaign in 1990 rejuvenated an ailing domestic game and encouraged phalanxes of wax-jackets into the sparkling new all-seater stadia that had sprung up post Hillsborough. Almost overnight footy had turned trendy and Davies' cultivated style appeared to be more in tune with the new chic. To the disappointment of Motson, who was apparently so disgruntled he sloped off on a year's "sabbatical", Davies was granted his moment in the spotlight. In a two-year stint as number-one, he commentated on the 1994 World Cup final, the FA Cup finals of 1995 and 1996 and the Euro '96 semi-final between England and Germany.

Unfortunately for the commentator dubbed by his colleagues "Lord Barrington of Davies", the scholarly dignity that the BBC bosses hoped he would bring to the coverage of football's showpieces turned out to be a double-edged weapon. Cup finals, which often turn out to be soporific affairs, were beginning to take on the bearing of a state occasion. "Davies is in danger of turning into the Tom Fleming of the BBC sports department," wrote Matthew Bond in *The Times*, "you can have too much of that quiet voice of calm." It didn't take long for Motson's more dependable cheer-leading qualities to be recalled from the wilderness.

Freed from the responsibilities of the top job, Davies indulged himself by stepping up his crusade to bring literacy to football commentary. During the 2002 World Cup finals he fired off some statements of particularly advanced verbosity. In Ireland's match against

BBC

## Multi-Broadcast Expert

Barry George Davies was appointed MBE in the 2005 New Year's honours list.

"Those two volleys really could be the story of this match summed up at the end of it."

"Poland 0, England 0, though England are now looking better value for their nil."

"During the Senegal game, I wonder if the French coach [Roger LeMerre] thought the spelling of his name has changed. They certainly had 'le mare'."

"The crowd think that Todd handled the ball. They must have seen something that nobody else did."

"Nicky Butt, he's another aptly named player. He joins things, brings one sentence to an end and starts another."

"No team has worked harder than the winners of this match...or indeed the losers."

"And Watford acknowledge the support of the crowd, indeed the crowd that supported them."

"A peep, peep, peep, another peep, and that's it."

"Cantona's expression saying the whole French dictionary without saying a word."

"The Dutch look like a huge jar of marmalade."

Cameroon, for example, he reported that the ball's proximity to the goal line "couldn't have been more *in extremis*". While a classical education certainly solves some of the puzzles he sets, a practical grounding in geometry is of no less use. When a Croat named Rapaic scuffed a looping shot over the head of the Italian goalkeeper, Davies offered an angle all of his own: "He didn't hit it cleanly but it took a parabola away from Buffon!"

Some viewers' brows furrow just as deeply at his tendency to emulate the gusto of a Moira Stewart in his attempts to pronounce tricky foreign surnames. Ukrainians tuning in would have undoubtedly applauded when the final two syllables of Mikhailichenko were correctly vocalised "chyenka", though how such pedantry can enhance the enjoyment of the remainder of his audience is moot. It represents another line of demarcation with Motson, who pronounces "Jean" like its female equivalent "Jeanne".

Like many of his colleagues, Davies feels the need to justify his complimentary ring-side by offering angles and observations that the camera's lens fails to pick up. To this end he suffers repeated bouts of "Slight Touch Syndrome", an affliction whereby commentators kid themselves that their magic eye has detected a tiny, unscheduled deviation of the ball. Often, however, the slow motion replay suggests that a bus towing a caravan could have easily executed a three-point turn in the gap between the ball and alleged deflector.

It would be unfair to overplay the odd indulgence considering how long Davies has been at the peak of his profession. After graduating from London University, he cut his broadcasting teeth in the late fifties with the British Forces Network in Cologne whilst serving as a lieutenant in the Royal Army Dental Corps. Concerned that his hands were too big for dentistry, he joined BBC radio in 1963 and became a football correspondent for *The Times*. In 1966 he left the corporation and joined ITV, where he made his first television commentary, a Fairs Cup match between Chelsea and AC Milan. The World Cup finals of that year were the first of ten consecutive tournaments to be covered by Davies, a record for a British commentator. He went on to underline his adaptability by covering a variety of sports at the Mexico City Olympics two years later but returned to the BBC. On 9 August 1969 he went to Selhurst Park to describe the first match of a 35 year association with *Match of the Day*.

In 1993 he lent his erudite tones to the University Boat Race, an event that held the personal resonance of his son Mark having coxed Cambridge's Goldie crew in 1992 and 1995. Despite it being a two-horse affair, Davies found it one of his most challenging assignments. "It's far from straightforward," he says, "in fact, the crews are rarely going in a straight line at all. We have to try and convey all the subtleties of steering and strike rate, and so on, as well as letting the viewer know something about the personalities of the crews in each boat." Andrew Baker in *The Daily Telegraph* wrote that the "combination of technical difficulty and tradition makes the Boat Race the Everest of television sports commentary." Davies is too unassuming to blow the trumpet however. "I just enjoy trying to find the right words to match the picture," he says.

With the BBC losing the broadcast rights, 2004 was the last boat race to be covered by Davies. It was a pity that the race was anti-climactic *in extremis*, and his mistake in falsely crediting Oxford with victory and his extended observations on the shape of willow trees suggested that the veteran wordsmith was finally approaching if not his "sell-by date" then possibly his "best before" threshold.

Such fears were dispelled, however, at the opening ceremony of the Athens Olympics when the dependable Davies was turned to as the BBC's only candidate capable of preventing a nation from nodding off at the spectacle of 150 barely distinguishable tricolours inching their way across the screen.

Davies' commentary on Arsenal's one-nil victory over Manchester City on 24 September 2004 was his last on the BBC payroll before leaving to concentrate on other sports as a freelancer. Signing off on a slightly precious note, Lord Barrington cited his increasing marginalisation by a garrulous new crop of commentators as the principal grounds for not renewing his contract. The BBC bade him a warm farewell from the gantry, however. Niall Sloane, the corporation's Head of Football, remarked that his "ability to sum up memorable moments succinctly had been one of the prime distinctions of *Match of the Day* down the years". The pastiche of classic lines that signed off his final programme was of a serenity to make even the "Ave Maria" backing-track sound flat.

What has been described somewhat gushingly as the "interpretative majesty" of Davies should really have been more wisely utilised, with England fans no doubt having been robbed of his informed rationality when the stakes were at their highest. His detractors may have labelled him a "frustrated poet" but, whatever happens, when he finally lays down the microphone for good, nobody will be able to question Barry Davies' status as the last of the great all-rounders.

'People always say to commentators 'What do you think's going to happen?' My answer to that is, 'I don't know, that's why I'm here.'

# Peter Drury

Super-slick Peter Drury is the bright new star of television football commentating. Judging by his vocational genetics, he is amply qualified for success. Like John Motson, he was born the son of a clergyman, like Brian Moore, he first watched football at Gillingham and like Richie Benaud and Raymond Glendenning, he trained to be an accountant.

In 1990, after leaving Hull University with a degree in politics, Drury joined BBC Radio Leeds, where he commentated and reported on football and cricket. Having changed his name to Peter from Cyprian, Drury added golf, tennis and the boat race to his broadcasting portfolio when he joined BBC 5 Live in 1993. During his season commentating for *Match of the Day*, his easy articulacy and a crystal-clear, if slightly tight-chested, enunciation caught the ear of ITV Sport, who enlisted him to help fill the gap on the gantry left by the retirement of Brian Moore.

Like most radio specialists, he struggled to transfer to television. "John Motson was my role model," he says, "I told him I reckoned it had taken me two years to make the change from radio to television – he said that was good because it had taken him five!" The transition's end product nevertheless bore little resemblance to the BBC's headline act. Where Motty sought to add value with factual flotsam, Drury chose to focus on premium phrase-making.

Known to his colleagues as "the man with the words", Drury has since turned the commentary box into dictionary corner. Brian Moore once said, "never use a sixpenny word when a twopenny one would do". Yet Drury's language is so florid, his is normally applying for an overdraft extension by half-time.

He is also that rarest of commentating birds - the committed grammarian. He delights pedants when he insists that "*fewer* than ten minutes have been played" and gets them positively hyperventilating with his efforts to avoid ending a sentence with a dreaded preposition: "Kitson's won his team a corner, on with which they get quickly."

Drury is at his prosaic best when setting the scene as the teams run out onto the pitch. The days of the clever sign off are fading fast, now it's all about jousting with Clive Tyldesley for the most poetic preamble. *The Guardian*'s Martin Kellner, who suggested that Drury had "ingested more back issues of the *Reader's Digest* 'Towards More Colourful Speech' than can possibly be good for you" also enjoys his

## PETER'S PEARLS

"It had to go in but it didn't."

"He'd almost adopted the right position, just half a yard ahead of himself."

"Daei's all alone here, with four Chelsea defenders for company."

"A smoked salmon sandwich of a game if ever there was one."

"And Tottenham ice their sublime cake with the ridiculous."

"And the team in midnight blue have effected an act of daylight robbery."

"The crowd, a cacophony of colour."

"The referee was only five or seven yards from that incident."

EAST KENT GAZETTE

### Off the Wall

Peter Drury, a keen village cricketer, poses while on tour to his old Kent club.

ability to "theme" a commentary. When Arsenal announced they were moving away from their Highbury home, Drury chose to make the stadium's iconic timepiece his *leitmotif.* As the Gunners raced into a two-goal lead against Charlton, Drury observed that "the clock can't catch up with a team it's watched for close on a century," and then fashioned a clever follow-up as their opponents got back into the game, "Down and out at five past three, Charlton are back in it at twenty past four."

Whether Drury's sumptuous phraseology and clever humour are able to compensate for his high-brow bearing and lack of genuine charisma is up for debate. You get the feeling, though, that the Barry Davies franchise is his for the taking.

Brought up in Kent, Drury lives in Hertfordshire with his wife Vicky and three children. When excused commentating duty, he takes in the odd Watford home game.

# Raymond Glendenning

The name Raymond Glendenning is synonymous with that halcyon, pre-transistor era of BBC radio sport. Conjuring flaky images of long shorts, Brylcreemed partings and wooden rattles whirling furiously amid oceans of flat caps, his commentaries are uniquely evocative of the post-war years.

Glendenning spoke as if by appointment to the *Boys' Own Annual*. "By Jove, what a rattling shot by Lawton!" he would typically exclaim in tones as fruity as grandma's summer pudding. As the voice of a bygone age, he seemed even to talk in black and white.

From the late thirties to the early sixties, Glendenning dominated the airwaves. His basic roster comprised rugby and football in the winter and tennis and racing in the summer. In between, he would also find time for boxing, table-tennis, motor-cycling, snooker, ski-ing, greyhound racing and even a spot of show jumping at the 1948 Olympics. The only sport that he declined to cover was cricket, as summer weekends were his only opportunity to rest his weary larynx.

"Handlebar Harry", as he was nicknamed by his colleagues, was born on 25 September 1907 and brought up in Newport, south Wales. He added a chartered accountancy qualification to his University of London Bachelor of Commerce before his theatrical urges took him to the BBC, where he began appearing in radio plays. In 1932, he joined the corporation staff as an announcer, later becoming the organiser of *Children's Hour*. Further career progression followed in 1936 when he was dispatched to Ulster to produce sport, current affairs and magazine programming. Whilst in the province, he became the first broadcaster to commentate on an entire season of football.

When war came, Glendenning was summoned to London to join the OBs unit. Away from the potentially lethal business of reporting the Blitz from the capital's roof-tops, he made his name commentating on sport. He was quick to notice, however, that government restrictions barely accommodated the requirements of the reporter, and artistic integrity rapidly went the same way as silk stockings and knicker elastic. The central problem was the ban on any mention of the weather. The War Department concluded, perhaps understandably, that the announcement of clear skies over southern England was tantamount to a personal invitation to the Luftwaffe. They even prohibited the phrase "greasy ball".

## Weapon of Mass Description

Glendenning's appearance may have suggested a genetic union between Harry Potter and Jimmy Edwards, but his 300 word-a-minute voice - the fastest in the business - was to prove inspirational to a generation of commentators.

There was no better illustration of the difficulties in commentating in wartime conditions than when the army met the Royal Air Force at football on Boxing Day 1942. A pea-soup fog had descended on Elland Road, Leeds, but it was decided that the game should go ahead nevertheless. Although the lack of visibility made commentating impossible, Glendenning was obliged to carry on with a broadcast, lest eavesdroppers in Berlin infer something by his absence. In a masterly piece of concoction, he compensated for the fact that he could only see half the pitch by basing his commentary on the reactions of the crowd.

"It's the Queen Mother's horse over first and now he's being chased by ESB. He's coming to the racecourse. It's Devon Loch for the Queen Mother with ESB in second place then Eagle Lodge in third and Gentle Moya coming very hard indeed. But Devon Loch is holding off ESB with 150 yards to go. And Devon Loch is about half a length ahead. He's stretching away. The hats are coming off. He's three yards clear. It's Devon Loch three yards clear with 100 yards to go! Oh he's gone down! Devon Loch has gone down! He's gone down and been passed by ESB, Gentle Moya in second place and Eagle Lodge coming up into third place, although he's just pipped at the post by Royal Tan. Well there was a man on the inside of the course and Dick Francis is just holding his hand to his head, he can't believe it."

Stanley Matthews was playing that day and at one point in the match, the oooohs and ahhhhs emanating from the far touchline suggested that the wizard of dribble was on one of his mazy runs. Backing his hunch that the full-back would be beaten, Glendenning ventured, "Matthews is centring!" He had got so far ahead of both himself and the crowd that when the cross eventually emerged from the gloom, the commentator was already congratulating the RAF centre-forward, who had been charging down the middle, on his headed goal. Fortunately the ball had read the script and obligingly hit the back of the net.

All too often Glendenning found himself being embarrassingly overtaken by events. Once he missed a goal because he was too busy lighting up one of his famous cigars. Instead of immediately conceding his error he decided to wait until the crowd roared loudly enough for him to be able to pass off as *bona fide* a completely fabricated account of the ball's passage into the goal.

Glendenning's Scottish equivalent, Peter Thomson, also remembered him at Hampden Park describing the flight of Billy Steel's 30 yard screamer for Britain against the Rest of Europe while the ball was being placed on the centre spot for the restart.

Those pieces of creativity summed up the Glendenning commentary philosophy. He was a crafty operator, a showman who was never afraid to ham up the action for the benefit of his audience. A young Harry Carpenter once tackled him about the way he was overdramatising a rather mundane bout of boxing. "Take your point, old boy," replied the senior man, "but it is my job to stop people reaching for that little switch marked 'off'." Notably, this admission did not tally with the official line he touted in his autobiography, where he insisted that "the good commentator only reflects what tension, excitement or emotion lives before him and doesn't attempt to create it himself."

Glendenning's postbag regularly bulged with listeners bemoaning his tendency for getting hopelessly carried away, but he argued that he was merely a helpless victim of the fervour of the crowd and the pace of the action. "Instead of writing to me, try asking the riders to slow down or the players to hold a move up, so as to give me the time to talk at your tempo," he griped in one of his more defensive moments.

Like all top commentators, Glendenning was expert in creating a mental picture for the listener using as few words as possible. He asked readers of his autobiography to consider this twelve-second piece of football commentary:

> "Now Arsenal are attacking and right-winger Kirchen has forced a corner way out on the far left-hand side of the field. He's going to make this one an inswinger; Walker's standing about a yard outside the Portsmouth goal - here it comes now - into the six-yard area - up goes Lewis with his head, and it's a goal, a beautiful goal, right into the corner of the net, and Arsenal have taken the lead."

From this carefully constructed piece of narrative, argued Glendenning, it was possible for the listener to glean ten key facts:

1. Who the teams were;
2. That they were level and that the corner put Arsenal ahead;
3. Who the goal scorer was;
4. That he scored it with his head;
5. The particular path the winger intended the ball to take;
6. The position it reached in front of goal;
7. Why it was ever there, i.e., from a corner;
8. Whose goal was in danger;
9. What the goalkeeper was doing about it, and finally
10. Where on the field this was taking place, looking at it through the commentator's eyes.

Despite his readiness to busk when circumstances demanded, getting right the "associative material" was important to Glendenning. He accumulated facts by getting to know personally many of the major sporting personalities of the day. Considering the huge variety of sports he covered and the lack of a handy internet search engine at his disposal, this was no mean achievement. One whom he could count among his closest personal friends was snooker legend Joe Davis.

In the snooker hall, Glendenning felt at home; when calling the horses he was far less comfortable. His first major commentary, the 1938 Cesarewitch, turned into a disaster when he missed his cue having not focused his binoculars properly. On another occasion he was hauled in front of the stewards for wrongly pre-empting the result of a tight finish.

How he envied the American commentators who, with the sun on their backs, were able to lazily list the dozen or so horses that orbited those tight Kentucky ovals. Things were so different in Britain; irregularly shaped courses, variable weather and occasionally huge fields. Glendenning's hoodoo race was The Cambridgeshire, the Newmarket cavalry charge in which 40-plus runners, some carrying almost identically uniformed jockeys, would split themselves into three or four separate contests across the width of the course. In 1951, Glendenning became so overwhelmed by the scale of his task that he

"Blimey, what's the worry now? He hasn't thrown a punch yet that has really hurt you. Raymond Glendenning said so."
(Daily Herald)

failed to make a single mention of the race's eventual winner, the appropriately named Fleeting Moment.

The occasional miscall of a horse race was brought into sharp context by Glendenning's involvement in the Randolph Turpin affair. One night at Wembley in 1951, he and his summariser W Barrington Dalby could hardly believe what they were witnessing. A game young Briton from Leamington Spa was taking on and more than holding his own against the fighter acknowledged as possibly the best pound-for-pound boxer ever. Despite Turpin's gradual domination of the word championship bout, Glendenning and Dalby's tone remained restrained, mindful as they were that the American could, at any second, unleash an assault that would cut the plucky challenger down in his tracks. When the final bell sounded and Turpin was declared the winner, the BBC switchboard went into warp-drive as irate listeners berated the commentators' "underplaying" of the home boxer's achievement. "A travesty of the truth," carped one correspondent.

The furore was such that the BBC rebroadcast a recording of the fight a week later in an attempt to set the record straight. "I know many listeners think that we gave the wrong impression. If we did I am sorry," said Dalby in a simpering preamble. "I should take the blame," he went on. "In the interval before the last round you remember I said that if Turpin could stage a grandstand finish, he would snatch the verdict. The word I had in mind was 'clinch' and not 'snatch'. 'Clinch' would have certainly represented my verdict at that stage."

In the aftermath, the commentary team was largely exonerated, being found guilty of nothing more sinister than "sitting on the fence". As Isidore Green wrote in the *Sporting Review*, "Glendenning probably based his broadcast on this belief: he did not want to fall into the trap of 'shouting' for Turpin and then suddenly finding himself acclaiming Robinson as the winner."

By the early sixties, the days of the all-round commentator were drawing to a close. Glendenning thought there would always be a place for a communicator who could combine sincerity, background knowledge, vocabulary and light and shade of expression. Unfortunately for him, the order of the day was for subject specialists, with a preference for those who had competed at the highest level.

From 1963, sports commentating's first icon faded from the scene after 24 years at the top. He kept active during his well-earned retirement, indulging his hobbies of water colour painting and snooker. An equally keen golfer, he spent a few years as editorial director of *Golf News*. He died on 23 February 1974.

# Alan Green

BBC 5 Live's Alan Green has the most instantly recognisable voice on British radio. The insistent Ulster tones of Britain's most dogmatic football commentator are guaranteed to bring any casual Saturday afternoon navigation of the medium wave band to an abrupt halt. Love him or loathe him, Green simply locks you on to 909/693: "Ince...midway inside the United half, moving forward..."

Green seems to believe that football's entrenchment in the national psyche gives him *carte blanche* to bite the hand that feeds. "This game is abysmal," he'd wail, "somebody get me OUTTA here!" He readily concedes he has no remit to sell the game. "No one ever tells me to imply that something is good when it patently isn't," he declares in his book *The Green Line*, "you must be able to trust me to tell the truth".

Unsurprisingly, Green's perceived negativity has left him isolated. *The Guardian's* Martin Kellner called him "the curmudgeon in the stand you don't want to sit behind" while other tender egos, mostly from within the game, contend he is Lucifer in headphones.

Aside from the referees - a profession he brands as being "populated by far too many poseurs and prima donnas" - Green is probably mistrusted most by the managers. Joe Royle, for one, took umbrage at accusations that he had sacrificed his Everton team's footballing soul in favour of a coarse "route-one" formula for Premiership survival. Green was later equally uncompromising about Royle's prospects of preserving Manchester City's status in the top-flight and, after the manager cried persecution in the media, became a victim of threats from disgruntled elements of the Maine Road faithful.

His relationship with Manchester United's manager Sir Alex Ferguson disintegrated from one of amicable co-operation to undiluted vitriol. Their mutual loathing, which elevated Green to hero status amongst United haters, is one of the most fractious sporting spats of recent years. According to the commentator, their bad blood goes back to an incident after a televised Cup match at The Dell when the Manchester United manager rounded on him with an unexpected burst of Glaswegian invective, "You don't pick my team you bastard!" They have hardly exchanged a word since.

Much of the rancour relates to a perception within Old Trafford that Green is a closet Liverpool fan. It is an accusation he emphatically refutes, insisting his only footballing allegiance is to Linfield of the Irish

> *Beckham places the ball on the spot... Oh that's awful. Absolutely awful.*

## Says it how he sees it

Alan Green won't be lamenting Sir Alex's Ferguson's retirement, when it eventually comes. "Football will undoubtedly miss him. I won't. I'm ready to crack open the champagne."

League. Insinuations of bias erupted into acrimony when Green branded United's rumbustious captain, Roy Keane, a "lout", leading him to be vilified in the club's fanzines. A tetchy feud ensued, with Ferguson refusing to grant interviews to 5 Live.

Green's conviction in the superiority of his own instinctive style chimes with his admission that he's not the easiest to work with. "I bridle against those who labour over commentaries for three days beforehand," he told the *Evening Standard* in a thinly-veiled swipe at television's John Motson, who had just rejoined the radio staff. "If a fact is important I should know it anyway. I'm not interested in telling listeners that this is the fourth goal scored by Smith on a Wednesday."

When BSkyB's Andy Gray railed against "opinionated radio commentators who had never played the game", Green robustly defended his position. "Through his arrogance he is offending 99.5 per cent of the football watching public, including his own audience," he countered. "He ignores one of the game's essentials, namely that it is about opinions."

In October 2004, the anti-Green lobby would no doubt have enjoyed the commentator's censure by the media regulator Ofcom after he put the words "Me no cheat" into the mouth of Manchester United's Eric Djemba-Djemba during a dispute with a referee. The BBC, while conceding that the insinuation that a black man could not speak grammatical English was ill-judged, defended Green, recommending that his laboured attempt at humour be seen in the context of his "commitment to eradicate racism from football." The satirical rottweilers at *Private Eye* were not to be thrown of the scent, however, promptly reminding their readers of a match a few months earlier when Green referred to Manchester City's Sun-Jihai as "number seventeen – that will be Chicken Chow Mein."

Yet this sledge-hammer subtlety conceals a surprisingly emotional dimension to Green's personality. The horrors of the Hillsborough disaster in 1989, for example, left him traumatised. His passion also manifests itself in his championing of the traditions of the game, whose great institutions, such as the FA and European Champions' Cup, he feels are being demeaned for the sake of greed and self-interest on the part of football's governing bodies.

The acidic subjectivity that has become his trademark is probably the reason that he never achieved his goal of reaching the top echelons of television news journalism at the BBC. While he concedes that he has the dream job of thousands, he bears the guilt that commentating was never his calling - his heart was set instead on the editor's chair of the BBC's *Nine O'Clock News*.

The path to meeting his lofty ambition started conventionally enough. After graduating in modern history at Queen's University in Belfast, he joined the *Belfast Telegraph*, where he filed weekly reports on hockey and cricket. With his career still smoking frustratingly on the launch pad, he almost took a job with the Inland Revenue before, in 1975, he won a much-coveted place as a BBC news trainee.

After four years treading water in various attachments to local radio and regional television, Green moved to BBC Northern Ireland Sport where he finally got his big break. Ulster's senior television football commentator, George Hamilton, was leaving and his boss was short of cover for the Irish Cup final. "Not a chance," replied Green. "I may be a presenter and a reporter, but I'll never be a commentator."

After eventually agreeing to step into the breach, he failed to share the conviction of his superiors that he was made of the right stuff. In February 1982, having moved over to BBC Radio Sport, he again had to be virtually frog-marched to the microphone, this time for the home international between England and Northern Ireland. He found sitting next to the masterly Peter Jones a wholly dispiriting experience and lamented that he never wanted to pick up a lip-mic again. The mandarins of radio sport nevertheless persisted with their reluctant charge and, in 1984, Green was entrusted with the final stages of a top-flight fixture for the first time.

On the retirement of Bryon Butler, the role of football correspondent was assumed by Mike Ingham, leaving Green free rein not only to vent his opinions, but to diversify into other sports, notably rowing and golf. Indeed, he cites his experiences green-side at the Ryder Cup and the exhilaration of calling home Steven Redgrave for his fifth gold medal at the Sydney Olympics as some of his most memorable commentary moments.

Green may have the face of a "well-fed weasel", as described by a *Times* profile, but his voice is definitely king of the jungle. Unalloyed by twenty-plus years' residence in Cheshire, his rich Northern Irish accent dilutes the homogeneous prefects' common-room tones that otherwise dominate 5 Live's football coverage. In fact, a scientific study found that, in standard trim, Green's voice had an "intimate quality" that "oozed sex appeal", although at full throttle, as at France '98, it takes on a much more primeval allure: "Owen with pace coming forward again. Owen is still going. Owen into the penalty area! Owen scores an absolutely fantastic goal by Michael Owen!"

The voice has probably grated on too many executives' ears for it to be promoted up the commentary food chain to television. Publicly, Green states that there is no reason why he would ever want to commentate on the box but, beneath the bravado, it is understood that he is irritated that the invitation has never come.

The common stock of football broadcasting would suffer, however, if Green left for television. Radio is the most effective platform for this self-confessed moaner to articulate the game's conscience and, thanks to his fearless dissension, his television counterparts are now finally finding it easier to tell it how it really is.

Few commentators polarise opinion more than Green. There will be those who bridle at a character who, after wallowing in so much self-doubt, now brags that commentating is an "easy job". There will be others, most exhibiting subconsciously the prickliness of the justly accused, who refuse to accept the painful home truths they are being administered. Yet, even his staunchest critic would have to concede that, in the twenty-first century, football undoubtedly needs its Greens.

'History is made! I don't care what you're doing, stop it! If you're not standing, get up on your feet! Applaud Tim Foster and James Cracknell, cheer for Matthew Pinsent, but take the roof off for the greatest British Olympian of all time, Steve Redgrave!'

# Tony Gubba

Tony Gubba has been "King of the Round-Up" since the early seventies. Yet despite boasting an eclectic portfolio that includes football, cycling, squash, table-tennis, ice skating and even bobsleighing, he has unfortunately so far failed to extend his repertoire to test cricket, thus denying a full generation of sports anchors the opportunity of introducing "Gubba from the 'Gabba".

Born in Manchester in 1943, Gubba grew up in Blackpool, beginning his career in local newspapers before becoming a staff reporter for the *Daily Mirror*. His first television work was as a newscaster at Southern Television in Southampton, where the influence of resident linkman and part-time *World of Sport* presenter Fred Dinenage presumably led to the adoption of the classic sweep-over Gubba coiffeur.

After moving back up north to become a Liverpool-based BBC correspondent, Gubba got himself noticed by the network when he reported on a local horse named Red Rum on the morning of the 1973 Grand National. Back then, highlights of the race were shown on *Match of the Day* and, with Red Rum having won, the programme's producer wanted Gubba's piece to head up the show. Unfortunately no sound had been recorded and he had to be flown to London to revoice his report live sitting next to David Coleman.

In the wake of that unconventional debut, Gubba became the Sam Kydd of commentators: familiar in myriad roles, but only ever a bit-part player. He has never had the opportunity to show all his moves as his typical C-list fixture allocation generally coincided with the bell for last orders at *Match of the Day*. While skips-full of his work have doubtlessly been bulldozed away from the cutting room floor over the years, he has occasionally struck gold. Most notable was the time he was sent to Hillsborough to cover an FA Cup replay between Sheffield Wednesday and Chelsea in the knowledge that *Sportsnight* would be designating it a paltry two minutes. In what Gubba describes as the most memorable game he had ever commentated on, Wednesday raced into a 3-0 first half lead. Chelsea then staged a remarkable comeback to lead 4-3, only for the home team to equalise in the dying seconds. *Sportsnight* stretched the two-minute slot to 36.

In terms of the World Cup, it has again fallen to Gubba to gobble up John Motson and Barry Davies' leftovers, a task he has undertaken for every finals tournament since 1974. Covering the lesser-known

## GUBBA GAFFES

"Nick Holmes also got two today as Southampton won 3-0 at Leeds. Nick Holmes got the other."

"…but Arsenal are quick to credit Bergkamp for laying on 75 per cent of their nine goals."

"The ball must be as slippery as a wet baby."

"He was in the right place at the right time, but he might have been elsewhere on a different afternoon."

"So often the pendulum continues to swing with the side that has just pulled themselves out of the hole."

"Wigan Athletic are certain to be promoted barring a mathematical tragedy."

"The ageless Teddy Sheringham, 37 now…"

## Sportsnight with Gubba

A 30-year-old Gubba in his *Sportsnight* publicity photo. He presented the programme full-time for a year from 1973 and then rotated with Harry Carpenter until 1978.

BBC

footballing nations presents its own difficulties, not least the pronunciation of exotic names and the identification of unfamiliar players. His most uncomfortable moment came during the 1998 finals, when the Rumanians emerged from the tunnel for the match against Tunisia sporting identical bleach blond hairstyles. Alas it is not always the case that it "takes one to know one".

With a voice that lacks the grunt of a David Coleman or the rasp of a Hugh Johns, Gubba has never quite been able to rid himself of the perennial bridesmaid tag. Nevertheless, as he winds down a successful career, Gubba has garnered a reputation as not only BBC Sport's most efficient and uncomplaining workhorse but also as perhaps its most incisive reporter.

In his own time, Gubba finds relaxation from fly-fishing and his photographs and articles often find their way into *Trout Salmon* magazine.

# Reg Gutteridge

Few understand the fight game better than Reg Gutteridge, ITV's boxing commentator for almost 40 years. His appreciation of the noble art is facilitated by the purest of blood-lines. His grandfather, whom he idolised, had been a famous bare-knuckle fighter, while his father and uncle were the best-known corner-men of their day. "I was almost literally born with a gumshield in my mouth," he says.

Young Reg, too, "coulda been a contenda" had he not lost half his left leg in Normandy in 1944. Ignoring the recommended procedure, he jumped off the front of a Sherman tank and landed on a German "Schu" mine. His nonchalant reaction, as he lay in the nearby flowerbed into which he had been blown, had "mere flesh wound" echoes of *Monty Python and the Holy Grail*. "Give Jerry an inch and he'll take a foot!" he recalls groaning to himself.

Gutteridge would go on to extract full comedy value from his disability. In an attempt to prove that not all Limeys were soft, he astounded Sonny Liston by plunging an ice-pick ten times into his apparently healthy limb. Further frolics followed when swimming in the sea on holiday. "Sharks!" he was wont to holler, as he hopped his way back onto the beach.

Having bought himself a wartime "Blighty", Gutteridge re-joined the London *Evening News*, where he had run errands before his army call-up. With "running" now not exactly an option, he became the paper's greyhound tipster and eventually its boxing correspondent.

A street-wise, if slightly displaced Cockney from Islington, he spoke the boxers' language. His rapport with Muhammad Ali was so strong that the champion even granted him an interview between rounds. In his 1973 fight against Rudi Lubbers, Ali called Gutteridge over to excuse his lacklustre performance: "I just want to apologise to all my friends in Great Britain for not putting this bum away yet…I'm getting old and tired, so you'll just have to excuse me please folks!" Their unlikely bond was not easily broken. In 1989, when Gutteridge was in hospital, close to death from blood poisoning, he woke to see the great champion on his knees at the end of the bed in prayer.

While Ali may have appreciated the Englishman's courtesy and good manners, Gutteridge was to prove himself one of commentating's straight talkers. When he told a ring interloper to "f__ off" while he was trying to secure a post-fight interview with Mike Tyson, there was the predictable flurry of complaints. A decade earlier he did far better, outraging an entire nation when at a Wembley greyhound meeting he commented on the plastic carpet used to protect the stadium against dog litter. "It's a pity they couldn't have done the same for those Scottish supporters," he suggested in reference to the tartan army's recent rampage at football's HQ. A long and successful commentary partnership with Scotland's former world champion Jim Watt was useful in rebuilding bridges north of the border.

An untrained ear would have assumed that Gutteridge had been in attendance for every headline bout of the seventies and eighties. The ITV coffers were, alas, not that capacious and he was obliged to dub many of his commentaries from a monitor back in London.

Superimposing the commentator's presence on transatlantic contests was an unscientific affair, and when a soundless recording of a fight in Puerto Rico had to be broadcast with Shoreditch crowd noises, *World of Sport* viewers could only have assumed that Dick van Dyke and family had taken ringside seats. ITV even went out and bought a bell for the contest, only for an over-eager floor manager to ring it a few seconds early. "They haven't heard the bell!" counter-punched the commentator, coming hard off the ropes. "As it was 9,000 miles away and a week later, I'm not surprised!" he later giggled.

Something similar happened when Ali fought Trevor Berbick in Bermuda. Although Gutteridge had again been advertised as being "ringside", audible public address announcements of "the hare is running" betrayed his true location as being a snowy Haringey dog track. Armchair fight fans would also have been surprised to hear the voice of a Jamaican refreshments lady interrupt another of his "live" studio commentaries. "You've got to have something, man," he remembers her saying as she thrust a banana into his mouth, "you look like you need it!"

This is what is known
in the trade as...

Dealing with inappropriate sound-effects was a cake-walk in comparison with the day in Maryland in March 1980 when he was required to commentate on four bouts – all from different venues – in one highly stressful session. While waiting at ringside for Sugar Ray Leonard's title defence against Britain's Dave "Boy" Green to start, he talked over picture feeds of Larry Holmes versus Leroy Jones, Eddie Gregory versus Marvin Johnson and Mike Weaver versus John Tate. Matters were complicated by the fact that commercial breaks left him dependent on visual prompts from technicians for descriptions of the usual inter-round close-ups. The Maryland crowd was making such a din during the Leonard-Green undercard, however, that he could only hear his instructions through his headphones by covering his ears in a towel.

Although Leonard was to do the commentator a favour by stopping Green in four rounds, a mentally exhausted Gutteridge had by that time already dubbed 34. "I still shiver and break out in a sweat when I think about it," he wrote.

The unique intensity of the fight game makes the boxing commentator's job one of the most hazardous. On an outing to New York's Yankee Stadium in 1976 for the Ali – Ken Norton fight, for instance, Gutteridge was almost crushed and suffocated in a *mêlée* caused by a strike at the local police department. On another occasion he was attacked by the umbrella-wielding mother of an amateur boxer, who had mistaken him for his BBC sparring partner Harry Carpenter.

There were nevertheless moments of light relief, such as the time he was in Rome for the world amateur championships and boarded an excursion bus that he though was going to a wine tasting. It turned out to be a service taking the Irish team to the Vatican and, before he could say "Jesus, Mary and Joseph", he was being ushered into a room for an unexpected audience with the Pope. "Forgive us our press passes," the non-practising Protestant remembers commenting to himself.

In 1980, the *Evening News* suffered a TKO at the hands of its rival the *Evening Standard* and a bitter Gutteridge was made redundant after 40 years. Yet the paper's demise allowed him to devote more time to a jamboree of televised mega-bouts featuring a trio of extravagantly skilled middleweights - Thomas Hearns, Roberto Duran and Marvin Hagler – who took it in turns to try to dethrone the regal Leonard. Gutteridge's profile was raised even further in the nineties when an exciting crop of home-grown talent in Michael Watson, Nigel Benn and Chris Eubank exploded onto the scene. In 1995, with boxing having reached a pinnacle of popularity, his 50 year stint as the sport's number one scribe was recognised with an OBE.

The tale of the tape had the BBC at a marked budgetary and technical advantage but, in Gutteridge, ITV had a commentator whose resilience and ingenuity helped the network punch well above its weight. It was fitting, then, that in 2002 he shared with Harry Carpenter the Royal Television Society's Lifetime Achievement award. When it came to bringing the nation the thrills and controversies of the fight game, whether at the microphone or at the typewriter, nobody gave better value for money than Reg Gutteridge.

# Brian Johnston

Brian Johnston was in his own way a commentating genius. His natural effervescence and irrepressible sense of fun helped to re-mould the BBC's coverage of cricket and turned *Test Match Special* into one of the great institutions of British radio. Some may have dismissed him as an overgrown schoolboy with an incorrigibly sweet tooth, but behind the image of a bumbling amateur lay a consummate professional whose contribution to broadcasting was immense.

"Johnners" was born in Little Berkhamsted on 24 June 1912 and brought up, in some style, in a Queen Anne mansion near Hitchin in Hertfordshire. The pivotal event of his early life occurred in 1922 when his City merchant father was drowned in the sea off Bude whilst attempting to save his sister. Johnners' biographer, Tim Heald, believed that the irrepressible jollity he subsequently radiated was partly his way of dealing with the tragedy and that a complicated, even mysterious personality lurked beneath the perpetually suave and urbane exterior.

Johnners was no scholar, but a combination of the old boy network and a talent for sport gained him entrance to read history at New College, Oxford. After three years of practical jokes and self-indulgence on the cricket pitch, he left with a class of degree that would inevitably propel him into the career *cul-de-sac* of the family coffee business. The young Johnners knew he would never aspire to the daily grind. After five years of menial paper shuffling – which included eighteen months of virtual paralysis after contracting acute peripheral neuritis in Brazil - he was granted a merciful release by the advent of war.

Johnners served with distinction in the Guards Armoured Division where, despite a tenuous grasp of the workings of a Sherman tank, he spent four years as a supremely popular technical adjutant. In 1945 he won the Military Cross for his part in keeping the Allied advance on track. "His own dynamic personality, coupled with his untiring determination and cheerfulness under fire," recorded his CO's citation, "have inspired those around him always to reach the highest standards of efficiency." With typical humility, Johnners turned untypically taciturn whenever asked to recall the gallant deeds of his past.

His war service over, Johnners, a frustrated music-hall artiste, sought to vent his thespian urges. First stop was the BBC and, after a successful audition button-holing passers-by in Oxford Circus, he joined the OBs unit in January 1946. The following month, his broadcasting career was

**Show me
your googly**

Johnners (*left*) with Jim Laker,
who was to succeed him in the
television commentary box.

to start quite literally with a bang. Armed with the roving microphone that was to become part of his apparel for the next 31 years, he was dispatched to the ladies' lavatory in St James' Park to flush out a story on the detonation of an unexploded bomb in the nearby lake.

Johnners cut his broadcasting teeth on "live" reporting from London's theatreland. In the process of spicing his half-hour dispatches from West End musicals with Terry Woganesque incidentals, he quickly picked up the fundamentals of commentary. "It was an admirable way to learn," he recalled, "because it was necessary to be slick and economical with words and to time one's comments so as not to clash with the music and singing."

The "Let's Go Somewhere" segment of the popular *In Town Tonight* programme, in which he performed all manner of daft and daring stunts, turned him into one of the first television stars. The variety of his escapades - one week he would be being lifted out of the sea by a helicopter and the next he would be singing in the street dressed as a tramp – gave him a useful practical grounding in live broadcasting.

In March 1946, Johnners had a call from Ian Orr-Ewing, the head of television OBs, asking him if he would like to have a try at commentating on the forthcoming test matches at Lord's and The Oval. He and Orr-Ewing had played cricket together before the war and

Johnners, a cricketing fanatic, could not believe his luck. The bug had first bitten him at prep school in Eastbourne, where he had looked on in awe at the batting exploits of fellow pupil and future war hero Douglas Bader. Suitably inspired, he developed into a competent wicket-keeper at Eton and was unfortunate not to be selected to appear in the annual fixture against Harrow at Lord's.

The fact that the summer of 1946 was damper than average meant that Johnners was obliged to take a crash-course in the art of filling. Although the MCC placed firm restrictions on the length of transmissions, he still found himself having to ad-lib his way through seemingly endless interruptions for rain. He may have been denied the fall-back of a well-stocked archive (the pre-war footage larder contained a measly four test matches) but Johnners proved himself to be a state-of-the-art talking machine.

During the fifties, the BBC-TV commentary team was led by the regular trinity of Johnners, Peter West and E W (Jim) Swanton. The first significant cricketing moment to be caught by the cameras had been Donald Bradman's final test match in 1948, an occasion judged by Johnners to have been one of the most poignant he had witnessed. Five years later, when England won back the Ashes, sentiment was set aside as Johnners ascended into delirium. "It's the Ashes, It's the Ashes! England have won the Ashes!"

In 1952, the new Holme Moss transmitter near Manchester became operational and all six test grounds came within range. Technology was improving rapidly and new angles and close-ups were now being routed through the commentary box. Cricket suddenly lost its mystery as a snooping zoom lens enabled an overjoyed Johnners to "pick" the wily Sonny Ramadhin's leg-break.

In regard to Lobby Lotbinière's first commandment ("thou shalt not speak unless adding to the picture"), Johnners' style was quite unsuited to television. But he was astute enough to realise that cricket was often dull and would require subtle repackaging if it were to retain the attention of the casual viewer. By selectively developing aspects of the wider spectacle and mixing it with his own brand of impish humour, Johnners earned the appreciation of his audience and, initially, the respect of his superiors. "A most satisfactory commentary," reported his producer Michael Henderson following a test match transmission in 1952, "without any fireworks or unnecessary talk, he is always able to lift our interest whenever he takes over."

As broadcasting techniques became more sophisticated, so too did the expectations of cricket's television audience. By the early sixties, the

'There's Neil Harvey standing at leg-slip with his legs wide apart waiting for a tickle.'

mood demanded less waffle and more analysis and Johnners, whose approach sometimes relegated the cricket to the status of backing-track to his personal meanderings down memory lane, was becoming increasingly exposed. Peter Dimmock, by then the General Manager of outside broadcasts, was beginning to lose patience with his commentator's flippant manner. Johnners' "unprofessionalism" when interviewing the glamorous wife of the commentary box scorer as an Ashes test petered out to a draw behind them turned out to be a damaging *faux pas*.

When Johnners was invited to become the BBC's first Cricket Correspondent in 1963, it appeared to be a promotion. However, in reality, the broadcasting mandarins were nudging aside the old guard ready to install the new order in the shape of former players Richie Benaud and later Jim Laker. In 1970, with the transition complete, Johnners heard on the grapevine that his services were, after 24 years, surplus to requirements at BBC-TV.

While he was bitter about the way the decision was handled, Johnners tried to remain philosophical about the reasoning that lay behind it. "(We) had become a happy group of friends who enjoyed our cricket and hoped that viewers did the same," he mourned. "It was natural that we probably gave an 'amateurish' atmosphere to the box with too many jokes and friendly asides and back-chat."

The long walk back to the pavilion was interrupted, happily, by an invitation to join BBC radio full-time. So began 23 years of organised mayhem with *Test Match Special* that were to be the happiest and most contented of Johnners' life. By assuming the juvenile lead (in mentality if not in years) of the *TMS* cast, he had finally satisfied his cravings to "perform". The *TMS* statistician, Bill Frindall, recalled Johnners' arrival in radio as being like a breath of fresh air: "Brian Johnston transformed the commentary box from a fairly dour and disciplined broadcasting studio to a cavern of cake and comedy."

The levity introduced by Johnners knew no heights. Rejoicing in their new nicknames, the *TMS* team began to swap *doubles entendres* and Christmas cracker jokes like a gaggle of fourth formers on summer camp. Cricket fans were quick to respond and followed Johnners over in droves, confounding the broadcasting gurus by keeping *TMS* turned up with the sound on their televisions turned down. Listeners enjoyed the banter so much that on many occasions *TMS*'s audience actually increased during the breaks for rain.

Johnners' chief co-conspirator was Jonathan "Aggers" Agnew, the former Leicestershire and England seam bowler who had arrived at

## THE ETERNAL SCHOOLBOY

"The bowler's Holding, the batsman's Willey."

"Bad luck on Peter. He's obviously in great pain and has probably sprained his ankle. It's especially bad luck as he is here on his honeymoon with his pretty young wife. Still he'll probably be alright tomorrow, if he sticks it up tonight."

"Henry Horton's got a funny sort of stance. It looks as if he's shitting on a sooting stick."

"Welcome to Worcester where you've just missed seeing Barry Richards hit one of Basil D'Oliveira's balls clean out of the ground."

"As you came over, Ray Illingworth has just relieved himself at the pavilion end."

**Crowning glory**

At Hyde Park with
Bernard Braden describing the
Coronation procession in 1953.

*TMS* via local radio. The pair were on such a dangerously similar wavelength that on one occasion their 40-second giggling fit activated an automatic fault detection system which switched off a transmitter in the Midlands. The trigger phrase had been Johnners' description of Javed Miandad "opening up his legs like a croquet hoop and tickling a ball down to fine leg."

The commentary box also ground to a halt the day Johnners received a copy of the Israeli Cricket Association's handbook, which happened to list the pair who had scored the record last-wicket stand for the national team. The names Solly Katz and Benny Wadwaker caused such an outbreak of mirth that Don Mosey, although oblivious to the joke, was unable to continue at the microphone.

Johnners' "corpsing" entered broadcasting legend in 1991 when he and Agnew reviewed the wicket of Ian Botham, who had trodden on his stumps in attempting to hook a Curtly Ambrose bouncer. "He more or less tried to do the splits over it and, unfortunately, the inner part of his thigh must have just removed the bail," summarised Johnners. "He just didn't quite get his leg over," added Aggers. The archives endlessly replay the meltdown that ensued as two highly educated men, who should really have known better, dissolved into hysterics. Long-suffering *TMS* producer Peter Baxter had to ban them from performing the close of play summary together.

Practical japery and leg-pulls became the new currency of the commentary box and Johnners revelled in testing the composure of his

**On the hair again**

Four TMS stalwarts on duty at Lord's. From the top, Trevor Bailey, Johnners, Alan McGilvray and statistician Bill Frindall.

colleagues. One story, surely apocryphal, concerned Rex Alston and a match between the MCC and Pakistan in 1962. Among the touring party was a bowler whose name, for Johnners, held category-A titter potential: Afaq Hussain. By the time the MCC's Barry Knight came out to bat, Johnners had confused Alston into believing that Hussain, although not selected, was coming on to bowl. "We are going to see Afaq to Knight at the Nursery End", promised the commentator with what should have been a nudge and a wink. "What am I saying?" wailed Alston as the penny dropped, "he's not even playing!"

In moving *TMS* down-market, Johnners resuscitated a sagging format. For the programme to survive, the tone had to remain populist and Johnners enjoyed gently teasing any perpetrator of pretence or unnecessary intellectualism. Christopher Martin-Jenkins was once brought to heel for using the word "apogee" to describe the flight of a ball. "Apogee?!" scoffed Johnners, "What a good word. I wonder what he is talking about?"

The relationship that developed between the *TMS* team and its audience bordered on the familial. One peckish commentator's throwaway remark about the general lack of sustenance brought out the mothering instinct in one listener, who sent in a cake. It was the first of a cavalcade of confections to compromise the waistbands of the *TMS* team. A dentist was so worried about their sugar intake that he sent in a toothbrush.

The tomfoolery disguised what an excellent commentator Johnners was. He may not have had the lavish phrase-making capability of John Arlott but he had the priceless knack of being able to decipher for everybody the infinite complexities of cricket. He spoke a universal language. If you couldn't tell the difference between short backward square leg and a slice of Victoria sponge, then Johnners was your man. What's more, he never missed a ball. Even at the age of 81, he showed himself to be as bright-eyed and perceptive as a man a quarter his age.

Johnners was also an extremely skilled interviewer. His ability to listen and appear interested on a broad range of topics was the secret behind the continued success of the *Down Your Way* programme which he presented on Radio 4 from 1972 (the year he was supposed to retire) to 1987.

Despite his years, Johnners seemed to draw on inexhaustible energy reserves. It was, therefore, with a sense of shock as well as sadness that the world of cricket and beyond learnt of the news of his heart attack in December 1993. Typically, he had been in a taxi en-route to yet another speaking engagement.

When he died in January 1994, prime minister John Major was moved to state that "summers would never be the same again". In some ways England would never be the same again either as Johnners, with his acute sense of tradition, manners and civility represented many of the things that were great about the old country.

Few commentators have been so sorely missed. Gone but never to be forgotten, as Christopher Martin-Jenkins' tribute makes clear:

"Brian's voice will forever be fresh in the BBC archives and his spirit, along with the message that cricket, like life, was a gift to be cherished, will live on."

# Peter Jones

The BBC's radio football commentators have never had it particularly easy. That they were allowed regular access to the national game in the first place was due only to a change of heart on the part of the Football League. In the pre-war years, live coverage had been banned in the belief it was a knife at the throat of attendances. The clubs even voted to prohibit live coverage of the FA Cup final and, bizarrely, numbers on players' shirts.

Describing a football match for radio can be one of the most exacting disciplines in commentary. The swashbuckling tempo of the English league habitually causes embarrassing misfires even in the most well-oiled oratory machine. Back in the more sedate days of the fifties, when the likes of Stanley Matthews and Tom Finney addressed the ball with the deference normally afforded only to a holy relic, the commentators still struggled to keep up with play. Like the flat-footed full-backs of the day, they bought every dummy, every shimmy. So overwhelmed was Raymond Glendenning, for instance, that he reckoned he was able to mention only one pass in three.

In the combat zone of the centre third of the pitch, commentators learned to make full use of the busk. This involved freewheeling through the midfield exchanges by offering the listener background paraphernalia as recommended by Lobby Lotbinière's commentary guidelines. At the other extreme was every commentator's nightmare: the non-event. Pity the individual who came to the microphone for the final quarter of a match whose outcome had already been decided.

The broadcaster who positively thrived on these challenges was the great Peter Jones of *Sport on Two*. Blessed with a wonderfully lilting Welsh voice, Jones was a high calibre wordsmith who painted such vivid aural pictures that the football was occasionally merely incidental. "He could make a dull game bearable and an exciting one almost unbearable," commented the producer David Hatch.

Jones was so fond of adding colour to dull passages of play that he would happily fabricate points of interest. During one match, his young apprentice Alan Green remembered the great care he took to describe a gentleman in a tall blue and white striped top hat a couple of rows in front of them. Green scoured vainly the seats in question, only to realise that this phantom fan was just another of Jones' decorative devices.

The Heysel and Hillsborough disasters of 1985 and 1989 illustrated the other side of Jones' great talent. His despairing descriptions of the tragedies as they unfolded not only graphically etched their horror on all those who heard them, but echoed the private heartache of a broadcaster who was witnessing his beloved game being brought to its knees. His sombre summary of that spring day when 95 Liverpool fans lost their lives in Sheffield was one of the most poignant of reflections on sporting tragedy:

I think the biggest irony now is that the sun is shining and Hillsborough's quiet. And over there to the left, the green Yorkshire hills. I don't necessarily want to reflect on Heysel, but I was there that night broadcasting with Emlyn Hughes. And he was sitting behind me this afternoon, and after half an hour of watching stretchers going out and oxygen cylinders being brought in, he touched me on the shoulder and said, "I can't take it any more." And Emlyn Hughes left. And two other items I think of sitting here now in the sunshine. The gymnasium here at Hillsborough is being used as a mortuary for the dead and at this moment, stewards have got cartons and little paper bags, they're gathering up the belongings of the spectators, some of whom died. And there are red and white scarves of Liverpool and red and white bobble hats of Liverpool and red and white rosettes of Liverpool. And nothing else out there on the enclosure where all the deaths occurred. And the sun shines now.

At a time when the national game was going through its gravest crisis, the BBC was understandably desperate to retain the talents of its most incisive correspondent. So, as Jones neared the compulsory retirement age of 60, the corporation broke with convention by offering him a new contract. Sadly, on 2 April 1990, just two months after his sixtieth birthday, Jones collapsed and died whilst commentating on the university boat race.

That day, the BBC lost perhaps its most natural broadcaster. Fluent, eloquent and knowledgeable, he had been given a voice that could communicate a hundred words with just an inflexion. His commentaries were uniquely tonal, almost choral in quality. It was as if he were speaking in chimes.

When they needed to be, they could be as dramatic as they were subtle. When Manchester United took the lead against Benfica in extra time in the 1968 European Cup final, Jones was almost Wagnerian in his delivery: "A chance here for George Best! George Best is through! He goes round Enriqué! He must score! George Best must score! George Best has scored!"

Jones, a Cambridge football blue, was recruited for BBC Radio by Angus Mackay while he was teaching at Bradfield School. A year after joining the *Sports Report* team as an assistant, Jones was posted to the north-east to cover the first round matches in the 1966 World Cup. He had the initiative to compile a dossier on the unknown North Koreans. "Not only did they all look alike," he recalled, "but their names - tongue-twisters indeed - all sounded alike." When the unfancied debutants progressed surprisingly to the next round, Jones, with his dossier, found himself to be "one of the most popular men in the sports room."

The disappointment at not being involved in the latter stages of the tournament was forgotten when he was promoted to join Maurice Edelston in the main commentary team for the 1970 finals following Brian Moore's departure to ITV. The 1974 final was particularly memorable. After commentating on West Germany's 2-1 win over Holland he was invited by Franz Beckenbauer, a personal friend, to join the Germans' table at the victory banquet.

Jones commentated on every FA Cup final from 1968 to 1989. He spoke his most famous line in 1983 when, with only seconds to go, Brighton's Gordon Smith stood poised to smite the winning goal past Gary Bailey in the Manchester United goal. The words "And Smith must score!" (followed in quick order by "And Smith hasn't scored") are worn almost as a badge of honour on the south coast, and indeed by fans of would-be giant killers everywhere who share the gnawing frustration of "what might have been".

Jones' other regular sports were swimming and Wimbledon tennis. He attended five Olympic games, five World Cups, and described numerous state occasions, from the funeral of Lord Mountbatten to royal weddings and the state opening of parliament.

One of his favourite expressions in football commentary was to describe a player "walking tall". Peter Jones bestrode BBC radio like a giant among broadcasters.

# Jim Laker

Jim Laker - the voice of English cricket in the seventies - was perhaps the greatest of all off-spinners. His feat of taking 19 Australian wickets for 90 runs in the fourth Ashes Test at Old Trafford in 1956 will live on as one of the most remarkable sporting achievements of the twentieth century.

Once he retired in the early sixties with 193 test scalps to his credit, Laker was surprised to be invited by Bryan Cowgill, the BBC's head of sport, to join the television commentary team. Although Laker was shy, modest and generally undemonstrative, Cowgill felt his vast technical knowledge and kudos as a national sporting hero would counteract the increasingly outdated Corinthian frippery of the likes of Brian Johnston. "Anyone who had taken 19 wickets against Australia can walk on water," commented the star-struck producer Nick Hunter. "We treated Jim, as was his due, with considerable respect."

Laker took his new role extremely seriously and quickly established a friendly but also highly professional partnership with his old Ashes foe, Richie Benaud. Their shared astuteness, dry wit and ability to recall a pithy anecdote at the drop of a hat set the benchmark for television cricket commentary for the next generation.

Although a Yorkshireman, Laker had played his cricket down south for Surrey and then Essex. With a foot in both camps, he was once sent a letter by a northern viewer accusing him of selling out to the southerners and another from Hove accusing him of being biased towards Yorkshire. His typically phlegmatic response was to send each correspondent a copy of each other's letter and invite them to sort it out amongst themselves.

Laker's presence at the microphone was easy-going to say the least. So in control of his emotions was he that some accused him of being soporific. "One viewer told me the other day that listening to my old mate Jim Laker and his new sidekick Bob Willis was better than taking two Mogadon," remarked Fred Trueman. The Somerset captain Peter Roebuck went so far as to label him "dirge-like".

Behind the placid exterior, however, lay true Yorkshire grit and Laker responded by commenting that watching Roebuck bat "was like being at a requiem mass." The ironic truth was that Laker's air of calm authority was ideally suited to television, being the rational antidote to the creeping hysteria of the new Australian model.

BBC

## Laker Airwaves

*"Oh dear oh dear oh dear oh dear..."*

*"He really threw the kitchen sink at that one."*

*"To date..."*

*"Four, from the moment it left the bat."*

*"Mornin' Richie..."*

Listening to Laker, there was no mistaking his origins. Flat vowels and an 'abit of droppin' the gee at the end of a word and losin' the aitch at the start of one betrayed his Yorkshire roots just as much as his willingness to speak his mind. Like Geoffrey Boycott, his talking occasionally got under the skin of under-achieving test players and, at one stage in the early 1980s, the English dressing room would turn off the sound on the television whenever Laker started his 30 minute stint.

Nevertheless, Laker's unassuming professionalism, perceptiveness and sense of perspective earned him the unqualified respect of his peers. "There was always the right emphasis," said Tony Lewis, "he did not hold back from praise but he would explain exactly how it lay in the firmament." John Arlott, never one to lavish unnecessary praise, summed up Laker's natural gift: "Among long-distance observers of a rapid incident, he is more likely than anybody to read it correctly."

Laker died on 23 April 1986 after contracting septicaemia following gall bladder surgery.

# Bjørge Lillelien

As well as being responsible for the creation of the "there are no easy games in world football" cliché, Norway's unexpected victory over England in a World Cup qualifier in Oslo in September 1981 prompted one of the most overblown rants in the annals of sporting verbiage. With the vanquished Englishmen shuffling off the pitch, their shaggy perms and proto-mullets hanging limp with shame, Norwegian radio's Bjørge Lillelien held up his microphone, seized the day, and let rip:

> We're the best in the world! We're the best in the world! We have defeated England 2-1 in football! It's completely unbelievable! We have defeated England, England the native land of giants! Lord Nelson! Lord Beaverbrook! Sir Winston Churchill! Sir Anthony Eden! Clement Attlee! Henry Cooper! Lady Diana! We have defeated them all! Maggie Thatcher, can you hear me? Maggie Thatcher, I have a message for you in the middle of your election campaign, I have a message for you: We have knocked England out of the World Cup! Maggie Thatcher! As they say in the boxing bars around Madison Square Garden, your boys took a hell of a beating, your boys took a hell of a beating! Maggie Thatcher! Norway has defeated England in football! We're the best in the world!

The ferocity of the tirade was a reflection of the esteem in which English football was held by Norwegians. English league matches had been transmitted live to Norway since 1969 and the fortunes of the likes of Leeds United, Arsenal and Manchester City (the first club to have its own Norwegian supporters' club) were followed with a nerdy enthusiasm simply not afforded to the domestic teams.

English football was tough, fast and uncompromising and the hardy types of the western half of the Scandinavian peninsula felt it talked their language. Moreover, the nationalist machismo that had lain waste to the monastic infrastructure of ninth century Northumbria had by now given way to a polite and almost sickly appreciation of other nations' achievements, sporting or otherwise.

By contrast, both population and media regarded the national football team with thinly veiled contempt. The shock at a victory over "the native land of giants", then, was seismic, as a director of Norway's

O H ANTHONSEN/REX FEATURES

premier league recalled: "That was one of the strangest days in my life. To think that Norway should beat England was inconceivable at the time. It was something which we believed could never happen. I didn't know what to think or feel. When I walked to Ullevaal Stadium that day I entered the end where the English were and…I mean what was Norway then? It was garbage, right? National team coaches saying things like 'oh shit, we got the Soviets in our group' or 'we got England in our group…well, well we better try to limit the defeats'. The national team was a joke."

It was a night that divested a nation of an overbearing footballing inferiority complex and the country's most well-known commentator, obviously not sharing the cynicism of many of his compatriots, was determined to extract full value out of his fantasy moment.

At the time Lillelien, who had been with the national broadcaster NRK since 1957, was the only universally respected voice of Norwegian sport. His years training as journalist in America (which accounts for his claimed familiarity with drinking establishments around Madison Square Garden) had taught him that Norwegian radio needed to be more audience orientated if it was to defend its position against television. "We had to develop a new Norwegian radio," he wrote. "It had to become more flexible, more entertaining and more personal to stand a chance of surviving." It was a controversial view at a time when the medium was seen exclusively as a public information platform focused on the people and the building of a nation.

## Just for the record...

Lord Beaverbook was a Canadian.

"Lady" Diana was by then a princess.

There was no election campaign taking place in Britain at the time.

Norway did not knock England out of the World Cup.

Norway's failure even to make the finals suggested they were some way off being the "best in the world".

In his quest to infuse sports commentaries with more excitement, Lillelien developed the "delayed action" technique by deliberately remaining a second or two behind the action. It was a cunning plan enabling him to "predict" what was going to happen and build up his intensity without the listener noticing.

Lillelien took the principle a stage further in the "test games" at Lake Placid in 1979 with the introduction of the "plausibly live" style. This time he fooled his audience he was describing in real time the victory of Oddvar Brå in the 15km langlauf, whereas in reality he was commentating over the telephone several minutes after Brå had already won.

As his Ullevaal outburst attests, Lillelien had a combustible microphone personality. While he seldom showed himself to be nervous before going on air, he could become extremely stressed if there was a technical failure. "He was very well prepared, but if things didn't go to plan when the game started he could partly lose control," explained his NRK colleague Dag Lindebjerg. "If the technical side wasn't ready, he could get really angry."

## They don't like it up 'em!

The fans of England's fiercest rivals, from Glasgow to Buenos Aires, have come to revere Bjørge Lillelien.

Unfortunately, Lillelien was not to inspire a noble commentating tradition in Norway. In fact, his successors have shown themselves to belong to a mercurial fraternity, capable of exhibiting the most woeful impropriety. There was, for instance, a character who apparently passed out drunk halfway through the first half of a Norwich City home game, while another silly Knut was reportedly sacked for offering this fragrant and subtle critique of a female gymnast doing the splits: "She's opening up her hot-dog stand - and who would want to be a customer there?"

Others seemed just plain sloppy. Terje Dalby, anchorman and occasional commentator, appeared to have immense difficulty differentiating players and clubs whose names started with the same letter. The Sheffield clubs were regularly interchanged as were, unbelievably, the ebony skinned Paul Ince and the wan Irishman Denis Irwin. He also believed that George Graham managed England and that there was a team from the Potteries called "Port Whale". But by the same token, inept British attempts at mastering the pronunciation of their very own "Solskjaer" doubtlessly inspire similar jocular contempt in Norway.

Had Lillelien not couched his whistle-stop tour of British history in the style of the quintessential Swedish chef, it is without question that his ramble would have passed into the ether unnoticed from these shores. Yet British audiences, suffocated by the robotic professionalism of their home commentators, habitually warm to muppetry from overseas. It caught the imagination so much that a journalist in *The Observer* estimated that Lillelien (erroneously given the semi-pornograhic moniker "Bjorn Minge") had spoken the "greatest bit of commentary ever". He argued it met all the criteria for greatness by being "dramatic, passionate, funny (where possible) and memorable enough to stay in the public consciousness for years."

The years have not dulled the lustre of Lillelien's inspirational moment, which has since been paraphrased in a variety of bizarre contexts. The front page of *The Sun* even used it to taunt the French in the run-up to a European Championships fixture. "Our boys are gonna give you one hell of a beating!" it bugled bravely. Perhaps predictably, the words would preface an identical outcome: a painful 2-1 defeat for England.

Sadly, Bjørge Lillelien wasn't able to dine out on his cult status for long. He died in 1987, aged just 60. His is nevertheless still warmly remembered in his homeland and in 2004 the television station TV2 used his name to title a talent-search for Norway's next star commentator. It promised to be one hell of a contest.

# Henry Longhurst

In the history of sports broadcasting arguably no name is spoken with more reverence than that of Henry Carpenter Longhurst. Blessed with perfect timing and an exquisite turn of phrase, Longhurst, with his gently gruff, port-soaked voice, established the rustic Scottish game of golf as a thoroughbred of television's sporting stable.

Talking golf was nevertheless just a detail in the rich tapestry of the life of this Bedfordshire retailer's son. Born on 18 March 1909, he grew up enjoying to the full the bounties that flowed from his father's success. After his schooling at Charterhouse and then Clare College, Cambridge, Longhurst spent the inter-war years traversing the globe on a quest for adventure. His seemingly insatiable thirst for thrills saw him try his hand at driving a train, skimming the Rockies in a helicopter, deep-sea diving in the Persian Gulf and tobogganing down the Cresta Run. In 1943, the serving Army captain was even elected Conservative MP for Acton.

Longhurst's politics, which were even further right than a Seve Ballesteros power-fade, stemmed from a fervent patriotism and an unshakable faith in the grace and goodness of the British Empire. Unfortunately, his potential to mature into one of the Commons' most wryly acerbic orators was submerged by Labour's election landslide of 1945. The prospect of him ever being returned to the Commons was, in fact, bleak from the very day of his election. In his autobiography, Harry Carpenter recalls the story of a taxi journey Longhurst and Arnold Palmer took through his old constituency. Passing Acton Central Hall he related to the great champion how he had outlined his grand parliamentary designs to the throng that had gathered on its steps. "What was their reaction?" asked a fascinated Palmer. "They just stood there muttering 'bollocks'," replied Longhurst.

The gospel according to Longhurst instead found prolific expression in the pages of the *The Sunday Times*, for which he set an astonishing record by penning an 800 word piece every week without fail for 25 years. His skills as a wordsmith, allied to his reputation as a wit and raconteur of the first order, equipped him well for the demands of describing golf on television. When the BBC sought to find a voice that could render comprehensible and stimulating the complexities and nuances of the stick-and-ball game to a new and largely uninitiated audience, Longhurst, himself a scratch golfer and former winner of the

> ' Jacklin has three more to win...oh it may drop in yet...and there is the shortest shot that ever won a championship. '

## An Englishman's home is his windmill

Longhurst lived at Hassocks, just north of Brighton, in a pair of windmills named Jack and Jill.

German Amateur championships, seemed as reasonable a choice as any.

The BBC made its first serious attempt at broadcasting golf in 1949[1]. The logistical problems involved in tracking the aerial progress of a white dot of only 1.62 inches in diameter was one of the stiffest challenges to face the BBC's OB producers. Football pitches, tennis courts and cricket grounds were accommodatingly formatted in their dimensions. A golf course, on the other hand, presented a miscellany of hillocks, lakes, gorse and other vegetation (not to mention swathes of rambling spectators) which stretched the boundaries of technical know-how to the limit.

The unpredictability of golf meant that thousands of yards of cable were occasionally unspooled in vain. In 1956, for example, it was decided that the BBC would devote half an hour to the final appearance in Britain of Ben Hogan. A slot in the schedule was set aside to coincide with the great American's appearance on Wentworth's seventh hole.

[1] The first Open Championship to be televised was Peter Thomson's victory at St Andrews in 1955. The BBC were granted permission to locate three cameras around the course - one at the loop, one at the 17th green and one behind the 18th green.

BBC

**Car park commentator**

Peter Alliss observes the master at work. Harry Carpenter sits in the background.

Unfortunately play was so slow that, by the end of the transmission, the only sight the viewers got of Hogan was the top of his white cap moving above the crowds back at the sixth green.

Commentating was hard and stressful work in the early days of golf coverage. The task of collating and processing the tide of birdies, pars and bogeys which converged on the commentary box from all corners of the course was performed not by the boffins at Hewlett Packard but on the hoof by the men at the microphone. As a tournament reached its climax, the commentary box became little more than a depository of scribbled arithmetic.

The absence of a talk-back facility with the production team compounded the problems facing the early commentators. In order to create a modicum of continuity, Longhurst and his colleagues were required to play producer by using coded prompts to steer the camera lens across the course. Comments such as "and when we've finished here, we will hopefully be able to see Oosterhuis on the twelfth" were actually just an optimistic invitation for a cameraman to man-handle his machine into position.

Longhurst was able to call the shots thanks to his ascension to the most precarious viewpoint in sports broadcasting: the golf commentary tower. The eagle's nest was introduced in the late fifties after swarming crowds, sent into frenzy at the sight of a picture on a monitor, had made ground-level reporting impracticable. The requirement to tackle 70 feet of ladders was, however, an unappealing proposition during inclement weather for a portly gentleman of a certain age and Longhurst eventually negotiated himself a berth at a safer altitude. But the elements still had their way. "At Wentworth one day somebody lifted the weight which was holding the scoresheet down," he recalled, "and the wind whipped it away into the heather a quarter of a mile away."

Brian Johnston observed that the golf commentator "has to speak against a background of silence, so that his every word is dropping like a pebble on to a still pond." Appreciating the canvas with which he was to work, Longhurst chose wisely to make a virtue of the overwhelming noiselessness. His assertion that "a second's silence is worth a minute's talk" made his reputation.

Longhurst's approach was the antithesis of what he called the "artificial and generally brassy style" of the US networks. The Americans, who loved his husky but always beautifully manicured English enunciation, were amazed that he could operate unbolstered by reams of statistics and background data. So highly regarded was the master communicator that his services were enlisted by both CBS and ABC, a division of labour that would be unheard of today.

Longhurst's natural, unforced manner complemented television golf perfectly. His was a born talent that his producers were wise to leave unmolested. It was ironic, though, that the great communicator felt unnerved by television. His lack of understanding of the new medium was exacerbated by his regular enjoyment of a pre-broadcast tipple. The habit so tickled the Americans that they dubbed him "Henry Longthirst". His determination not suffer the embarrassment of a booze-induced howler was highlighted during a tournament in the sixties which featured two of Britain's best-known players. To a query as to his "well-being" a worse-for-wear Longhurst responded, "I shall be fine as long as I don't have to say 'Hunt and Coles' too often!"

He also showed himself to be vulnerable, even when not "under the influence", to the advent of any new technology. "Gosh, he's done it again!" he gasped in genuine incredulity as a repeat showing of a Jack Nicklaus putt announced the arrival of the action replay machine.

Like cricket's John Arlott, Longhurst's brilliance was in his ability, through the tone of his voice, to reflect human frailty by observation.

'Nothing is more maddening than the commentator who talks as you are watching the shot, whether the player is trying to hole a putt or convert a try or score from a penalty.'

"And there, but for the grace of God..."

## THE SAGE OF GOLF

Therefore, despite his sublime phraseology, it was Longhurst's ability to identify and empathise with the players' struggle against their mental demons that earned their regard. Having consigned his own set of clubs permanently to the garage after his putting stroke was terminally afflicted by the "yips", Longhurst sympathised fully with the golfer's plight. "We know the feeling," he wrote in 1964. "So when some other luckless fellow does it, our reaction is not 'You _____ fool!' but 'There, but for the grace of God, went I.'" They were words he used famously six years later when Doug Sanders missed the three foot putt that would have won him the Open at St Andrews.

Longhurst's fatalistic summation of Sanders' misfortune made for an iconic piece of television. As the leader, desperately fighting off the challenge of Jack Nicklaus, addressed his approach putt, needing to negotiate "The Valley of Sin" and get down in two for victory, Longhurst's voice was pregnant with foreboding. Intuition was nagging that Sanders hadn't the making of a true champion.

"Of all the greens that I wouldn't want a long downhill one from the back of to get down in two from to win the British Open, this is the one." The ball, adhering to the script to the letter, pulled up agonisingly short: "Oh Lord…well that's not one I would like to have…and they clap little knowing what is to come for Sanders." As the American stooped over what he prayed would be the final putt, Longhurst summed up the magnitude of the moment: "And so now this is it. And this is what people dream about, that you've got this one, with a left-hand borrow, downhill, on the last green at St Andrews to win the Open."

As the brisk wind blew an imaginary piece of fluff across the line of the putt Longhurst gasped melodramatically as Sanders bent down to remove it. The nervous jab that pushed the ball below and past the hole confirmed his grim premonition. "Missed it. Certainty. Yes, that's the side you're bound to miss it. And there it is. And there, but for the grace of God…"

Longhurst died of cancer on 21 July 1978. His fight against the disease may have been debilitating, but it never dented his appetite for a witticism. "The one good thing about me going first," he reassured his friend Peter Alliss, "is that at least it will afford me the opportunity of finding the sponsor's hospitality room."

The prime exponent of the observational style, "the Great" Henry Longhurst is rightly lauded as the most civilised, informative and unobtrusive of commentators.

# Ted Lowe

The rise of snooker from its genesis as an obscure English lounge-room pastime to one of British television's most popular and bankable phenomena is due exclusively to the drive and dedication of "Whispering" Ted Lowe. There can be no personality who has been more influential in the development, promotion and indeed survival of their sport than he.

By rights, Lowe should have been a jockey as he was born and brought up in the Berkshire racing village of Lambourn where his father Ernest was head lad at a local stables. His mother's family, however, was in the licensing trade and Lowe allowed himself to be packed off to Streatham to learn the art of pint-pulling at one of his uncle's pubs. The shy country boy struggled to adapt to life in the big city but his boredom was relieved by the occasional expedition to the West End to watch the great Joe Davis play snooker.

The green baize had held Lowe under its spell ever since his childhood when he built break after break on his quarter-size table. His out-of-hours access to a full-size version at the pub turned him into a player good enough to reach the semi-final of the English amateur championship and the new friendships he forged whilst taking on all-comers enabled him to slowly overcome his loneliness. One of Lowe's snooker connections even found him a job and he spent the war years in a reserved occupation, estimating and fixing rates for a gas meter manufacturer.

At Smith Meters, Lowe took his first steps as a snooker impresario. As the founder of the company's first social club, he invited Joe Davis to give an exhibition on the newly acquired billiard table. He made use of a 28 point handicap to beat his hero soundly.

In 1946, Lowe was invited to become general manager at the new Leicester Square Hall, a cosy 200 seat venue in the heart of London that had been designed to host the country's headline snooker and billiards competitions. As chief cook and bottle-washer, Lowe worked tirelessly to organise all the world championships and major tournaments of the day. He ran a hectic programme of charity, fund-raising and novelty events, one of the most memorable being a 48 hour non-stop snooker marathon attempted by a gentleman who rejoiced in the name of Dickie Flicker.

Snooker's headquarters and shop window closed in 1955, leaving the

**Hands in pockets**

Ted (*right*) with occasional left-hander Fred Davis.

sport in crisis. With no sponsorship, few promoters and the BBC turning a deaf ear to Lowe's pleas for regular television coverage, interest in snooker dwindled to such an extent that the world championships were uncontested from 1958 to 1963. But while snooker languished, Lowe, who had been recruited as a sales manager for the brewer Ind Coope, found unexpected celebrity as the voice of the pools panel, which "guestimated" football results in the event of weather wreaking havoc with the Saturday fixture list.

Snooker didn't emerge from the wilderness until 1969. It got its big break with the arrival of colour television, which the BBC was naturally

"Well, the shot would have been safe if the red hadn't ended up over the pocket."

"Oh and that's a brilliant shot. The odd thing is his mum's not very keen on snooker."

"Higgins first entered the Championship ten years ago. That was for the first time, of course."

"Just enough points here for Tony to pull the cat out of the fire!"

"And it is my guess that Steve Davis will try to score as many points as he can this frame."

"Steve Davis has a tough consignment in front of him."

"And Griffiths has looked at that blue four times now, and it still hasn't moved."

"A little pale in the face, but then his name is White."

"That pot puts the game beyond reproach."

"There is, I believe, a time limit for playing a shot. But I think it's true to say that nobody knows what that limit is."

"The formalities are now over and it's down to business, Steve Davis now adjusting his socks."

"Steve, with his sip of water, part of his make-up."

eager to showcase. The fairy godmother was Philip Lewis, a BBC2 producer who commissioned Lowe to devise a 30-minute snooker series to run for eight weeks. *Pot Black*, which was introduced by Alan Weeks with Lowe as commentator, was an instant hit. A new breed of players, resplendent in their Peter Sutcliffe-issue bow ties, appealed to a rapidly expanding television audience that was discovering the game for the first time.

Lowe was a clever marketeer. His suggestion that players should adopt evening attire drew in female viewers by their droves, while his regular invitations to less well-known foreign players caused an explosion in the game's popularity overseas. When the Australian Eddie Charlton took the title in 1972 and 1973, the series was snapped up and networked from Perth to Brisbane.

The new sophisticated image attracted sponsorship from cigarette companies and a new cachet attached itself to the world championships. When the tournament moved to the Crucible Theatre in Sheffield in 1977, snooker's annual showpiece rapidly became a staple in the BBC's sporting calendar. Ultimately it would rival golf's Open Championship as its largest outside broadcast.

Nobody was more qualified to lead the coverage than Lowe, snooker's one-man life-support system for a full 30 years. As a commentator, his "softly-softly" style became as much a signature to the sport as the catchy ragtime number that introduced *Pot Black*.

He adopted his famous whisper when acting as prompter for Raymond Glendenning during the occasional broadcast in the fifties. The microphone was as little as six feet away from the table, so Lowe kept his timorous style when Glendenning's lost voice gave him his opportunity. The BBC suggested he make more use of the commentary box they had given him in 1958 but Lowe retained his whisper, bowing to the consensus that it formed "part of the atmosphere".

As one of the foremost authorities on snooker, Lowe's primary commentating role was as an educator. "In the early days of TV it was necessary to explain shots and even the value of the colours," he recalled. But as his audience became more knowledgeable, Lowe concentrated on eking out the tension as much as possible, occasionally with the assistance of some gloriously strained metaphors: "The audience are literally electrified and glued to their seats."

Together with his first co-commentators, John Spencer and Rex Williams, Lowe would try to anticipate shots in order to assist the director in his organisation of camera angles. When Steve Davis once opted to slam home a long straight green when a cut into the centre

pocket appeared the obvious option, Lowe, like all experienced commentators, calmly turned the error to his advantage: "Davis has fooled me. It was a brilliant shot."

Lowe's attempts to stay at least one shot ahead of the game once brought an amusing response from John Pulman. In a match during the days when his commentary position was not much more than a cue's length from the table, Lowe was correctly forecasting each pot of a large break until the world champion (and future ITV rival) unexpectedly ran out of position. "Ted," said Pulman in a mock whisper, "do you mind if I play my own bloody game now?"

As the sport's most influential grandee, Lowe would reserve for himself a tournament's keynote observations. When it became clear that the championship-winning break was being made, he would adopt a familiar ritual: "To the runner-up…£75,000…to the winner…£150,000". It was Lowe's way of reminding the viewer how far his players' earnings potential had advanced from the £244 that comprised the entire prize pool for the first series of *Pot Black*.

How seriously Lowe took the business of snooker was illustrated by his priceless comment as coverage of the 1980 world championship final was interrupted by live news footage of the SAS liberating the Iranian hostages. Without the merest hint of irony, he welcomed BBC viewers back to the Crucible with the words, "And so from one Embassy we return you this Embassy – world snooker final."

## TED LOWE'S
## SNOOKER BALLS
### (PART TWO)

*"He's going for the pink, and for those of you with black-and-white sets, the yellow is behind the blue."*

*"And Alex Higgins has literally come back from the dead."*

*"Ninety-nine times out of a thousand he would have potted that ball."*

*"One mistake here could win or lose the match either way."*

*"This young man Jimmy White celebrated his 22nd birthday literally four days ago."*

*"Alex, unlike many other professionals, adds a bit on his cue rather than put on an extension."*

*"He's 40 points behind and there's only 51 points left on the table."*

*"That's inches away from being millimetre perfect."*

*"Jimmy White has that wonderful gift of being able to point his cue where he is looking."*

*"He's lucky in one sense and lucky in the other."*

*"Cliff Thorburn has been unsettled by the erratic but consistent potting of Perrie Mans."*

*"Fred Davis, the doyen of snooker, now 67 years of age and too old to get his leg over, prefers to use his left hand."*

The BBC and ITV now regarded snooker as a key battleground. The two networks' rivalry crystallised into the race to be the first to broadcast a maximum 147 break. In 1977, the BBC producer Nick Hunter video-taped every shot in major tournaments in the hope of capturing the consummate frame, but it was ITV who were on hand for John Spencer's maximum a year later. Sadly for them, their cameramen were on their tea break as Spencer delivered perfection. There are few more compelling moments in sport than a 147 and, although Steve Davis' maximum at the 1982 Lada Classic gave ITV the first, the BBC's Jack Karnehm made Cliff Thorburn's maximum at the world championships a year later much more memorable. As the Canadian stooped over the final black, Karnehm spoke snooker commentary's most celebrated line: "Good luck mate!"

In the eighties, snooker had become huge box office. The pallid, vitamin starved complexions of the sport's headliners may have been the antithesis of conventional athletic wholesomeness, but they attracted television audiences so vast that some foreign observers commented that snooker had replaced football as the national game. ITV and the BBC indulged snooker addicts with blanket coverage of all ranking tournaments. To add to the orgy of over-exposure, the Crucible cameras even transmitted live pictures of Cliff Thorburn grinding his way to victory over Terry Griffiths at four o'clock in the morning.

Snooker reached the zenith of its popularity in 1985 when Dennis Taylor deposed the apparently invincible world champion Steve Davis in a remarkable Embassy final. The deciding thirty-fifth frame was watched by an estimated 18.5 million spellbound viewers, more than any other non-footballing event apart from Torvill & Dean. It was easily the largest audience to tune in after midnight.

As the players anxiously shunted the final decisive black around the table, Lowe did well to keep himself in check: "I have never known an atmosphere like this... John Williams, the referee, trying to keep our crowd in order." As successive errors racked up the tension still further, Lowe even allowed himself a little chuckle as Taylor's outrageous attempted double fortuitously rolled safe: "I'm sure Dennis wouldn't mind me saying he chanced his arm and came up lucky."

Few will forget Lowe's gasp of "No!?" when Davis missed a straightforward opportunity to deliver the *coup de grace*. It proved to be the unkindest of cuts for "The Nugget" and Lowe garnished the Irishman's winning pot with laudable understatement: "He's done it! Dennis Taylor, for the first time, becomes Embassy World Snooker Champion, 1985. He is *so* thrilled."

In 1996, Lowe's retirement from commentating after nearly 50 years as snooker's guiding light left a vacuum that was filled by scandals and internecine bickering on the part of the game's administrators. Penning his memoirs in 1983, he was already forecasting "trouble in paradise caused by pure greed". When Lowe's successor, Clive Everton, wrote a series of stinging articles in his *Guardian* column about expenses abuse and creative accounting within the governing body, the WPBSA, he received a seven month ban from all tournament venues. Only after the snooker writers' association threatened to omit all names of sponsors from reports was it eventually lifted.

By the end of the nineties snooker's popularity began to tail off as researchers indicted the game's "staid" and "funereal" image. As Jessica Hodgson noted in *The Guardian*: "A sport that in the eighties commanded the fascination of the nation and made heartthrobs out of middle-aged men with charisma by-passes is reduced to little more than late-night wallpaper for insomniacs."

Although for the moment the BBC appears to remain smitten, snooker's life-blood - the financial benevolence of the cigarette companies - is due to be withdrawn after 2006. For the game that Ted built, does a new dark age beckon?

# Archie Macpherson

Archie Macpherson is sufficiently celebrated north of the border to have had his sheepskin coat inducted into the Scottish football museum at Hampden Park. One of the most opinionated of "fitbah" commentators, he has built his popularity on his ability to modulate his impish voice extravagantly to make his point, as quoted by one viewer: "The man who I see as the weak link in this Rangers defence - Porini - needs to show fulllllll...concENTRATION FOR THE FUUUUUUULLL NNNnnniiiine-ty minutes!"

Glasgow-born Macpherson, the son of a professional footballer, got into the BBC on the strength of his talents as a short story writer. Drawing on his talent for flowery prose, he made his first radio reports in 1961 before moving to television three years later.

During his first televised football match at Fir Park, Motherwell, in August 1964, he immediately discovered how vulnerable a commentator could be to the limitations of first generation technology. Being forced to stop every ten minutes while a technician changed the film canister on the single camera, he cold only hope that no goal was scored during the eternity it took to perform the reload. During one of the enforced breaks, he remembers a home forward blasting a shot over the bar and out of the ground: "A Motherwell supporter just in front of us shouted, 'Ya mug.' I felt like shouting, 'Stay there, ya beauty!'"

Shortly after his television debut, Macpherson was invited to move to London to join BBC radio's *Sports Report* team. The tempting offer was only refused on the advice of Brian Moore, who warned him that the regime of his fellow Scot Angus Mackay could be cruel and unforgiving if a reporter's face did not fit. Besides, by staying in Scotland, Macpherson knew that he would be on hand to report on that most white-hot of sporting stand-offs, the uniquely bitter rivalry of Celtic and Rangers.

For the commentator, the sectarian cauldron of the "Old Firm" demands implacable impartiality. Baptised a Protestant, Macpherson was well aware that each time he opened his mouth, the ears of one half of Glasgow would be scanning his every syllable for the merest inflection of bias. Spite-laden correspondence would follow habitually any "injudicious" remark, with ominous threats being issued by extremists from both camps. One Celtic director warned of "dire consequences" after calculating that Macpherson referred to Rangers

> I predicted in August that Celtic would reach the final. On the eve of that final, I stand by that prediction.

## Archie Academical

Macpherson was rector
of Edinburgh University
between 1985 and 1988.

players more often by their first names than he did to Celtic's, while a Rangers fanatic, disgruntled at hearing his team criticised, vowed to bomb the commentator "to f_____ eternity."

Supporters of both teams enjoyed trying to tease a gesture of partisanship out of Macpherson. "Archie, Archie cross yersel!" they'd chorus at Celtic Park; "Gie us the Sash, Archie!" they'd implore at Ibrox. Careful to decline each invitation, he managed to regulate his tone sufficiently to steer a relatively safe course through the sectarian minefield.

Even so, Macpherson had a tempestuous relationship with Celtic's forceful manager Jock Stein. Stein, who was to lead The Bhoys to nine consecutive Scottish league titles from the 1965/66 season, refused to co-operate with the "bigoted" BBC Scotland due to its apparent failure to give his team the credit it he felt it deserved. The corporation, which had "lost" five Celtic goals in the 1957 League Cup final, was now accused of editing a league review to make it appear, falsely, that Rangers had won. Stein was incensed and on the warpath.

The BBC's head of sport in Scotland, Peter Thomson, was said to be terrified of Stein so Macpherson took it upon himself to try to forge some sort of workable relationship with the manager. Despite the dressing-room door being regularly slammed in his face, literally and metaphorically, Macpherson's persistence eventually paid off and gradually an understanding was built. "Within the sports corridors of the Beeb in Scotland he was regarded almost as being the Great Satan," he wrote. "Later, though, he would give me invaluable advice at critical junctures in my professional life and work with relish with me on several outstanding broadcasting occasions."

In 1969, Macpherson left Swinton School in Lanarkshire, where he had been headmaster since 1965, to join the BBC full-time. He quickly found himself sucked into the *maelstrom* of drama and controversy that was seventies football in Scotland. It was a decade that started with what was then British sport's worst ever tragedy. For Macpherson, the sight of 66 fans who had died on Ibrox Park's Stairway 13 on 2 January 1971 was an overwhelming emotional experience. "We were weeping before we went on and during the programme," he recalled after his interview with the Lord Provost. "I had to keep nipping my thigh hard to keep some semblance of order in what I was doing."

The World Cup offered little respite. In 1974, Scotland's gallant failure to qualify to the second stage in their first ever finals set a painful and frustrating precedent for tournaments to come. The commentating fraternity shared the burden of crushed expectations and Macpherson remembers the disgusted reaction of his STV counterpart, Arthur Montford, who "sped back to the hotel without talking to anybody, jumped in his car and headed for the North Sea ferry."

There was the odd moment of sweetness and light, however. In 1978, Archie Gemmill's wondrous dribble past a succession of flat-footed Dutchmen led to one of the most memorable goals in World Cup history and brought 30 commentators to their feet in rapturous appreciation: "It was a goal of perfect commentating symmetry with a distinct beginning, middle and end," he recalls. "Will he do it? Can he get there? Yes, he's scored!!" It was a moment of some contrast to the despair of the Peru match, when Macpherson was forced to sit helpless as Scottish viewers took David Coleman's commentary because somebody in Glasgow had forgotten to reserve the satellite time.

The seventies saw a raising of Macpherson's profile south of the border. On the then rather stuffy "Football Focus" segment of *Grandstand*, English viewers became accustomed to his chirpy reporting style. When a talking snowman appeared before the camera, for

'That's the kind he normally knocks in in his sleep - with his eyes closed.'

instance, it was guaranteed to be Macpherson playing the fool. The BBC network warmed to his easy presentational manner and his famed "Shredded Wheat" haircut soon found its way, appropriately enough, onto breakfast television. The Scottish newspapers were even starting to refer to him as "London's pet Jock".

While his career in England was blooming, relations with BBC Scotland were souring. Peter Thomson, his mentor and inspiration, had tolerated his chief commentator's maverick tendencies. When Macpherson was pilloried for remaining uncharacteristically silent as Scotland and Northern Ireland submerged themselves in a Hampden Park mud-bath, Thomson was supportive. Under James Hunter, the new Head of Television in Scotland, the leash was to tighten.

Matters came to a head during the Costa Rica *debâcle* in the 1990 World Cup when Hunter, via his producer, instructed a morose and exasperated Macpherson to be more positive towards Scotland. The commentator, incensed that he should be forced to abandon his objectivity, ignored the appeal. "In conversations afterwards with experienced broadcasters," he wrote, "we reached the view that it was probably the first time a senior BBC figure had actively encouraged a commentator to be biased." Retribution was swift. On his return, Hunter cited Macpherson's "bad attitude" as grounds for not renewing his contract.

Although Macpherson's banishment to the wastelands of the Eurosport satellite channel and the slop and gruel of the UEFA Cup after 23 years at the BBC represented a grim demotion, STV eventually brought him back to Glasgow and the Old Firm. The wry grin on his face can only be imagined as he picked up the microphone to commentate live on the Champions League, whilst the BBC found itself frozen out almost completely.

Writing in *The Scotsman*, Alistair McKay suggested that, like Morecambe & Wise, Macpherson had lost something by going to ITV. Yet at the same time he felt obliged to recognise the comforting and reassuring appeal of that most familiar of lowland baritones:

> "The Archie Effect is not entirely unpleasant, because Archieville is a kinder place, full of new-build homes on fresh-field sites, their walls smelling faintly of paint and their carpets gently swirling. Archie-time was the time before choice, a pre-decimal age when there was only This or That, and you could count yourself lucky to have either, sonny Jim."

Few commentators enjoy that special knack.

# Howard Marshall

Howard Marshall, known popularly as "the Voice of England", was the most illustrious of the BBC's early broadcasters. From 1933 to 1945, he was the commanding presence on the nation's airwaves, delighting vast audiences with his cosy fire-side chats on home and family and vivid descriptions of the ceremonials and pageants of the day. His voice was also the linchpin of the Empire, chiming in with Big Ben to bring tens of millions around the world evocative dispatches from the mother-country.

Marshall was a broadcaster of many achievements. Not only did he establish ball-by-ball cricket commentary as a viable proposition, but he also developed youth programming and ground-breaking social reporting. It could be argued that Marshall's readiness to scratch away at the veneer of British society helped the BBC come of age.

Marshall, who was born in Sutton in Surrey in 1900, came from prime Establishment stock. Educated at Haileybury School he continued his studies at Oxford, although he left before completing his degree to join the merchant navy. He served for a time in the Essex oyster fleet before leaving to join his father's magazine publishing house.

He could have been shunted into the career siding of *Model Railway* magazine had his mother not suggested he write speculatively to the BBC. Her hunch that his journalistic background, extravagant vocabulary and fine speaking voice constituted the ideal curriculum vitae for a broadcaster proved well founded. In 1927, Marshall was interviewed by Lord Reith, who promptly salaried him at £300 a year.

A former Oxford rugby blue who had captained Harlequins and represented London versus the All Blacks, Marshall was a strong candidate to front the corporation's sports output. He had also been a useful cricketer, having played for his school at Lord's, and it was with the summer game that Marshall was to make his greatest impression.

Up until the early thirties, the BBC had believed that cricket, with its languid meanderings, was quite inappropriate for broadcasting. Yet producer Lobby Lotbinière was to employ his legendary vision to reappraise the game's suitability. As his successor Peter Baxter noted, "He realised that it was the structure of cricket – the slow build up to a moment of violent action – that actually make cricket the best commentary sport, not the most impossible."

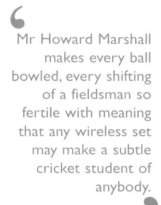

But the concept of ball-by-ball coverage would not have been feasible without the unique vocal skills of Marshall. Described by Brian Johnston as "slow, deep and burbling", his voice established the intimate and conversational commentary formula that was later to be the cornerstone of the success of *Test Match Special*. But it was not simply its aural qualities that were turning the format into a success – it was Marshall's ability to maintain a pauseless loop of unembellished, functional description that convinced his superiors that commentary on cricket could be just as immediate as football, rugby or racing. And, unlike those other sports, Marshall performed his early commentaries entirely on his own, not even with the assistance of a scorer.

In 1934, the BBC finally gained permission from a sceptical MCC to broadcast the first running commentary on a test match in England. Lord's, the high temple of cricket, had been previously off-limits to

## Boys' Own Commentator

*"I had to make a minor journey by road at night in pouring rain back from the battle-front, with no lights, over mountain passes, then hop on a plane to Algiers, where I got to the microphone just five minutes before my broadcast."*

broadcasters, with Marshall and his engineers having been forced to file their reports from a room in one of the neighbouring houses. Marshall's close of play summary was once even interrupted by a young piano student in the flat above performing her scales.

With admittance through the hallowed portals finally granted, the controversial concept of broadcasting cricket live was vindicated with one of the most remarkable days in test match history as Hedley Verity took fourteen wickets in one day to bowl out the Australians. Listeners and journalists came to revere Marshall's thoughtful style, but his decision to laud the bowling of Bill "Tiger" O'Reilly by bursting into a song that included the line "Gor Blimey, O'Reilly, you are bowling well" caused a furore. "We know you're not the Archbishop of Canterbury but need you descend to blasphemy?" wrote one of the 300 complainants, "I hope they ex-communicate you!"

Marshall would be no stranger to controversy. In the late thirties, his first-hand investigative accounts of deprivation in the north-east of England and the East End of London – which were the first of their kind – led to accusations of his being "a lying Bolshevik".

Marshall also courted unpopularity when, after war broke out, he moved back to the BBC as Director of War Reporting after a spell as Director of Public Relations at the Ministry of Food. His appointment upset the established war correspondents and Marshall fuelled their resentment by assigning himself the best scoops.

His work on D-Day was nevertheless masterful. Accompanying the troops onto the Normandy beaches, his landing craft was twice hit by mortars. With his recording equipment lost, he somehow got himself back to Broadcasting House that evening to present his account. He began with a most memorable rider:

> "I've just come back from the beaches and I've been in the sea twice and I'm sitting in my soaked-through clothes with no notes at all. All my notes are sodden and at the bottom of the sea."

D-Day was the high point of Marshall's career at the BBC. Several weeks later, when bringing the world the first news of the liberation of Paris, he was to lose his reporter's accreditation for filing his report without a censor being present. Some believed it to be the day he also lost his enthusiasm for broadcasting.

Having achieved just about everything at the BBC, Marshall left the staff after the war to become director of personnel at the Steel Company of Wales. The retreat into relative obscurity was perhaps understandable given the increasing turbulence of his private life. While his wife and two sons were sitting the war out in America, Marshall had been carrying on an affair with Nerina Shute, daughter of the writer Nevile. Following a divorce, he married Nerina in 1944, only to discover she was a bisexual who had been conducting an affair of her own with the French housekeeper. With a second divorce under his belt, Marshall eventually set up home with Jasmine Bligh, television's first announcer.

Marshall continued to make the occasional contribution to radio into the fifties, with his work on Queen Elizabeth's coronation being regarded as amongst his best. Yet it was television that was generating the brightest new stars and Marshall's refusal to concede its growing status - he said it was called a medium "because it's neither rare nor well done" - confirmed him as yesterday's man.

Considering the scope of his influence on broadcasting in Britain, it is incredible how easily his name has faded from memory. He not only pioneered an astounding range of programmes, but he acted as a model for future broadcasters with his effortless fluency and complete imperturbability. A Radio 4 portrait of the "Forgotten Broadcaster", remarked that what really set Marshall apart was the way he dispassionately set aside celebrity, something that few of his successors would countenance: "It is, after all, a brave, even great man, who can put fame behind him with a snap of the fingers."

Having suffered for some years from Parkinson's disease, Howard Marshall died at his home in Easton, in the Lambourn Valley, in 1973.

# Dan Maskell

Dan Maskell, whose gentle tones were no less complementary to that sporting high-point of the English summer than the dollop of cream on the obligatory strawberries, will always be remembered with great affection as the voice of Wimbledon. Anything else just wasn't tennis.

Yet the plumminess with which Maskell gasped his way though 45 All England Championships masked a relatively modest upbringing. Born in Fulham on 11 April 1908, he endured, along with his seven siblings, the privations and austerity that followed the first world war.

As the second youngest of the brood, Maskell reacted to the scarcity of parental attention by expressing himself through sport. He was an enthusiastic and talented footballer and keenly followed the varsity rowers, whose blades flashed though the waters close to his home.

Maskell's love affair with tennis was kindled when he got himself a holiday job as a ball-boy at the nearby Queen's Club. Having climbed the academic ladder no higher than the local elementary school, he was short of challenging career options. But his enjoyment of the "good breeding and orderly management" that pervaded Queen's and the discovery of a natural ability to strike a tennis ball convinced him he had an aptitude to teach the game professionally. Relishing the glamour of the playground of the well-heeled, he made quick progress and, after becoming a full-time ball-boy in 1923, joined the coaching staff.

The teenage professional moved within the most exulted of circles. During his career he was to practise regularly with legends of the game such as Jean Borotra, Fred Perry and Helen Wills Moody. He would even step into Katharine Hepburn's pumps as Spencer Tracy's doubles partner. Thirty years later he would appear by royal appointment, too, keeping a regular Buckingham Palace date to give instruction to the Queen's children Anne, Charles and Andrew. Not even Sir Peter O'Sullevan could claim to be so well connected.

All the great champions were amateurs in those days and Maskell's status as a professional meant he had to forego his share of the limelight. Within the ranks of his fellow pros, however, he was dominant. In 1928, the first of his sixteen British professional championships alerted the All England Lawn Tennis and Croquet Club to his talents and they moved quickly to enlist his services. Having broken new ground as Wimbledon's first professional coach, Maskell was tasked with grooming the future stars of the British Davis Cup team. Success was

## Just a Mo

In conversation with Maureen Connolly, affectionately known as "Little Mo", who in 1953 became the first woman to achieve the Grand Slam.

swift to follow under his guidance. In 1933, Great Britain regained the Cup after defeating the French in Paris and went on to defend it successfully for the next four years.

When world war intervened once again in 1939, the All England Club was turned into an air-raid precautions centre and tennis shut itself down altogether. Maskell, eager to make his contribution, joined the RAF and was dispatched to Hastings to help instruct pilots at an Initial Training Wing. From there he would transfer to Torquay and then Loughborough, where he dedicated himself to the rehabilitation of injured aircrew. "I shall always remember my days at Torquay with great humility," he recalled, "I counted it a privilege to be working among men who showed such depths of courage in great adversity."

Maskell's broadcasting career began in 1938 when the BBC, whose regular television service had started in November 1936, asked him to make a coaching film. It was probably the first ever instructional broadcast on tennis. (Maskell would also be on hand for another first when, in August 1967, at Wimbledon's first professional tournament, the BBC made its first outside broadcast in colour.)

## OH I SAY!
### TEN UNFORCED ERRORS

"When Martina is tense, it
helps her relax."

"And the British boys are
adopting the attacking position,
Cox up."

"There is Peter Graf, Steffi's
father, with his head on his chin."

"You can almost hear the silence
as they battle it out."

"He slips . . . but manages to
regroup himself."

"The spectators behind the roller
have got a good view of Martina
Navratilova receiving service."

"And here's Zivojinovic, six foot
six inches tall and fourteen
pounds ten ounces."

"The Gullikson twins here. An
interesting pair, both from
Wisconsin."

"Lendl has remained
throughout as calm as the
proverbial iceberg."

"Oh, that cross-court angle was
so acute it doesn't exist."

The first radio commentaries at Wimbledon had been made in 1927 by Teddy Wakelam and Colonel Brand. At the time there were doubts as to the worth of trying to translate the cut and thrust of the tennis court into a coherent audio narrative. Frenetic rallies would often descend into farce. During one long exchange, Brand became particularly excited: "Smash, recovery, smash, recovery, smash, recovery, gosh! It's gone hurtling into the royal box at toque height!" On another occasion Wakelam had more genuine reason to be animated. Commentating on a men's doubles at Wimbledon, he ignited some old papers while lighting a cigarette. The fire spread to his trousers, although he managed to extinguish the blaze without interrupting his commentary. This self-incendiary approach was later purloined and perfected by motor racing's Murray Walker.

Maskell made his first Wimbledon radio commentary in 1949 when the BBC asked him to perform a summariser's role for Max Robertson. Two years later he teamed up with Freddie Grisewood, "the man with the golden voice", who invited him to attempt his first stroke-by-stroke commentary. From that moment in 1951 until his final championships in 1992, he would not miss a single day's commentating at Wimbledon.

When Maskell moved to television he had to reinvent himself as a commentator. Radio commentating demanded Olympian vocal dexterity allied to Vulcan mental alertness. It was challenging enough enunciating baseline rallies on clay let alone rapid-fire volley duels at the net. The television screen, by contrast, said almost everything by itself. Framing the court perfectly from behind the baseline, the camera caught every aspect of the action and relegated the commentator's role to one of embroidery. "Instead of describing in words a winner that they have just seen anyway," explained Maskell, "I try to say why it was a winner."

His golden rule was to never speak during a rally and the sound of silence was to become his trademark. The Americans, whose broadcasters felt obliged to force-feed their viewers with scores, statistics and graphics during the brief intervals between their commercial breaks, found his approach startling. When the US network NBC switched to the BBC output to show their viewers "how they do it in England", commentator Bud Collins had to constantly reassure his viewers that the 45 second pauses between points were quite normal: "Don't worry folks, we really are tuned to the BBC commentary – they just don't happen to be saying anything at the moment!"

While he may have made other habitual Trappists such as Henry Longhurst and Richie Benaud seem verbally flatulent by comparison,

**Strike a pose**

Game, set and match to David Vine (*left*) in the knitwear stakes.

Maskell still got letters complaining that he talked too much. But in whining about the regular interjection of "gosh!", "oh I say!" and "what a peach!", the complainants failed to appreciate that these exclamations reflected perfectly the refined understatement that made the All England championships unique.

Maskell brought to the commentary box the immense wealth of knowledge that had been gleaned from decades of involvement at the highest level of the game. He prided himself on the accuracy with which he profiled the players and their records. Petrified that he would one day be compromised by insufficient homework, he gave himself two hours' preparation time before each broadcast. Once the transmission was over, he would go home and review his commentary on video-tape to check he had not foot-faulted on his phraseology.

Maskell always tried to avoid the trap of suffocating the viewer with the minutiae of technique and strategy. "There is a delicate balance between being informative and lecturing to an audience," he wrote. He did dip his toe into the jargon of the game but would wait for a spectacular winner before really letting go: "Oh what a superb running two-handed top-spin pass down the line! And such disguise, too!"

A contributory reason behind his silence during play was his meticulous note keeping. In order to keep an accurate tally of the rally, Maskell used his own system of shorthand, the nib of his pencil marking time with each sweep of the racket.

"He's now letting Chang play
his own game - and he does
that better than anyone."
(Christine Janes)

"That shot knocked the
stuffing out of his sails!"
(Fru McMillan)

"Noah always beats Curren.
He has a sort of Houdini
against him." (John Lloyd)

"She puts her head down and
bangs it straight across the
line." (Ann Jones)

"Even when he has to move
back, he moves back so that
he's moving forwards!"
(Mark Cox)

"Chris Lloyd came out of the
dressing room like a pistol."
(Virginia Wade)

"Zivojinovic seems to be able
to pull the big bullet out of
the top drawer."
(Mike Ingham)

"Martina, she's got several
layers of steel out there like
a cat with nine
lives." (Virginia Wade)

"These ball boys are
marvellous. You don't even
notice them. There's a left-
handed one over there.
I noticed him earlier."
(Max Robertson)

"And when Chrissie is
playing well I always feel
that she is playing well."
(Ann Jones)

Maskell's was an old colonial style that was totally in keeping with a championships that, in its 1930s time-warp, forbade advertising, dressed its players in virginal white and referred to all married women players by their husbands' names. But while classic British reserve set the tone, it would be wrong to say that emotion never got the better of Maskell. When the Centre Court crowd sang "For She's a Jolly Good Fellow" to Virginia Wade following her ladies' singles triumph in the jubilee year of 1977, the commentator, tears welling in his eyes, was overcome and speechless.

The late seventies were the swansong for the great stroke-players. Muscle-bound serve-and-volleyers were about to unzip their graphite-framed weapons of mass destruction and blow away the purveyors of guile and subtlety. Before they departed the scene, they bequeathed Maskell his two most memorable Wimbledon matches.

The veteran believed that Bjorn Borg's titanic five set victory over Vitas Guerilitis in a 1978 semi-final would never be eclipsed, but in the final two years later, the Swede defeated John McEnroe in a yet greater epic. Maskell described the fourth set tie-break, which McEnroe won 18-16 after more than twenty minutes as the most remarkable set of tennis he had ever witnessed. "Their physical and mental speed, plus their controlled power and accuracy – the result of perfect timing – was almost beyond belief," he wrote. Borg won the deciding set 8-6 to take his record fifth consecutive Wimbledon title.

Maskell rated Rod Laver as the best player he had ever seen. It was not just his technical brilliance that Maskell admired, it was his indestructible temperament and his humility. John McEnroe's lack of grace did not preclude his appearance on the list of all-time greats. At Palm Springs in 1978 for a Davis Cup match, Maskell had been served early notice of the New Yorker's rudeness when he was told to "shut up" half way though the first set of the opening rubber. Nevertheless, his tennis was sublime and Maskell felt his demolition of Jimmy Connors in 1984 was the most complete performance in a Wimbledon final.

Away from the commentary box, Maskell continued to take a broader role in the development of British tennis. In 1955 he left his coaching duties at Wimbledon to become the training manager for the Lawn Tennis Association. Until his retirement from the LTA in 1973, Maskell dedicated himself to the promotion of the game, travelling the country to spread the gospel and completely restructuring the amateur coaching set-up.

In 1970, Maskell suffered the first of two crushing personal tragedies. His accountant son, Jay, was killed when the light aircraft he

BBC

was piloting crashed when coming in to land on the Bahamas. Nine years, later his wife, Con, was drowned in Antigua while taking her early morning swim. That Maskell was able to survive the double trauma was due in no small part to his marriage in 1980 to Kay Latto, who had turned to him for advice when writing her book on the rehabilitation of the mentally handicapped. What he had learned in the war about rebuilding the lives of wounded airmen was now, indirectly, sustaining him in his own hour of need.

Maskell's morale was raised further in 1982 with the award of the CBE to add to his earlier OBE. The unintentionally apt citation read for "services to tennis". He was also granted an honorary degree from the University of Loughborough. He died on 10 December 1992.

# Bill McLaren

Thirty mud-caked hulks, half of whom are mostly visible only from their shorts down, and a book of laws as impenetrable as the constitution of a banana republic make rugby union one of the most challenging sports for a commentator to describe. Teddy Wakelam, the first to attempt it, bemoaned the checklist of peril that awaited the man at the microphone:

> "Continuity, clearness, co-operation with 'Dr Watson', correct tally of score and scorers, visibility, raising of voice and consequent blasting when the crowd begins to roar, accuracy of summing up at half-time and at the end, filling up gaps during stoppages or unseen incidents, picking out celebrities who may be present, watching for changes of position on the field, or alterations when a man goes off or returns after temporary absence, summing up the whys and wherefores of the referee's whistle, watching the touch judges' flags to see whether a goal is kicked, keeping going, keeping going, keeping going."

When searching for a new voice to take up the gauntlet and bring popular appeal to this "ruffians' game played by gentlemen", the BBC decided to look away from the traditional spawning grounds of the Home Counties to find a personality with the knowledge and enthusiasm to fire the imagination of the viewing public *en masse*. Their quest ended at the bastion of Scottish borders rugby, Hawick, and a 28-year-old local newspaper journalist blessed with a voice in a million. His name was William Pollock McLaren.

Here was a real gem. Not only did a passion for the game course through his veins (he received a rugby ball for Christmas every year from the age of six) but he also possessed in abundance the other two indispensable attributes of a potential commentating great: a talent for accumulating and retaining information and an effortless ease of expression.

The first signs of a journalistic desire to communicate appeared when, as a youngster, he appointed himself Hawick's unofficial correspondent to the Scottish XV. Punting a ball back and forth across the local rec, this young Walter McMitty would conjure reports of his heroes humiliating all-comers before disappearing into his room to recount their heroics in the voices of the radio commentators of the day. When not sitting on walls, spinning vivid descriptions of his

### Home Lovin' Man

"I took one look at the traffic in London and decided it wasn't for me."

schoolmates replaying the Olympics, he would spend hours cramming data on rugby and cricket (he enthusiastically followed the fortunes of Yorkshire) into scrapbook after scrapbook.

But McLaren yearned for more than just third-party involvement; his dream was to pull on the navy blue shirt of his country and run out onto the hallowed turf of Murrayfield. "I would have given it all up to have played just once for Scotland," he mused when looking back over the considerable aggregate of a lifetime's achievements. The pillar of the Hawick back row certainly had the ability, but his call up into the army at the age of eighteen was to kick his ambitions temporarily into touch.

A couple of years after returning from service in the artillery in Italy, he had been again on the verge of international selection when he broke down with what turned out to be a life-threatening illness.

It was with unfortunate irony that, having survived unscathed the shelling and the snipers' bullets in the bloodbath of Monte Cassino, McLaren should be struck down by a disease picked up right at the end of the war during a three-week stint in charge of a military prison in Milan. At the time, tuberculosis was tantamount to a death sentence and McLaren's doctors warned him that, with a hole in his lung "the size of an old half crown", the best he could hope for was to spend four years confined to a hospital bed. Yet, after agreeing to be a guinea pig for a new wonder drug called streptomycin, he stunned his physicians by walking out of the East Fortune Sanatorium after just 19 months.

Knowing he wouldn't be able to play rugby seriously again, McLaren got a job as a junior reporter at his local newspaper while he waited for a teaching post to become available in the town. International rugby honours aside, he had always harboured ambitions to be a teacher and had trained in physical education on leaving the army. In 1959, he became supervisor of sport and PE for Hawick's five primary schools, a post he would hold until 1987.

As far as his entry into broadcasting was concerned, it wasn't McLaren's hospital radio commentaries on inter-ward putting and table-tennis competitions that got his foot in the door, it was his skills as a statistician. The editor of the *Hawick Express* noted his dedication and wrote to the BBC suggesting they consider employing him as a commentator. Having thrown away the invitation to audition, dismissing it as a joke, McLaren eventually made his trial broadcast in 1951 as part of a six-man team covering a match between the South of Scotland and South Africa. Despite being almost consumed by nerves, he did well enough during his ten-minute slot to be asked to cover the inter-city match between Edinburgh and Glasgow the following week. McLaren stayed on radio for the remainder of the decade, not making his television debut until 1962.

In the meantime, McLaren had passed up a golden opportunity to become the voice of BBC athletics. The corporation had been sufficiently beguiled by his knowledge and professionalism to offer him a staff post, with a view to him leading the coverage of track and field, which at the time was the jewel in its sporting crown. But the requirement to move south would have frayed the emotional ties with his beloved home town. True to his belief that "a day out of Hawick is a day wasted", he declined and let the baton pass to David Coleman.

BBC

As McLaren began his television career he must have rued his decision to forego the Olympics. When the cameras arrived at rugby union matches in the early sixties, they were greeted by a bland spectacle, with most internationals offering the on-looker little more than grim kicking and scrummaging duels. In 1963 he described a Scotland-Wales clash featuring 111 line outs.

It was hardly the kind of fare that complemented the incessant rhythm of McLaren's "melodic Borders baritone" and he had to wait until the seventies and the emergence of thrilling new Welsh stars such as Gareth Edwards, Barry John, Phil Bennett and JPR Williams to be given the opportunity to communicate the joy of fast, skilful, flowing rugby.

"Weir's romping up there like a
mad giraffe!"

"Gagan Huth: all arms and legs
like a mad octopus when he
goes in there!"

"The ball is being laid back like
a hen laying an egg."

"He's as slippery as a baggy
in a Border burn is Brian
Redpath there."

"I'm no hod carrier but I'd be
laying bricks if he were running
at me."

"He's so solid you'd need
dynamite or a Highland Light
Infantry to shift him."

"He didn't hit it very well. It
went over like a pound
of mince."

The men in red were joined by players of stunning flair and invention from all quarters. The swashbuckling Australian David Campese and the prodigiously talented Scottish full-back Andy Irvine caught McLaren's eye particularly. "They were two players who always made the spectator sit up and take notice every time they got the ball," he recalled. McLaren rated Ireland's Mike Gibson as the most complete rugby footballer he had ever seen. Gibson, who was as at home at scrum-half as he was in the midfield "had a forest animal's instinct for what was going on. He would sniff a try quicker than anyone else."

Bizarre animal similes would develop into the stock-in-trade of McLaren's work. During a typical commentary a whole menagerie of deranged creatures would slip onto the field of play. A "mad giraffe", "niggly rhino", "animated meercat", "startled whippet", "enraged water buffalo", not to mention a "demented tsetse fly", all took their bow at some stage or other. It was all part of his ploy to use slang and everyday language to bring a humorous dimension to the game and lure in the casual viewer. "At times I have to switch off my mike because I'm laughing so much at his fantastic imagery," confessed his occasional co-commentator, Gavin Hastings. Viewers, too, warmed to McLaren's refreshing informality; in the heat of battle, phrases like "shilly-shallying", "jiggery-pokery" and "argy-bargy" were like a gust of fresh air amid stifling technical jargon.

McLaren concedes that not all of his analogies were off the cuff and that he would usually have three or four lines up his sleeve "to get him out of trouble". In fact, every eventuality was covered with a clinical fussiness matched only by horse racing's Peter O'Sullevan or football's John Motson. The process for a Saturday match would start on a Monday, when he would take a deck of cards, one for each player, and practice randomly matching names to numbers. It was rarely before Thursday that recognition became automatic.

By mid-week, McLaren's mother-of-all-crib-sheets would be nearing completion. He jam-packed this A3-sized labour of love with multi-coloured mini-profiles of all the players, including replacements, plus the referee, touch judges and their replacements. In all, they contained potted biographies of over forty individuals. There were data and vital statistics to cover virtually every scenario and he never missed an opportunity to reap full value from his preparation: "They'll be chortling down at Poynder Park at that one, Alan Tait, who used to play for Kelso." The regular "and they'll be dancing in the streets of _____" name-checks for the outposts of the Scottish game also served as a clever PR exercise that helped underpin his enormous popularity back home.

The "big sheet", as he called it, counted for nothing when McLaren was confronted by his most implacable enemy: heavy rain. Pitches dissolved into morasses and the players became, as he puts it, "creations from a sculptor's table brought to life." Another problem was the growing fad for players to wear scrum-caps. In the old days, only the occasional lock felt precious enough to adorn his brow with a hoop of precautionary bandage. As time went on, not only half the pack but even the scrum-halves upgraded to these feature-distorting devices.

Like several other commentators, notably Murray Walker, McLaren thrived on nervous energy. "Don't worry about being nervous, in fact don't broadcast unless you're nervous," he advises. "You have got to be keyed up like the players and let the adrenalin flow. Just trust in your ability and experience." Fifteen minutes before each kick-off, those nerves translated into a quick dash down the blind side to the toilet - a ritual he would perform prior to every game, whether he needed to or not.

Whatever nerves may have been present were totally untraceable once the first whistle sounded. From the kick-off his vocal handling was sure and his judgement almost never strayed offside. When play was at its most expansive, he maintained a constant pitch all the while the ball stayed live, only dropping his register and pausing for oxygen when touch was made or the referee's whistle blew.

'Hikka the hooker from Nongataha puts an end to it for the All Blacks with a brilliant try!'

In John Allan's facsimile of a typical passage of McLaren commentary, his ability to weave luscious imagery and associative material into a metronomic rhythm is neatly illustrated:

"Armstrong to Chalmers, who pops it inside like clockwork to John Jeffries, known to his friends and foes as the White Shark, who hails from a wee town in the Borders known as Kelso. Jeffries sets up the ruck and the Scottish forwards – like a pack of hyenas – clean up over the ball – Armstrong digs the ball out like a demented mole and gives a peach of a pass to Gavin Hastings, who hoists a Garryowen deep into the English half."

Only once the try-line was sure to be breached would he allow himself the luxury of a crescendo, granting himself only a moment's respite before drawing on amazing powers of recall to expertly dissect the action replay.

It is impossible to find a bad word said about Bill McLaren. Within the game he was held in universal affection, with players being especially appreciative of the tender terms in which he couched any criticism. "The great thing about him is that he'll never ridicule your mistakes, and that's why the players love him so much" observed Andy Irvine. "If someone drops a pass or knocks on, he'll simply say, "…and Andy will know he could have done a wee bit better there.'"

There may have been no prouder Scot than McLaren, but he was almost unique amongst commentators in never receiving mail accusing him of bias. For commentary purposes he was a rugby enthusiast first and a patriot second and it was a tribute to both his impartiality and popularity when a group of red-swathed supporters from the Valleys unfurled a banner at Murrayfield proclaiming "Bill McLaren is a Welshman".

McLaren's neutrality was never to be more sorely tested, though, than in 1976, when his son-in-law, Alan Lawson, touched down against England to finish a move that had started from Scotland's goal line. "I was so excited," he recalled, "I almost fell out of the commentary box!" It was to be his most exhilarating moment as a commentator.

The 1990 grand slam decider against the auld enemy was another highlight, especially as the crucial score in Scotland's emotional win was scored by Tony Stanger, one of his former pupils at Hawick. Some Scottish players even regarded him as their unofficial talisman, with one even using his absence from the commentary box as an excuse for a defeat.

Few people are better qualified to pass judgement on the evolution of rugby union in the last fifty years than McLaren. "From school days

> And Clive Norling, running backwards, just like a football referee, looking forward to make sure nothing is happening behind him.

158

to college days and beyond, from black and white to satellite, players would come and go. But there would always be one constant," eulogised John Inverdale in a television profile. It was unfortunate, then, that the final years of his broadcasting career would see the spirit of Barry John and company eroded by the arrival of the money men. "The essence of rugby to me is that it is sporting and fun and I don't believe there is another game that brings out the best in people like rugby does. But we have definitely lost something in the move to professionalism," he noted sombrely. As the eminent sports scribe Hugh McIlvanney pointed out, "To many in these days of mercenary imperatives and cynical ruthlessness, he is the voice of sport's lost innocence."

In his last Calcutta Cup match with the BBC in February 2002, McLaren belied his 78 years to deliver a typically vivid and mellifluous commentary. The only clue he gave that it was time to blow the whistle on a definitive career was when he committed an uncharacteristic verbal knock-on by referring to Scotland being set to win the match when they were in fact twenty points behind. "Wishful thinking, Bill?" asked his co-commentator, the former England hooker Brian Moore, "working the oracle", with a skilful piece of invisible mending.

"The Voice" retired in April 2002, acknowledged from Dundee to Dunedin as the world's best rugby commentator. His status as a legend in the game was confirmed by his induction into the International Rugby Hall of Fame, the only non-international to receive the honour. He was even offered an honorary cap for Scotland but, with typical shy modesty, declined.

"McLaren has the gift to spread his own enthusiasm through his audience like a contagion," wrote Alasdair Reid in *The Times*. Sadly, the sanitised environment in which the game of rugby now operates is unlikely to breed a worthy successor to this uniquely gifted professional whose golden voice both entranced and enthralled.

# Brian Moore

Brian Moore, the voice of ITV football for over thirty years, was one of the most respected and widely liked commentators of his generation. Generous and self-effacing, he brought a reassuring presence to football presentation without which the network would have struggled to challenge the BBC's position as the sport's dominant terrestrial broadcaster.

Brian Baden Moore was born on 28 February 1932 in Benenden, a chocolate box village set amongst the meadows and hop gardens of the Weald of Kent. Despite his contented, if modest, upbringing, the farm worker's son yearned for more challenging horizons. His escapism manifested itself in his love of sport, and the commentaries of Raymond Glendenning, which crackled through on the family's old Bakelite wireless, inspired his ambition to enter sports journalism.

Moore may never have been granted any such opportunity had he not won a scholarship to Cranbrook public school. There, he excelled at sport, becoming captain of cricket and hockey and ultimately head boy. His rise from the ranks was all the more impressive as his "village green grammar" at first alienated him from classmates from more well-heeled families. His early experiences left him with what he described as a "crippling inferiority complex" which, together with his natural affinity for the working man, helped lay the foundation of his life-long allegiance to the Labour Party.

Psychometric tests concluded that Moore was "too sensitive and diffident and too easily discouraged" to pursue his dream and instead recommended the "trading departments such as water supply or gas". It was during his two years' national service with the RAF that a chance event would nudge him towards commentating. After an injury had side-lined him from a sports gala, he was asked by his commanding officer to perform the announcements over the tannoy. One of his officer friends' wives informed him he had "such an attractive voice" and recommended he made use of it when he was demobbed.

Back on civvy street, the possibility of a lifetime's futility in a utility prompted Moore to mothball his socialist principles and tap into the old boy network. Peter West, the cricket presenter and fellow Old Cranbrookian, dipped into his little black book and got him a job as the driver and personal assistant to E W Swanton, the eminent *Daily Telegraph* journalist, BBC cricket commentator and Kent stalwart. Swanton may

**What a sheepskin!**

Moore brought an
audience to the edge of
its collective seat more
often than most.

have been testy and demanding but he taught Moore some harsh though critical lessons in the art of sports writing. Having learnt the hard way, he was able to progress to *The Times* where, in 1958, he joined the anonymous legion of "football correspondents".

As a talented batsman who once proudly shared a partnership with the great Colin Cowdrey, it was natural that Moore's first love should be cricket. Yet football prised its way into his affections when, in September 1947, he took time out from visiting his Aunt Mary to take in a match at Gillingham's Priestfield Stadium. The Southern League encounter, in which the Kent club triumphed 4-1 over Bath City, may have had the glamour of Ena Sharples in a G-string but the experience fired his imagination. For the boy from the sticks it was, as he put it, "like a trip to another and more exciting world". He would later serve for ten years on the club's board of directors.[1]

Covering amateur football had whetted the appetite of the ambitious young reporter. In a fit of dogged persistence that his psychometric counsellor would have found hard to fathom, Moore successfully petitioned Angus Mackay, the Generalissimo of BBC radio sport, to

[1]In 2002 Gillingham named a new stand after him which, perhaps in tribute to his famously thin pate, came without a roof.

offer him a job on the *Sports Report* desk. The meticulous Scotsman would shape his whole broadcasting life, instilling in him first and foremost the importance of preparation and attention to detail. Having completed the best possible apprenticeship, Moore went on to commit remarkably few errors of detail in the course of his commentating career, although he did once tell 15 million viewers that "Hamburg win the European Cup" just minutes after John McGovern had lifted the trophy for Nottingham Forest.

The tutelage of Mackay culminated in Moore's first radio commentaries and soon the BBC's first "Association Football Correspondent" was exchanging the modest terraces of Walthamstow Avenue and Kingstonian for more exalted perches in the grand theatres of European football. When the World Cup came to England in 1966, BBC-TV invited him to join their commentary team. To Moore's deep disappointment, his somewhat cupidinous agent managed to scupper the contract negotiations, leaving him to trudge back to his desk at Broadcasting House fearing his opportunity to break into television had eluded him forever. But then a chin hove into view.

By the late 1960s, Jimmy Hill, the luxuriantly jawed ex-Fulham utility player, former chairman of the Professional Footballers' Association and successful abolitionist of the footballers' maximum wage had resigned as manager of newly promoted Coventry City to become Head of Sport at London Weekend Television. While his number two, John Bromley, had expressed a preference for Barry Davies to be the station's lead football commentator, Hill, or the "silver-tongued persuader" as Moore christened him, was firm in his conviction. "I want you to climb a mountain with me," he schmoozed over lunch. "I can't promise an easy climb, but one thing's for certain - it'll be an exciting one!"

Suitably beguiled, Moore forsook a lifetime's security in radio and buckled on his crampons. The culture shock was significant as he was obliged to swap the splendour of his West London abode not for LWT's state-of-the-art studios on the South Bank, but a dingy concrete base-camp just off the North Circular.

ITV's sports coverage in the 1960s, like its accommodation, was hopelessly outgunned by the BBC. The proudly independent regional stations that comprised the network had not been able to establish a pooled sports unit to take on the corporation in terms of resources, negotiating power and, most importantly, credibility. Under the brash and ambitious Hill, the worm started to turn and LWT, in the vanguard of the ITV sports revolution, introduced a refreshing new edge to sports

### Fanzine Fame

Brian Moore's Head Looks Uncannily Like The London Planetarium, according to the Gillingham fanzine of the same name.

## ARSENAL SNATCH THE 1989 LEAGUE CHAMPIONSHIP

*"Arsenal come streaming forward in what surely will be their last attack. A good ball by Dixon, finding Smith. Thomas, charging through the mid-field. Thomas...it's up for grabs now! An unbelievable climax to the league season! Well into injury time, and the Liverpool players are down, absolutely abject! Aldridge is down, Barnes is down. Dalglish just stands there. Nicol's on his knees, McMahon's on his knees. Suddenly it was Michael Thomas, bursting through. The bounce fell his way. He flicks it wide of Grobbelaar and we have one of the most dramatic finishes maybe in the history of the football league!"*

coverage. *The Big Match*, LWT's Sunday afternoon equivalent of the BBC's *Match of the Day*, signalled the company's intentions as it reinvigorated the highlights package concept with readers' letters, oddities from around the world and innovations such as the Golden Goals competition.

When Hill began to spice up the post-match platitudes with opinion and analysis, the concept of punditry was born. For the 1970 World Cup, the lone expert expanded into a panel of four and a quantum leap in television football presentation was made.

In its drive to dent the ratings of its rival, ITV was pushing back the frontiers of broadcasting and, some would say, taste. In the role of ring-master to Bob McNab, Pat Crerand, Derek Dougan and Malcolm Allison, Moore presided over a quartet of feisty personalities whose opinions were often even more raw than their fashion sense. The off-the-cuff debate spawned the legend of the bar-room footballing cliché and Moore looked on like a bemused clergyman at the font as "the boy done great" and "over the moon" received their baptism into the parlance of the game. As their foil, "Brian" would also remain indelible in the vernacular.

In 1970, ITV's principal football commentator was the effervescent Hugh "one-nothing" Johns, with Moore deployed to the studio to marshal his temperamental back four. As a broadcaster from the gantry, Moore's skills were still developing as his first match in tandem with the cameras had been an early season encounter between Queen's Park Rangers and Manchester City only two years earlier.

"My commentaries from those early days still fill me with embarrassment," he conceded in his autobiography, "I shouted far too much." His fondness for stating the obvious by hollering "GOAL" whenever the onion-bag bulged was a throw-back to his radio days and drew comment from "wiser" old heads amongst the production team. Yet Moore saw it as his commentary remit to "milk the drama for all it was worth" and, after reining himself in for a few weeks, he subtly reasserted his clamorous style. Playbacks proved that the crowd shouted "GOAL" when the ball hits the net, so why, he reasoned, shouldn't he?

In the early years of his television career, Moore found himself pondering a learning curve that challenged the vertical. Mexico was the technical nemesis for many a television executive as the era of satellite communications dawned, but ITV knew that they had to be in the vanguard of the revolution. In 1969, Moore was dispatched westwards in the role of commentating *conquistador* to cover England's World Cup warm-up game against Mexico. It was almost a disaster. First, Jimmy

## THE STRIFE OF BRIAN

Hill's live preamble was drowned out by a marching band so belligerent that it could easily have been re-routed from the gates of The Alamo and, second, Moore had been confined to a sweltering glass-house with no view and a microphone straight out of Marconi's attic.

By the time the World Cup returned to Mexico sixteen years later, the commentator's lot had barely improved. This time, although the commentary position was satisfactory, the audio feed to London went down, forcing Moore to retreat to the back of the box to describe the whole 90 minutes on a public telephone. Yet even this was a paltry inconvenience compared with events at the tournament proper the following summer. When Spain met Brazil, the Mexican technicians had hopelessly confused the plugs for each country's sound feed, resulting in the world's broadcasters receiving commentaries in random languages. While the words of ITV's commentator, Peter Brackley, were unwittingly illuminating living rooms somewhere in Asia, Moore made ready to describe the action from a monitor in the studio back in London. He and his co-commentator Brian Clough were clever enough, though, to own up to their predicament and turned the episode into an unexpected "bonding" opportunity with the viewers.

While Moore enjoyed a harmonious relationship with all of his co-commentators, his partnership with Clough was, for him, the most memorable. They made an odd couple, sharing little more than sincerely held socialist convictions, but they forged a compelling partnership in the early seventies that threatened to seize the initiative from the BBC. Clough's wilful contrariness and sometimes black-hatted indignation (not to mention masterly analytical skill) complemented Moore's rational even-handedness. For the first and possibly only time, viewers hovered over their channel selectors as they pondered their provider for the FA Cup final.

By dividing his time between presentation and commentary, Moore had become the face of televised football, as well as one of its premier voices. The BBC, duly noting his versatility and reliability, attempted to lure him back to the corporation with the succulent offer of a cricket presentation role similar to that of Peter West. Although he would remain behind John Motson and Barry Davies in Saturday night's *Match of the Day* pecking-order, Moore made up his mind to accept the offer. Only the intervention of his agent and the promise of his own sporting documentary series (dubbed *Brian Moore Meets*) deflected him from his intention. Later, Sky Sports invited him to lead the satellite channel's Monday night football coverage but by the time he got round to registering his interest, the wind had changed direction.

"Commentators don't boost ratings," proclaimed David Hill, Sky's Head of Sport, and the Monday evening franchise was passed to ITV's ever-reliable second-stringer, Alan Parry.

The arrival of the image-fixated eighties sounded the death-knell for the old guard. Television executives were starting to clamour for the youth, sophistication and Hollywood smile of a Steve Rider over the high forehead, saggy eyes and toothy grin of a Brian Moore. Yet despite the inevitability that youth would at some stage supplant experience, Moore's sacking from the *Midweek Sports Special* chair in 1986 came as a bitter personal blow. An assault to his self-esteem it may have been, but it was a decision that was possibly to save his life as later that year he was diagnosed with a heart condition that, if left untreated, would have been fatal had he maintained his unforgiving work-load.

For the last dozen years of his career, which coincided with the renaissance of the game in England following the relative success of the 1990 World Cup, Moore was able to concentrate on commentary. He was rewarded by some matches of quite breathtaking drama.

Surely there will never be a more thrilling climax to a championship season than in 1989. In the days before Sky had annexed the phrase "live and exclusive", ITV was on hand to relay the excitement of the title decider between Liverpool and Arsenal free-to-air. As Arsenal's Michael Thomas bore down on Bruce Grobbelaar's goal and prepared to dispatch the fateful injury time dink, Moore spoke one of the most famous lines in football commentary: "It's up for grabs now!" It most definitely was - and so was the video, which sold 25,000 copies within a week. Moore, whose second team was Arsenal's arch rivals Tottenham, was subsequently fêted by Gunners fans wherever he went.

One of Moore's cleverest pieces of commentary was for the infamous Ronald Koeman goal which helped condemn Graham Taylor's hapless England to non-qualification for the 1994 World Cup. To prepare for the crucial match against Holland in Rotterdam, Moore had taken a taxi to the Dutch training ground, where he observed the full repertoire of Koeman speciality free-kicks. As the clock ticked down on an evenly matched contest, Koeman, who should not have been on the field having earlier committed a crass professional foul on David Platt, placed the ball down just outside England's penalty area. The kick, which had been leathered with all the Dutchman's might against an encroaching English wall, had to be retaken and Moore knew from his reconnaissance that Koeman, whose neatly cropped, bright-blond hair caused him to resemble an escapee from *The Village of the Damned*, would have something more sinister up his sleeve. "He's going to clip it,

## Kipper Hell

Moore is joined on the 1974 World Cup panel by fashion victims (right to left) Malcolm Allison, Jack Charlton, Brian Clough and Derek Dougan.

he's going to clip it," flustered the commentator as the man in orange hesitated at the end of a suspiciously truncated run-up. They turned out to be cruelly prophetic words and the ball flopped over the wall into David Seaman's net, thus condemning England to another four years in the World Cup wilderness.

The France World Cup of 1998 was to be Moore's last tournament before slipping off into a well-deserved retirement. It was a pity that England couldn't have done him the courtesy of at least reaching the last four. In the end, their dramatic penalty competition exit at the hands of old foes Argentina on a balmy night in St Etienne left a memorable career not quite consummated. What is worse, most of his thunder was stolen by his co-commentator, Kevin Keegan.

As a footballing exponent, he was top drawer, but when it came to imparting incisive third-party wisdom, King Kev was propping up the Conference. The chickens came home to roost at the end of England's first phase match versus Rumania. England had equalised and were looking to snatch a late winner. Then, on 87 minutes, Keegan failed to heed one of commentating's cardinal rules (to remember that *anything* can happen) and uttered the most memorable sound-bite of the whole tournament: "When a game goes like this, Brian, there's only one team gonna win it, that's England." On 89 minutes, the ball looped into the box and Moore was onto it quickly, the rising intonation of voice indicating that another humiliation was in the offing: "A little chip in again. It's Petrescu right in there. Oh, he's scored!"

A professional of Moore's experience should have realised that Keegan was cursed. Nevertheless, eight days later, as David Batty placed the ball on the penalty spot in order to keep England alive in the penalty competition against Argentina, he needlessly reactivated the hex: "You know him much better than anybody. Do you back him to score? Quickly, yes or no?" "Yes", replied Kevin. England flew home the next day.

Although Moore was haunted by the hospital pass that he had lobbed Keegan, the match, which turned out to be the most dramatic of the tournament, was a personal triumph. The broadcast attracted 27 million viewers, an audience bettered only by a Christmas edition of *Only Fools and Horses* (itself an apt descriptor of several England squads in the nineties) and, owing to a strike at ITV, an episode of *To the Manor Born*. Moore had finally reached the summit of his personal mountain.

He had hoped to spend a long and satisfying retirement indulging his passion for cricket from the stands of the St Lawrence Ground in Canterbury. But, in September 2001 at the age of 69, Moore died suddenly from a heart attack. With the saddest of ironies it was just a few hours before England's 5-1 World Cup qualifying triumph over Germany in Munich. The tributes were fulsome and sincere. The minute's silences, held at grounds up and down the country, were observed impeccably. Quite simply, he was held in universal esteem.

"I've listened to you a lot," said Jimmy Hill, "I like your voice and, more importantly, you don't offend anyone". That may have sounded like damnation with faint praise but it neatly summed up the essence of good commentary, a craft which Moore, the broadcaster with the human touch, had off to a tee.

Brian Moore would never permit personal opinion, forced humour, trivial asides or, heaven forbid, statistics to clog the conduit between the field of play and the nation's living rooms. Unimpaired by the constraints of ego he was able to communicate fully the passion, excitement and emotion of football.

For almost a generation, he remained true to his own definition of football commentary: "finding the right delicate balance between describing the action, imparting information and adding that dash of drama that draws it to the realms of entertainment". As befits a master communicator, it is probably the most succinct interpretation of the art that there is.

# John Motson

Every citizen of the United Kingdom, save perhaps the more insular elements of the Hebridean crofting community, has heard of John Motson. Frequently lampooned but held in great affection by the viewing public, "Motty" has been virtually unassailable as BBC-TV's voice of football for a quarter of a century.

"Golly, you have to say it's been quite an astonishing career," as Motson-speak would probably have it. Owner of the best overcoat in the business – a knee-length sheepskin number that wouldn't have looked out of place on the set of *Shaft* - this broadcasting institution has presided over a more lucrative exchange of silverware than Arthur Negus and Hugh Scully combined. Between 1979 and 1994 he covered 29 consecutive major cup finals and, in all, has chronicled over one thousand matches. He also holds the distinction of being the only broadcaster to commentate on the final of five World Cups.

Motty, who was born in Salford in Lancashire but grew up in London, was introduced to football by his Methodist minister father, who took him to The Valley to watch Charlton Athletic reserves. In April 1952, at the age of six, he remembers being mesmerised by the experience of seeing his first competitive game, a 1-1 draw against visiting Chelsea.

As Motson senior's flock-tending duties took him all over the city, Motty junior became an avid accumulator of match-day programmes. These treasure-troves of trivia, gleaned from all corners of the capital, fuelled the fascination for factual fluff that has since made him an irritant to some but an engagingly obsessed "anorak" to the game's rank and file.

The devotion could have easily withered once the eleven-year-old had been packed off to a rugby-playing boarding school in Bury St Edmunds, but he was able to feed his habit through the occasional Saturday afternoon bunk-off to Portman Road to watch Ipswich. Between lessons he passed the time by pasting statistics into his fastidiously maintained scrap-books. Particularly eagerly awaited was the weekly Saturday night classified results paper which he acquired - at a price - from school-mate and later head of sport at Central Television, Gary Newbon.

When he was 18, Motty joined the *Barnet Press* newspaper as a junior reporter, later moving to the *Morning Telegraph* in Sheffield where he first covered league football. A short freelance spell with BBC Radio Sheffield was followed by a switch to network radio in 1968, where on Radio 2 he made his name as a sports presenter as well as a commentator on football,

tennis and boxing. The second half of Everton against Derby County in December 1969 was the first piece of football he described for the BBC.

At the age of 26, Motty won himself a season's trial on *Match of the Day* following the departure of Kenneth Wolstenholme to ITV. Halfway through his first season, in February 1972, he was lucky enough to be allocated the celebrated FA Cup tie between Southern League Hereford United and first division Newcastle. As a much delayed third-round clash being played on fourth round day, the match was hardly top of the bill fare. "I'd been sent down on the basis that Newcastle would probably coast through and it would be three minutes at the end of the show," he recalls. "They promoted that match to the top of the programme and ran it at about 40 minutes. I think that convinced people for the first time that I could handle the big game."

"Middlesbrough are withdrawing Maccarone the Italian, Nemeth the Slovakian and Stockdale the right back."

"He's got those telescopic legs that turn a Leeds long ball into an Arsenal one."

"And Seaman, like a falling oak, manages to change direction."

"Wimbledon head the ball forward in the shape of Robbie Earle.

"That's an old Ipswich move – O'Callaghan crossing for Mariner to drive over the bar."

"This could be our best victory over Germany since the war."

"Gullit…turned to find he had someone standing on his toes."

"The world cup – truly an international event."

"Nearly all the Brazilian supporters are wearing yellow shirts. It's a fabulous kaleidoscope of colour."

"And I suppose they [Spurs] are nearer to being out of the FA Cup now than at any time since the first half of the season, when they weren't even in it anyway."

"For those of you watching in black and white, Spurs are in the all-yellow strip."

"It's a football stadium in the truest sense of the word."

"And what a time to score. 22 minutes gone."

Handle it he could. The clip that starts "…and Tudor goes down for Newcastle" and ends with Hereford's Ronnie Radford prancing around with arms aloft and muddied shirt flapping around his navel after scoring one of the most explosive thunderbolts in the history of the competition is one of the most repeated items from the BBC archives. Motty's shrieks of "What a goal! What a goal!" were as vociferous an expression of exhilaration as had yet been heard in football commentary and armchair fans immediately welcomed him into their living rooms as one of their own. The canny ability to express what the average fan is thinking has indeed been the key to his enduring popularity.

Science has deconstructed the Motson formula and also ratified it as a winner. In a Barclaycard-sponsored project to establish which television or radio voice struck the most harmonious chord with football's ten million lounge-based spectators, the voice patterns of eight well-known commentators were examined. The findings revealed that, in terms of speed range and volume, Motty's came closest to matching the "first ever blueprint for perfect vocal commentary". A speech therapist attached to the project said, "Close analysis of the commentators showed many similarities in their capacity to inspire enthusiasm, trust and excitement, but John Motson has the biggest impact on fans, simply due to the use of his voice."

Ever modest, Motty prefers to say that keeping things simple has been the key to his success. "I'm commentating for the bloke in the pub really," he says, "it's a working man's sport. You can't take a terribly intellectual view of Wimbledon versus Aston Villa on a cold Saturday in November."

The armoury of statistics with which Motty equips himself before every commentary is for his own "satisfaction and protection" as he puts it. Obscure substitutes who come on and grab glory are singled out as being particularly dangerous. "You never know who is the story," he warns, "the papers can check. I have to have it filed away." His determination to cover every base and leave no stone of triviality unturned paid particular dividends in 1977 when the captain of Manchester United went up to receive the FA Cup. "How fitting that a man called Buchan should be the first to climb the thirty-nine steps!" Motty remarked gleefully. He could hardly have suspected that his out-of-hours fondness for reading thrillers would ever have assisted him in his day job.

Motty's lieutenant in all things statistical is his wife Anne, who every season compiles an almanac of matches, scorers and appearances to complement her husband's vast library of cuttings, videos and reference works. The lengths to which he goes to avoid being caught out know no bounds. Just before the 1990 World Cup, he took a course of lessons in

Italian from a woman in Watford. He's even been known to study footballers at adjacent dinner tables.

In domestic football, Motty is admirably unpartisan. Indeed, you'll do very well to pin him down to any particular club allegiance. He gets a regular postbag from cretins up and down the country accusing him of holding scab-like loyalties to hated rivals. True, he held a Chelsea season ticket in the days before five Lotto numbers were needed to buy one, but his professional detachment as a journalist has bestowed on him, so he claims, the most diplomatic of neutralities. He admits to having more than a soft-spot for Barnet, no doubt safe in the knowledge that hell will freeze over before he would ever be called on to commentate on north London's men in amber.

When England are playing, however, Motty gleefully bins his Henry Kissinger raincoat to drape himself in the cross of St George, his accompaniment being vibrant and effervescent when things are going well, dispirited and deflated when they are not. His partisanship has been deemed jingoistic by some critics, who scorned his need to mention that the Ireland versus Norway match in the 1994 World Cup finals (for which England did not qualify) featured seventeen players from the Premiership. The stat-man refutes the allegations, stating that in the previous FA Cup final, he happily named the fourteen non-English players who were included in the Chelsea and Manchester United line-ups.

The predictability of Motty's rhetoric is not to the connoisseur's taste. Regular fillers such as "I wonder", "I fancy" and "surely" and the gratuitous little chuckle he employs between clauses to buy himself a second's thinking time (or to tone down a comment that could be viewed as controversial) are all essential, if rather mechanical, ingredients of the unique Motty mix.

In 1998, Motty gift-wrapped some further ammunition for his detractors in the press corps when he let slip an injudicious comment during an interview on Radio 5 Live. When asked about the particular difficulties faced by a commentator he conceded that, from a distance, it wasn't easy to tell some black players apart. Motty's career was plunged into a mini crisis when intellectuals from within the game and without formed a disorderly queue to demand that the planet's most inoffensive broadcaster be sacked him from his £140,000-a-year post.

Motty made the mistake of digging his pit yet deeper by attempting to justify his comments (with claims that many black players actually agreed with his sentiments) rather than offering an immediate apology. In the end, rain forests of testimonials from his many friends within the game saved the day, leaving Motty culpable of naivety but thankfully

> Gascoigne takes over. The crowd was pleased about that. It was going nowhere that attack. It is now! Walsh, Gascoigne! It really *is* going somewhere now! It's a brilliant goal! And that's what he can do! And the crowd loved it!

BBC

**Early Starter**
Motty always ensures he is at the ground three hours before kick-off.

not racism. How true was David Coleman's warning of some 25 years earlier - commentating was "all about survival".

But Motty was not off the hook and his rough ride continued during the 2002 World Cup. While England fans were chewing their fingernails to the elbow during the Japan/Korea finals, he sought to find light relief in references to the eight-hour time difference. As the monumental lunchtime grudge match against Argentina loomed, he bemused millions with a series of laboured analogies involving food, plates and cutlery. It was a tournament in which Motty unwisely attempted to embellish his successful formula of infectious exuberance by trying to emulate the slick rent-a-quote style of ITV's Clive Tyldesley and Peter Drury. When England took the lead against Brazil in the quarter-final, he splattered further egg on his face with another culinary parallel: "Michael Owen and England are sizzling in the heat of Shizuoka, and back home the bacon and eggs will be sizzling too!"

By the time Euro 2004 arrived, Motty was in danger of turning into a caricature of himself. His distracting wittering during England's quarter-final about the derivation of an obscure Portuguese midfielder's nickname while men in white shirts were spilling blood and guts in the cause served only to estrange the more partisan elements of his audience, many of whom were becoming convinced that the commentator was a Jonah. By the end of the evening, the most predictable of all Motty lines, the one that starts "And England are out of the World Cup/European Championships", had received its customary biennial airing.

Yet despite the minor frustrations that are part and parcel of listening to a Motty commentary, his status as the voice of football will no doubt guarantee his seat on the gantry for as long as he can sustain his appetite. Writing in *The Times*, Robert Crampton described why Motty's populist style has remained in vogue for over three decades. "…we love him because beneath what even the most fashion-conscious fan wears in these days of intellectual postmodern, post-Cantona football theses, intelligent post-Italy football memoirs, impressive post-Hillsborough football self-criticism and unprecedented post-match football analysis, there still lies, very close to the skin of every fan, a smart, sensible anorak, equipped with lots of useful pockets for pens, notebooks, sandwiches and memories."

John Motson habitually finds the right words, for the right audience, at the right moment. Perhaps his most memorable was his summation of the 1988 FA Cup final victory of the truculent upstarts of Wimbledon over the aristocrats of Liverpool: "And the Crazy Gang have beaten the Culture Club!" A quality line by a quality commentator.

# Michael O'Hehir

Michael O'Hehir, remembered as Ireland's premier commentator, had arguably the most distinctive voice in sport. Suggestive of a helium-infused leprechaun hollering through a long metal pipe, his tones simply reeked of the Emerald Isle and the Gaelic Athletic Association.

In Britain, O'Hehir was known as the voice of the Irish turf, with his commentaries from deep green oases such as Fairyhouse, The Curragh and Punchestown being a regular feature of *World of Sport*'s Saturday afternoon line-up. From 1946 to 1984[1], he was a member of the BBC Radio team covering the Aintree Grand National, taking his station between Becher's Brook and the Canal Turn. In 1967, he won plaudits for his brilliant description of the famous *mêlée* at the twenty-third fence. From his vantage point just 50 yards away, O'Hehir managed to unpick the chaos of unseated jockeys and riderless horses that left 100/1 no-hoper Foinavon with a free canter to the line. O'Hehir was not so lucky two years later, however, when he called Highland Wedding, the eventual winner, as a faller at Becher's Brook. Despite the landing side of the fence being obscured from the commentator's view by the spectators who had been allowed into the inside of the course for the first time that year, Peter Dimmock removed him from the team for the following year.

This was but a relatively minor stumble in a remarkable 47 year career. It began in 1938 when the eighteen-year-old radio ham, still in his school cap and blazer, successfully auditioned as a hurling commentator for Radio Eireann. As the "Voice of Gaeldom", O'Hehir would commentate on 99 All-Ireland football and hurling finals, the most memorable being the 1947 football final which was played at the Polo Grounds in New York. With thousands back home hanging on to his every word, he had to beg on air for the transatlantic line to be kept open past its allotted slot so the end of the match would not be missed. His plea was granted and his commentary won rich praise on both sides of the pond.

[1] But not in 1952. That year there was no BBC radio coverage of the Grand National because Lobby Lotbinière could not agree terms on broadcasting rights. The coverage, which was performed by five amateur commentators appointed by race controllers Topham's, was a classic botch from start to finish. Bemused listeners had to contend with overlapping voices, embarrassing pauses and appalling identification. Teal, the eventual winner, was described as having fallen at fence number three but seconds later was back up leading the race, while Wot No Sun somehow managed to survive a "fall" at the last to finish third. The BBC enjoyed further *Schadenfreude* as Miss Dorothy Paget's horse Legal Joy was referred to variously as "Dorothy's Joy" and "Legal Paget".

## People's Commentator

O'Hehir used to have his name listed in the Dublin telephone directory: "I'm in the communications business after all."

In his first commentary - a Gaelic football semi-final between Galway and Monaghan – O'Hehir quickly learned one of the perils of the profession after he gave the name of a linesman who had only been able to escape from his day-job courtesy of an expired sick-note.

It set something of a precedent as, over the years, the Dubliner would find himself in hot water of varying depths, often being the innocent victim of inflamed tribal passions. There were those who read bias into his every word, deed and even into his choice of car. He was once berated on his doorstep by a Dublin fan complaining that his vehicle sported the same maroon colour as arch rivals Galway, while another supporter pilloried him at a football final for having his car registered in the town of his team's opponents. Sometimes it turned malevolent, such as when a group of Dublin fans vented their frustration at a defeat by Meath by pelting his commentary box with stones and other projectiles.

But at least O'Hehir had the luxury of a dedicated box. At a hurling match at Kilkenny in 1950, his commentary position was a car that had been placed on top of a lorry. A clever piece of improvisation it may have been but, by the time the 37,000 crowd had filed into the ground, O'Hehir found his view had been reduced to just thirty yards. He

# Twenty-Third Fence, 1967 Grand National

"…they're turning now to the fence after Becher's and as they do the leader is Castle Falls with Rutherfords along the inside. And Rutherfords is being hampered and so is Castle Falls. Rondetto has fallen. Princeful has fallen. Norther has fallen. Kirtle Lad has fallen. The Fossa has fallen. It's a right pile-up. Leedsy has climbed over the fence and left his jockey there. And now with all this mayhem, Foinavon has gone off on his own. He's about 50 to 100 yards in front of everything else. They're all pulling up, having a look now to see what's happening at the fence. Auzzie is jumping over it now. Quintin Boy is climbing over it as they go now to the Canal Turn, well the one that went to the Canal Turn happened to be Foinavon. He's 100 yards in front of Kirtle-Lad. Then came Quintin Boy and Auzzie together, Greek Scholar is next. They're coming to Valentine's, at least when I say they're coming it's Foinavon who's coming. He is nearly 200 yards in front. And over to Michael Seth-Smith…"

thought he had solved the problem by climbing onto the car's roof, only for it to start to collapse under his weight once the game was underway.

When it came to commentating on horses on television, O'Hehir went against convention by shunning the assistance of a monitor. He preferred to scour the field using his favoured Zeiss 10x50 binoculars, trusting to fortune that rain, fog and, worst of all, the glare of the sun would not render useless his hours of painstaking preparation. For O'Hehir, everything was secondary to the committal to memory of owners' livery, a task he undertook with the help of a deck of coloured cards and the hours he spent hovering around the paddock.

Problems arose when one owner had two or more horses in a race, with caps sometimes being the only differentiating feature. O'Hehir remembered the day at Longchamp when one owner had four horses running in the same race. The coloured sashes worn by the jockeys were of no assistance and, by the home straight, neither he nor Peter O'Sullevan, who was also commentating on the race, had a clue as to which one of the quartet was battling it out with the leaders. Using their commentator's intuition, they both happily guessed correctly.

During the forties and fifties O'Hehir filled his schedule with journalism – he was the racing correspondent of the *Irish Independent* – and freelance radio work for Radio Eireann. His career advanced a notch in 1960 when he was persuaded by Eamonn Andrews, who was chairing the committee to set up Irish television (RTE), to become the station's head of sport. In his dozen years in the post, he became the voice of Irish sport world-wide, working not only with the BBC but also the American networks NBC, CBS and ABC. One of his greatest professional achievements with RTE was his commentary on the funeral of John F Kennedy in 1963. During the four gruelling hours he was on the air, he worked in isolation, asking for no interruptions from his producer in case it would "disturb the flow and mood of the commentary". O'Hehir left RTE in 1972 to become manager of Leopardstown racecourse, although he resigned shortly after joining due to a dislike of having to deal with non-racing matters.

O'Hehir continued to broadcast as a freelancer until a stroke forced him to retire in 1985. When he died in December 1996, aged 76, the tributes flowed for a man whose intimate, folksy style had, in the words of Ireland's president Mary Robinson, "entered the subconscious of a nation." O'Hehir was uniquely "the people's commentator", a broadcaster who saw himself "as the representative of many thousands of people all over the country, particularly the old and the not so well off, who couldn't get to the big sporting occasions".

# Sir Peter O'Sullevan

For those who have never attempted the narration of a horse race, it is all too easy to underestimate the skill required to interpret the kaleidoscope of colour obscured in that *mêlée* of flying hooves and bobbing sea of flaring nostrils. Yet any *faux* notion of its simplicity relates solely to the expertise and dedication of equine broadcasting's dominant personality over the second half of the twentieth century, Sir Peter O'Sullevan.

Born on 3 March 1918 in County Kerry, O'Sullevan was brought up at the sprawling Surrey seat of his maternal grandparents following the divorce of his mother, a volatile Englishwoman, from his father, a tranquil Irish colonel. A racing stable was attached to the estate and, from the moment the mischievous seven-year-old succeeded in cajoling his grandmother's head groom to let him ride a horse round Epsom's Tattenham Corner, "Master Peter" yearned to become a jockey. He would come within a sheepskin noseband's width away from realising his ambition, but a bout of pneumonia on the eve of his debut ride in a novices' chase at Plumpton meant that his preferred career never came under starter's orders.

A sickly, asthmatic child, O'Sullevan had his formative years disrupted by long periods of hospitalisation. Attempts to ease his condition were many and varied and he was even packed off to Iceland to test the healing powers of the sulphur springs. At sixteen he was taken out of Charterhouse School to complete his education in the sweeter air of Switzerland, an adventure that afforded him a fluency both in French and on skis.

The combined effects of his prolonged confinement to a hospital bed and his affliction by a most virulent form of acne brought about a shyness which accompanied him into adulthood. But while many have grown to regard him as a natural loner who does not cultivate a wide circle of friends, those who have succeeded in breaking down the outer stockade report warmth, charm and a sprightly sense humour.

As the second world war began, O'Sullevan was ineligible for the call-up on medical grounds and instead elected to join the Chelsea Civil Defence Rescue Service where, as an ambulance driver, he sampled at close hand the grisly realities of life and death during the blitz. After a flaring appendix cut short his war-time service in 1944, O'Sullevan took a job with a publishing company to help fund the upkeep of his

## Race Reader

O'Sullevan (*right*) in his initial role as Peter Dimmock's trusted prompter.

various thoroughbreds, both equine and canine, and his enthusiasm for a flutter. As the hankering grew to be involved with horses on a daily basis he was offered a job as an on-course representative with the Press Association. His first involvement with broadcasting came when the BBC Overseas Service invited him to become a "race reader", a keen-eyed racing insider who would interpret the action and prompt the main commentator.

In the early days of commentating, it was the race reader alone who brought any degree of integrity to the proceedings. Many broadcasts were little more than a busk from start to finish. At the off, Peter Dimmock, who by his own admission knew nothing about racing, would assume that the lighter weights had made the cleaner start and arbitrarily reel off the runners from the bottom of the card upwards. O'Sullevan, stationed at a vantage point out on the course, would then try to unravel the mayhem before passing a coherent version of events through to the main stand where the principal commentator, Raymond Glendenning, would garnish the run-in with a characteristically generous slice of ham.

It soon became clear that the race reader had also to be the commentator and, with Dimmock having sought the sanctuary of the producer's chair, O'Sullevan was offered the chance to show his mettle with a trial at Cheltenham. Although nerves lifted his voice several octaves, the young tyro's castrato performance failed to assault his appraisers' ears sufficiently for him to be refused his opportunity. At Kempton Park on 31 January 1948, he made his first television commentary.

The viewing public were not slow out of the stalls in offering criticism. He was accused of speaking too quickly, droning like a sozzled blue-bottle and accelerating into incoherence as the winning post came into view. Yet O'Sullevan was pragmatic enough to realise that he was in a no-win situation with the punting fraternity. "The most a racing commentator can hope for," he sighs in his autobiography, "is to annoy as few people as possible. As an inevitable purveyor of unwelcome tidings, he is not only an intruder upon private grief but is liable to be held partially accountable for it."

As he left behind his precarious vantage points on lofty scaffolds to assume the lead commentary position in the grandstand, O'Sullevan became acutely aware of the pressure that comes with being granted the perfect view and of his responsibilities to the watching audience: "The day you give the wrong result from the number one position is the one commentary you'll be remembered for." It is a testament to him that the day never came. "I've worked with O'Sullevan, man and boy, for

over 25 years," effused his BBC boss Bryan Cowgill, "and I've never known the bugger to be wrong."

As with all master exponents of the commentator's art, the trick was in the groundwork. His paranoia over mis-identifying a horse led him to prepare himself extraordinarily assiduously for each race. He chose the osmosis approach, surrounding himself with race cards and colouring in silks by hand in the hope he could absorb the critical clues in the horse-rider-owner equation.

The scope for error is indeed huge in horse race commentating. While the requirement to be able to distinguish crimson cross-belts from bright pink polka-dots may not appear too daunting, external variables such as rain, mist and fog can queer the pitch at almost a moment's notice. Depending on the prevailing meteorological extremity, his monitor - providing it was functioning - offered him, as he puts it, "white mice in a snowstorm or black mice in a coal mine". Little wonder, then, that nerves routinely afflicted him with bouts of pre-race diarrhoea.

Then there were the horses' names to contend with. O'Sullevan's knowledge of French stood him in good stead for some of the more pretentiously named runners, although not even the tongue of a professor of elocution would have emerged unknotted following a photo-finish involving the American horse Yakahikkamikkadola.

The full use of the maximum permitted allocation of letters - eighteen - was not the only ploy used by frolicsome owners to ambush unwary commentators. Some tried to sneak outrageous schoolboy *double-entendres* past the authorities. One such name submitted for approval by the Irish scrutineers was "Norfolk And Chance" - a phrase potentially lethal in the larynx of a Michael O'Hehir.

The virtues of an immaculate short-term memory and flawless articulation were of little use without the lung capacity of a Domingo and the respiratory talents of a Cousteau. In this regard, O'Sullevan was again a good two lengths clear of his rivals as, year after year, he cruised through fields of sometimes over fifty Grand National runners without even a hint of hesitation, deviation or repetition. As one wag chortled, "He has the apparent ability to breathe only on alternate Tuesdays".

Amongst sports commentators, only rugby union's Bill McLaren rivalled O'Sullevan in terms of vocal allure. Those uniquely velvet tones, lauded variously as "Savile Row" and "honeyed gravel", always built a smoothness of crescendo attributed normally only to Rossini. It was a voice that oozed class and breeding but that crucially retained the common touch.

‘ His voice carried authority, the context was conveyed concisely, and every word was delivered with a fluency and accuracy that were a marvel to witness at close hand. ’

(PETER BROMLEY)

## RED RUM'S THIRD
## GRAND NATIONAL

"And it's Red Rum and Tommy Stack now from Churchtown Boy, The Pilgarlic and Eyecatcher as they come to the last fence in the National. And Red Rum with a tremendous chance of winning his third National! He jumps it clear of Churchtown Boy. He's getting the most tremendous cheer from the crowd. They're willing him home now, the twelve-year-old Red Rum, being preceded only by loose horses, being chased by Churchtown Boy, Eyecatcher has moved third, The Pilgarlic fourth. They're coming to the Elbow. There's a furlong now between Red Rum and his third Grand National triumph. And he's coming up to the line to win it like a fresh horse in great style. It's hats off to a great reception - you've never heard one like it at Liverpool! Red Rum wins the National!"

The commentary style of O'Sullevan was equally inclusive. The race was narrated in linear fashion with pitch and pace adjusted perfectly as the positional jockeying of the opening furlongs merged into the frantic denouement. Yet the excitability was never bogus, with hype being used in measures "not enough to exasperate the aficionado but sufficient to keep the uncommitted awake." The content was always perfectly tailored and never defaulted to the bargain-bucket "identikit" descriptors such as "being ridden on" and "getting reminders" so regularly relied upon by lesser practitioners.

Broadcasting was, and would remain, a relative sideline for O'Sullevan as his main energies were devoted to filling columns of the racing press with news, hard opinion and often sublime tipping. From 1947 he penned regular pieces for *The Racehorse* under the pseudonym Patrick Moore (considering the telescopic power of his huge, tripod-mounted, navy-issue binoculars, this was perhaps appropriate) and in 1950 he joined the racing staff of the *Daily Express*.

Through his regular "Off the Record" column, he became a vociferous crusader on racing matters ranging from the adoption of the photo-finish in National Hunt races to the rights and remuneration of stable lads. He also argued insistently on safety and animal welfare issues and was instrumental in the introduction of the patrol car camera. Somewhat controversially, he lent his voice to the campaign to temper the severity of the fearsome Becher's Brook fence on the Aintree Grand National course.

His relationship with the *Express* was occasionally uneasy as the paper wanted his work to be unfettered by commentating commitments. Peter Dimmock at BBC-TV also petitioned hard for his undivided loyalty, but O'Sullevan would resolutely maintain a foot in both camps, insisting that newspaper reporting gave him greater scope for reflecting the horse racing scene.

In 1954, an invitation to commentate on a trotting race in Milan offered O'Sullevan the opportunity to sample live European sports broadcasting in its full ante-diluvian glory. His Eurovision colleagues were the motliest of crews. One declined to bring binoculars with him because they gave him a headache while another begged assistance due to his total colour-blindness. French television coverage had crawled little farther out of the swamp. While at Longchamp to cover the Prix de l'Arc de Triomphe meeting, O'Sullevan discovered with unease the limitations of the local producer. The indiscriminate sprinkling of cameras across the course had left several blind-spots which he attempted to conceal by filling the screen with a graphic of a mannequin.

During the early 1950s, the BBC may have enjoyed a clear run in its sporting coverage but the tentacles of puritanical Reithian doctrine still held racing in a vice-like grip. Unsurprisingly, the dogma forbade any reference to betting and the O'Sullevan post-bag was invariably replete with complaints from irate viewers that he had forgotten to make his tactical pause while the on-course public address cackled the starting prices. Commentators did manage to find a way of side-stepping the embargo by employing parade-ring chicanery such as "and there's everybody's second favourite", but it wasn't until 1958, when the new ITV network began to announce prices with abandon, that the BBC Board of Governors finally lifted the prohibition.

It still took the BBC a further two years before it could compromise its morals sufficiently to allow mention of pre-race betting and, by that time, ITV had seized the initiative. The network had already begun snapping up long-term broadcasting contracts on several top courses and, as the decade drew to a close, it was clear that BBC-TV's racing coverage options would become increasingly limited. The BBC's creeping ambivalence towards racing became all too obvious to O'Sullevan as the corporation gradually surrendered all five English classics, the majority of Group 1 races and virtually all racing from abroad.

Horse racing is anathema to the large number of armchair sports fans for whom it appears to be scheduled merely for the gratification of the

**Under starter's orders**

Introducing the day's coverage from Kempton Park.

## Byt between his teeth

Commentating on the first computerised horse race during the foot and mouth crisis of 1967. Julian Wilson supplies the data.

chinless elite, bookie-bound desperados and octogenarian telly-addicts. Yet O'Sullevan spent much of his BBC career fighting his employer's perception that racing was unpopular with the viewing public. After BBC cameras absented themselves from the 1975 Derby, the coverage of Europe's premier flat race became something of a *cause célèbre*.

Two years later, while negotiating his new contract, he secured a tacit agreement that coverage would resume that year and, in 1977, he was back at Epsom to call home Lester Piggott on The Minstrel. There was no Derby coverage in 1978 for "financial reasons" and when the 1979 Hennessy Gold Cup was dropped because its delayed start clashed with the preliminaries of a Twickenham rugby international, O'Sullevan finally vented his ire. As *The Sporting Life* blared, "O'Sullevan slams BBC over 'lost' race".

It is an attestation to his sense of loyalty that he never seriously contemplated crossing the Melling Road to ITV. In 1967, Jimmy Hill, then Head of Sport at London Weekend Television, cupped under the BBC thoroughbred's nose a tasty handful of Polo mints in the shape of a trio of English classics, but O'Sullevan refused to nibble. He was not to be prised away from the "old firm".

He also showed laudable fidelity to the *Daily Express*, despite the tetchy disputes that punctuated his 36 year relationship with the newspaper. The closest he came to joining the *Daily Mail*, which had previously courted him in the early fifties, was in 1973, when the *Express*'s abrasive new sports editor downgraded his customary Jaguar to the lowest category of self-drive. This affront to the famed O'Sullevan sense of style compounded the deeper indignity of having to have his articles vetted prior to publication. It was only when the chairman of Beaverbrook Newspapers, Max Aitken, suggested, a touch melodramatically, that his departure to their principal rival could deal the newspaper a crippling, even mortal, blow that his resolve weakened.

Having survived another dozen years of what he described as a "police state", O'Sullevan wrote his last column for the *Express* in January 1985. He signed off on a high note, scooping the biggest story in years - the news that his long-standing friend, Lester Piggott, was about to announce his retirement. In doing so he stole the thunder of the *Daily Star*, who had apparently already secured, on a not insubstantial retainer, the exclusive views of the "housewives' favourite".

Prior to joining the new *Today* newspaper, where he enjoyed a most satisfying swansong to his journalistic career, O'Sullevan continued to offer tips to *Express* readers. On the occasion of the publication of his final selections in January 1986, *The Sporting Life*, as part of a gushing tribute, saluted the bookmakers' nemesis:

> "His naps have shown a profit in 46 out of the last 71 Flat and National Hunt seasons. His best sequence being 22 out of 24 over jumps in 1965-66. We will miss him."

It did not appear that his prowess as a tipster would be matched by his success as an owner. By 1960, 21 horses in 149 races had worn his black and yellow silks, yet he had visited the winner's enclosure on only four occasions, each time in a selling-plate. But his patience was repaid with dividends in 1966 when a colt named Be Friendly blazed a trail across the sprinting scene. At Haydock Park in the November, the two-year-old chestnut, ridden by an apprentice, accelerated clear of the country's top sprinters to become, at 15/2, the middle leg of a succulent 57/1 *Daily Express* treble. Just to round off the triumph, O'Sullevan was in the commentary box exhibiting what John Oaksey called "super-human *sang froid*" as his horse passed the post.

Commentating on his own horses was never less than nerve-wracking but, when fences or hurdles were involved, the potential for tragedy would ratchet up the tension still further. A year earlier, when at the microphone at Cheltenham for his very own Peter O'Sullevan Chase, his horse Friendly Again fell, leaving her jockey, Stan Mellor, crumpled and motionless on the turf. Although both horse and rider would emerge unscathed, it demanded uncommon professionalism for O'Sullevan to maintain his composure to accompany the leaders to the finish while a possible personal disaster lay out of shot. The ability to defy any vested interest and retain those calm, imperturbable tones, come triumph or adversity, was a mark of his unique talent.

Races that held a personal interest naturally stuck in the memory. Yet it was the notorious 1993 Grand National that brought O'Sullevan his most extraordinary and, indeed, surreal commentary experience. The world's greatest steeplechase had been for some years targeted by animal rights activists and on this particular running the antics of a group of demonstrators just in front of the first fence caused the National to be false-started twice. Knowing full well that the race, which had nevertheless got itself underway, would be declared void, O'Sullevan was compelled to go through the motions and then somehow contrive a "finish": "and so Esha Ness wins the Grand National that never was!"

Colleagues regarded his performance as a *tour de force*. Typically the commentator eschewed praise, preferring, characteristically, to focus on professional and humanitarian concerns. "(My) reaction was a blend of frustration and relief," he wrote. "Frustration that such a disaster should have been presented worldwide. Relief that there was not a single casualty among horse or rider."

While he may have been winding down his journalism career in the mid-eighties, O'Sullevan showed no inclination to relinquish the microphone. Yet the introduction of SIS (Satellite Information Services) coverage direct into betting shops in 1986 placed the veteran's commentaries under the remorseless and unforgiving scrutiny of full-time gamblers. High street punters, who did not appreciate that the master never commentated from his monitor under normal conditions, noticed on one occasion that O'Sullevan had missed a horse that had fallen in full view of the cameras. *The Sporting Life*, sensing a story, overplayed the incident and suggestions began to be made that the veteran, in career terms, should be dispatched to the glue factory.

The criticism he received spurred O'Sullevan into even more diligent preparation, but it wasn't until a meeting at The Curragh in 1993 that he discovered that he had been struggling with seriously impaired vision. With 17,000 colours on the Weatherby's register, 20/20 vision was a pre-requisite for swift and accurate identification and the commentator was stunned to learn that his eyes were 40 per cent below par. Immediate (and clandestine) double cataract surgery proved successful and, with the assistance of his new blinkers, he was able to ease through the final furlong of his career with his senses reinvigorated and his reputation intact and unsullied.

At the age of 79, after almost exactly 50 years and an estimated 35,000 races as a television horse-racing commentator, O'Sullevan made his final broadcast in November 1997 when he called home Suny Bay in the Hennessy Cognac Gold Cup at Newbury.

Few television personalities have been so regally celebrated on their retirement. The Queen and the Queen Mother were moved to pay special tribute, as was the President of Ireland, Mary Robinson. Yet the most vivid homage came from the venerable sports journalist Hugh McIlvanney, who wrote:

"Peter O'Sullevan is widely accepted as the best horse racing commentator in the history of broadcasting and possibly the most accomplished reader of action active in any sport in the English-speaking world. His admirers are convinced that if he had been on the rails at Balaclava, he would have kept pace with the Charge of the Light Brigade, listing the fallers in precise order and describing the riders' injuries before they hit the ground."

Peter O'Sullevan was awarded an OBE in 1976 and CBE in 1991. The citation for his knighthood would no doubt have commended a contribution to his sport that no other commentator (with the possible exception of snooker's Ted Lowe) has thus far achieved. He was pivotal in adding to the popularity of it, the prestige of it, the safety of it and the humanity of it. What is more, he helped a few punters make a little profit out of it.

As an admiring colleague of the press corps put it so pertinently, "Precious few commoners have exerted greater influence on the sport of kings."

# Ron Pickering

Ron Pickering wasn't just a popular and knowledgeable television commentator, he was a driving force behind the development of track and field in Britain. Although only a moderate athlete in his own right, the boxer's son from Hackney in London's East End proved to be a talented coach and inspirational motivator. As John Goodbody noted in *The Times*, "You felt you could bunny-hop up Everest if Pickering were alongside you."

In 1960, at the age of 30, he was appointed the national athletics coach of Wales and quickly made his mark. The long jumper, Lynn Davies, recalled the day he saw a tall man with a distinctive black quiff and a Great Britain athletics blazer striding towards him: "I'm Ron Pickering," he said, "and you could be one of this country's great athletes." Pickering's eye for talent was certainly needle-sharp and he went on to transform the raw Welsh triple-jumper into a gold medal winning long-jumper at the 1964 Tokyo Olympics. "I could never have done what I did in athletics without him," confessed Davies. "Ron had the rare ability to communicate with people. It shone through whether he was talking to a group of school children or broadcasting to millions of people."

In his promotion of athletics as a force for good in disadvantaged communities, Pickering was almost evangelistic. He campaigned hard for the facilities that would allow the young and underprivileged to enhance their lives and started up Haringey Athletics Club to help foster race relations. The support and encouragement he gave to black athletes in particular was acknowledged by Linford Christie, who dedicated his gold medal in the Olympic 100 metres at Barcelona to the man whose enthusiasm had infused so many.

Pickering talked so uncompromisingly on ethical issues that he was denounced by some as a pontificating zealot. Yet his arguments on the morality of South African apartheid and politics in sport were as lucid as they were sincere. He reserved his most emotive language, however, to denounce the drug cheats. "This is evil that is being exposed here," he pronounced as Ben Johnson's gently fermenting urine sample sent the Seoul Olympics into a hysteria of doping allegations.

Pickering's broadcasting career began in the mid-sixties, when the BBC enlisted the former decathlete to unpick for the viewers the technical complexities of track and field. He would go on to forge a

> I believe that sport without its ethic of fair play would not have survived 33 weeks let alone 33 centuries.

## BOB BEAMON LEAPS INTO HISTORY, MEXICO CITY, 1968

"On the long jump runway, Bobby Beamon of the United States. The man most feared by every competitor in this competition. Erratic but highly talented. Here he goes for his opening leap. Oooh, it's an enormous one! My goodness me, it's an enormous one! That's surely shattered the Olympic record. This is what everybody is here for. It's been said that if he hits the board right he could go out the end of the pit. And that's an enormous one....it's the greatest leap, by the greatest margin there has ever been."

BBC

fruitful 25 year partnership with David Coleman, whose authoritative style was complemented well by the more sympathetic and supportive register of his new colleague. Together they established a tone and style for athletics commentary that has been clearly carried on by their successors, Stuart Storey and Paul Dickinson.

Untypically for a British commentator, Pickering was unashamed to wear his heart on his sleeve as far as the home competitors were concerned. When Mary Peters was battling through for potentially gold medal winning points in the 200 metres of the 1972 pentathlon, he suspended all impartiality to urge his compatriot on: "Now come on Mary, you need the run of your life...keep going - Rosendahl on the outside - Mary, come on! COME ON! You've got two yards to make!"

His paternalism shone through no brighter than when decathlete Daley Thompson found himself under intense pressure in the discus competition at the Los Angeles Olympics. Hardly able to bear the tension, he gave a commentary that was quirky, undisciplined, cliché-saturated yet gloriously uninhibited and compelling:

> "The world champion gets a tremendous cheer as he goes into the circle. Everyone knows that the chips are down and for the first time in the competition he really needs 45 metres...It's a better one, it's a better one, it's a better one, it's a BETTER one! And the man comes good! And he's dancing in the circle! For those who gave up on me, he said, oh ye of little faith! The iron man comes through. When the going gets tough, the tough get going!"

Translating the thrill and excitement of competition into logical, well-constructed prose was, indeed, never particularly high on his list of priorities and he committed many an entertaining howler:

> "Watch the time – it gives you a good indication of how fast they are running."
> **"And if he goes clear here, he'll really take the competition by the scruff of the throat."**
> "Ernest Vettori: the man of the moment last year."
> **"You were treading where no man fears to go."**
> "And the hush of anticipation is rising to a crescendo."
> **"The French are not normally a Nordic skiing nation."**

As that last observation attests, Pickering's voice could also be heard in competition with the clanging cowbells of Olympic ski-ing. His breathless description of Franz Klammer's storming second run in the downhill at Innsbruck in 1976 drew such an audience reaction that it persuaded the BBC to launch *Ski Sunday* two years later.

Pickering was also partly responsible for one of the most bizarre phenomena of the modern Olympic movement. When an unknown goggle-eyed plasterer from Cheltenham by the name of Eddie Edwards defied the technique manual to achieve a safe landing in the ski-jump, Pickering's ironic comment, "The eagle has landed", caught the moment and triggered the unlikeliest of feeding frenzies across the world's media.

Away from conventional competition, Pickering lent Olympic gravitas to the BBC's *Superstars* programme and unpatronising enthusiasm to the souped-up kiddies' egg-and-spoon racing that was *We Are The Champions*. The closing ritual, which involved him inviting several dozen ten-year-olds to throw themselves into a swimming pool, spawned one of the most fondly remembered catchphrases on seventies children's television: "And *away* you go!"

Pickering inspired great respect and affection among his colleagues. Archie Macpherson admired his "sharp intellect and passion", recalling him as a man's man who "could hold his booze with the best, converse on your terms as well as his and was one of the best dispensers of a risqué joke in the business." When David Coleman stood up at his memorial service, he remembered him more simply as "the brother I never had".

Following the commentator's untimely death after heart bypass surgery in February 1991, his wife Jean set up the Ron Pickering Memorial Fund to give permanent expression to his ideals. "Sport is the most precious commodity we have to pass on to the next generation," he said. The countless young athletes who have since been given the opportunity to express themselves and realise their potential make this one of the most meaningful bequests in British sport.

**In the Arena**
At an indoor meeting, watched by Mitch Fenner.

# Clive Tyldesley

Clive Tyldesley is the BMW of football commentators. Painstakingly engineered, scrupulously reliable, highly polished, yet arguably lacking the frailties of personality that would endear him to the genuine enthusiast. That said, he wafts his fellow travellers through 90 minutes with luxurious smoothness, regularly spicing the ride with some of the cheekiest humour in the business.

Lancashire-born Tyldesley began his commentating career on independent local radio in Nottingham and Liverpool where, it is said, he developed a fondness for Everton. In 1987, he joined Granada Television and commentated on rugby league as well as football before leaving for the BBC in time for the 1994 World Cup. After Euro '96, ITV tempted the slick B-teamer back to the fold on the understanding that he would assume Brian Moore's position as the network's principal commentator once the grand old campaigner retired.

While the lure of regular "live" Champions League football was too succulent a proposition for the ambitious Tyldesley to resist, it has nevertheless probably led to his over-exposure. Good commentators, like the proverbial fine wines, are best sampled in moderation and UEFA's determination to wring every last euro out of the world's premier club competition resulted in a seemingly endless procession of bland round-robin encounters that inevitably left some of his word-plays seeming just a mite corked.

In Tyldesley's defence, an hour and a half of live Manchester United or Arsenal every fortnight would drain dry the creative juices of even the most resourceful wordsmith. Sympathy is required for his constant struggle to generate new metaphors for that Giggs run, Keane tackle or Scholes thunderbolt. Inevitably, a few hackneyed descriptors slip through the net, notably United's desire to "double their money" in search of a second goal, or Thierry Henry's ability to "pick the pocket" of leaden-footed defenders.

Instinctive and articulate, Tyldesley makes a decent stab in convincing the viewer that his elaborately constructed observations are all off the cuff. Freeze-dried the night before or not, many of his lines do impress with their lyricism. When Senegal stunned France in the opening game in Korea in 2002, for instance, he was not to be wrong-footed: "This world cup has started with a bang and it's the bang of an African drum!"

Sometimes events develop in such a way as to allow Tyldesley to assemble one of his trademark proclamations, such as when England capitulated in injury time to France in Euro 2004: "The finest midfielder in the world has equalised, the finest forward player in the world has won a penalty, and just about the finest midfield player in English football this season, Steven Gerrard, has gifted it to Thierry Henry!" You can't complain that our Clive never gives it the big un.

Tyldesley, with his flowery and extravagant caveats, is arguably the commentary box's answer to Laurence Llewellyn Bowen. He is particularly dandy-ish in his fussy pronunciation of foreign players' names. Every syllable of "Zin-e-dine Zi-dane" gets deliberate, meticulous enunciation whenever the Gallic virtuoso takes receipt of

## EXCLUSIVELY CLIVE

the ball. You feel he yearns for Sergio Conceiçao to be brought into the game. He's most enthusiastic, however, when Italian players are strutting their stuff. Di Livio becomes a flourished "deee Leeevyo" and Baggio turns into "Baaajjo'. For a few games di Canio even became "di Caarnyo".

But Tyldesley has his bravura moments, let there be no doubt about that. His finest hour came in the 1999 Champions League final when Manchester United came back from the grave against Bayern Munich. Not since the Kursk salient had a troupe of Germans suffered a more debilitating reverse. One nil down and with no time on the clock, United won a corner and a final chance to equalise. Tyldesley then uttered a line of bewildering prescience: "Can Manchester United score? They *always* score." Fifteen seconds later, the ball was in the back of the net courtesy of Teddy Sheringham. A boyhood United fan, Tyldesley then allowed the excitement of it all get to him. "Oh Teddy, Teddy...,"[1] he crowed, mischievously mocking (but mercifully not completing) the Arsenal fans' infamous taunt that the former Tottenham striker "went to Man United but he won f___ all".

Tyldesley, then, is not averse to taking a figurative leap from the gantry to join the punters in the stands. When the luck of the draw facilitated the Germans' progress to the 2002 World Cup final, he voiced amusingly the frustrations of their by-then eliminated package tour foes: "Look, if Germany win I don't know what I'm gonna do," he huffed at the end of the semi-final, "they've already got their towels down".

Being that Tyldesley is the sort of commentator that prefers to be the star of the show, it is not too surprising that his partnership with the equally extroverted Ron Atkinson, while amiable, never really bloomed. Brian Moore had been happy to let his co-commentator steal the limelight, but his successor, employing the occasional witty put-down, showed himself to be of the breed that prefers not to be upstaged. "What do you say to a team that's 5-0 up at half-time?" Tyldesley asked his side-kick during England's rout of Luxembourg in 1999, "though I don't suppose you know!" As well as taking sideswipes at Atkinson's so-so managerial record, Tyldesley enjoyed making the occasional ironic reference to Ron-Speak. "'Cool panic?' I like that," he chuckled in response to Atkinson's oxymoronic description of a piece of hurried defending, "*Cool* panic or *blind* calm?"

In terms of his delivery, Tyldesley is quite an interesting case. The same propeller-heads who dismantled the vocal styles of John Motson

---

[1] Alan Green, commentating on BBC 5 Live, used the same words at virtually the same moment.

and Alan Green also noted the way their ITV rival constricted his voice when trying to convey excitement. "Constriction," so they say, "(is) the 'squeeze' factor or harshness heard in the voice. It is made by tightening the band of muscle in the larynx and also the soft palate, the opening between the nose and the mouth; the tighter these are, the more constricted the voice will sound. It is also what gives a voice its 'edge' or makes it sound sexy." Whether deliberately or not, Motson seems to have followed Tyldesley's lead by introducing a harsher, almost serrated tone to his commentaries when things heat up in the attacking third of the pitch.

During the 2004 European Championships, Tyldesley stepped out of character by dangling his toe over the vipers' nest of impropriety that had got Atkinson the sack so spectacularly just two months previously. In England's match with France, his jibe that the referee, being a German dentist, was "probably not the sort of character you would want to mess with" raised a few eyebrows in the press, as did the curious "my, what big eyes you have" remark he made in reference to the bulging minces of the French manager Jacques Santini.[2]

It wasn't turning out to be the slickest of nights for ITV's number one, particularly when moves involving Pires, Vieira and Henry prompted him to call France "Arsenal". Worst of all, he committed the schoolboy error of prejudging the result. His rash assumption that Premiership fans would be singing "1-0" at the new Spurs manager (Santini) next season prefaced the gruesome injury time turnaround, leading to suggestions from some in the press that Mr Tyldesley consult the commentating handbook at his earliest convenience.

It cannot be easy being the standard-bearer for ITV's coverage of major tournaments and Tyldesley's poise has occasionally faltered under the constant pressure to deliver the show-stopping, ratings-winning performance. The trophy cabinet doesn't lie, however. He has twice won the highest accolade in his field, the Royal Television Society's sports commentator of the year award.

Clive Tyldesley is the jive-talking, wise-cracking, verse-reciting embodiment of the new "robo-commentator" generation. Arguably a watershed figure in the development of the profession, his rise has signalled the unseating by the "players" of the "gentlemen" from their eyries in the main stand.

---

[2]Other amusing, if unnecessary, remarks made at the expense of managers/officials include Peter Drury's "and the Fat Controller runs from his box" (of Uruguay's rotund coach Victor Pua) and Steve Wilson's "that referee's assistant used to run the Daleks."

# Sid Waddell

Since the late seventies Sid Waddell has striven to kid the English speaking world that darts, the traditional British *modus operandi* for burning off a four pints of lager and a packet of cheese and onion, shares the same sporting integrity as nobler athletic recreations. It is a crusade that has been wholly unconvincing yet, it has to be said, immensely entertaining.

Few commentators make more racket than Waddell. In *The Daily Telegraph*, Giles Smith wrote that his adrenalin-drenched rantings matched "the urgency of a man whose briefcase had just snapped shut on his genitals." His colleague Martin Johnson added appositely, "When Sid Waddell gets behind the microphone, dogs start howling and the cat arches its back behind the sofa."

"Hissing Sid" is relaxed enough to admit his caterwauling is not to every viewer's taste but remains unrepentant: "What did Willy Wordsworth say about emotion recollected in tranquility? Well just you try being tranquil when the fun starts up on the oche!" But it is not only the punters who occasionally take exception to his rocket-motored rhetoric. At a tournament in Rochester, Phil "The Power" Taylor had launched seven consecutive arrows of classic sobriety and was teetering, wrist cocked, on the cusp of the coveted nine-dart finish and a £25,000 booty. Convulsed with anticipation that he may be about to witness only the third ever televised nine-darter, Waddell yelled, "He wants treble 17!" from his vantage point right next to the oche. With his concentration broken at the critical moment, Taylor stepped back to vector a look towards Waddell that would have melted tungsten. Although he regained his composure to hit the treble, the bull proved to be a bed too far and the ransom went begging. Not only was this to be Waddell's most embarrassing moment, but it was also possibly the only occasion that the words of a commentator had a material impact on the action he was describing.

"The Geordie Lip" puts the development of his unique patter down to "the conflicting desires to be the brainbox of the Remove and the king of the local billiard hall". Whether his penchant for extracting bewildering analogies from the cream of English literature and classical antiquity (e.g. "His physiognomy is that of a weeping Madonna") is simply a handy canvas for comic irony or some surly statement of class envy is unclear, but it is obvious that Waddell is keen to stress his

> ' Jocky, on the oche, lookin' cocky! '

Oxbridge credentials (he has a degree in modern history from Cambridge) despite a much-trumpeted working-class background.

The clever thing about Waddell and his pseudo-intellectual gibberish is that he always keeps the darts fan guessing. Does the man actually believe his own propaganda? Could the spangle-shirted likes of Cliff Lazarenko, Eric Bristow or Bobby George justifiably stand belly to shoulder with Ali, Pele or Fangio in the sporting hall of fame? Are they truly "a lot fitter than footballers in overall body strength"? The fact that he sometimes comes close to achieving this outrageous hoodwink underlines his wizardry.

If his mother Martha had had her way, Waddell would have entered the priesthood and the greatest schism to befall Christianity since the day Luther nailed up his theses would undoubtedly have come to pass. Choosing an alternative path to righteousness, he worked as a brewery rep and then as road manager for The Animals before trying his hand as a television producer. Although he created the popular children's football saga *Josse's Giants*, his most influential contribution to seventies TV was the format for *Indoor League,* a "raucous, low-brow, red-neck" homage to pub games.

The BBC was dubious as to whether the thick Geordie twang and bizarre cadences employed by Waddell set the appropriate tone for the inaugural world championships. When Leighton Rees shook Alan Evans' hand and claimed the first title in 1978, Waddell was obligingly reverential, almost in awe that his saloon bar pals were having their skills showcased on network television. But a year later he turned up the volume and courted controversy for the first time when he compared the atmosphere in the crowd to "Ayatollah Khomeini coming to town". His fast-talking, gag-a-minute style helped win plenty of new viewers but left his BBC bosses, who had never seen the like, bewildered. "That's ridiculous!" huffed his exasperated director during an early final. "In two minutes you've flung in the Old Testament, Rod Stewart, the Koran, half of Shakespeare and some of Milton. For God's sake spread it out!"

World darts were at their peak in the eighties and the sport threw up a set of characters so unlikely that they sent Waddell into a state of allegorical nirvana. His feeding frenzy was at its most ferocious when a pale, panda-eyed 100-1 qualifier named Keith Deller made his way to the oche for the 1983 final. Deller, an unemployed 23-year-old from Ipswich, was so pallid of complexion that Waddell was moved to observe that "all he needs is fangs and a Transylvanian passport!" Pitted against the mighty "Praying Mantis" himself, Eric Bristow, the

> I've been accused of trying to start wars, corrupting the English language, screaming like a banshee with piles and even having Tourette's Syndrome.

youngster wasn't given much of a sniff. "Keith Deller's not an underdog," hollered Sid, "he's an underpuppy!" Deller's ultimate victory was one of the highlights of Waddell's commentating career. It had been "a clash between sheer innocence and the psychological tricks of Bristow, who was like a burglar picking pockets."

For Waddell, Bristow (or "Bristoerwah" as he tends to call him) has always held a certain mystique. He had been king of the roost in the world championships' early years and, for many, had the arrogance to match his talent. "When Alexander of Macedonia was 33," eulogised Sid, "he cried salt tears because there were no more worlds left to conquer. Bristow's only 27!" As his powers waned into the nineties Waddell, along with many dart fans, finally warmed to Brissy and his newly acquired vulnerability.

Other gladiators to drive Waddell's decibel threshold to beyond sub-stratospheric levels included Cliff Lazarenko, a dartsman whose aim was allegedly so accurate "he could hit the nucleus of a proton"[1]. But it is twelve-time world champion Phil Taylor for whom the greatest reverence is reserved. "They won't have to play outta their skin to beat Phil Taylor," he once remarked, "they'll have to play outta their essence!" True enough as, for over a decade, Taylor has towered over the sport like a sequin-studded Colossus of Rhodes. He is so lethal in his finishing that he "can pin a fly to tops by its eye". One of the only players to have threatened to keep pace with Taylor's "inter-ballistic" darts has been Dennis "The Menace" Priestley, and even then the strain has left his eyes bulging "like the belly of a hungry chaffinch".

The start of the Taylor era coincided with Waddell's migration from the BBC to Sky TV. In 1993, the top sixteen players led a revolt against the World Darts Organisation (or "blinkered dinosaurs" as he calls them) in a bid to organise their own tournaments. The razzmatazz of the PDC events, whipped up by Sky, made the BBC's Embassy Championships look like Tuesday night whist with Darby and Joan. The Geordie mullah converted to Sky in 1994 and has been calling home the faithful to the alternative championships in Purfleet ever since. "I loved the Beeb", he sighs, "but, apart from the final, it was only ever highlights. So, some of my best lines hit the cutting room floor."

Since being let off the leash a grateful Waddell has sought to reward his satellite paymasters with a tidal wave of ever more outrageous similes and metaphors ("He's like D'Artagnan at the scissor factory" being a notably ridiculous example). He claims, sometimes almost defensively,

---

[1] Which is no mean feat considering a proton doesn't have a nucleus.

# The Bard of Darts

## The atmosphere

"There hasn't been this much excitement since the Romans fed the
Christians to the lions!"
"There's less noise than when Pompeii was swamped with lava!"
"The dart echoes like soil on a coffin!"
"You couldn't get more excitement here if Elvis walked in
eating a chip sandwich!"

## The drama

"He's got one foot in the crematorium, Dennis,
and the other is very near thin ice!"
"It's the nearest thing to a public execution this side of Saudi Arabia."
"He's about as predictable as a wasp on speed!"
"The players are under so much duress, it's like Duressic Park out there!"

## The players

"Bob [Anderson] came up like The Laughing Cavalier, now he looks like
Lee van Cleef on a bad night."
"Big Cliff Lazarenko's idea of exercise is sitting in a room with the windows open,
taking the lid off something cool and fizzy."
"Steve Beaton: he's not Adonis, he's THE donis!"

## The skill

"That was like throwing three pickled onions into a thimble."
"Phil Taylor's got the consistency of a planet…and he's in darts orbit!"
"He's playing like Robin Hood in the Nottingham Super League."
"Eyes like a pterodactyl…with contact lenses."

that all his puns are totally off the cuff. With lines such as "He's as slick as minestrone soup" or "He's as cool as a prize marrow" you can believe it. Yet it's stretching the limits of reason to suggest that "Bristow reasons, Bristow quickens...aaahhh, Bristow" was not the result of some concerted late-night pencil chewing.

When it comes to relating the dramas and palavers of a clash between two darting heavyweights, Waddell leaves his co-commentators dawdling. But while his Sky colleague John Gwynne occasionally tortures the viewer's ear with sub-standard efforts such as "Even Captain Spock can't have seen stars like these in his travels", he does seem to be learning a trick or two from the master. During a match at the Circus Tavern between Dave Askew and Chris Mason, Dave Lanning, the third member of the triumvirate, commented that Acker Bilk was a "considerable dart player". Gwynne's brain then engaged in several seconds of laboured processing before contriving the retort: "Well neither of these two are strangers, for sure."

It is problematic, though, to attribute genius to a commentator in such a one-dimensional sport. Is Waddell merely a rabble-rouser with a poetic licence that should have been endorsed two decades ago? After all, what value can a darts commentator add for the viewer, save to advise on the wisdom of a "cover-shot" or the cleanest way to check out from 142?

His skill lies in the sheer infectiousness of his enthusiasm. He's a salesman extraordinaire who could flog bacon butties in a synagogue or prophylactics in the Vatican. You need look no further than the comparatively funereal atmosphere of the Embassy Championships since his departure to appreciate Waddell's ability to galvanise "two blokes throwing lumps of metal at a mat" into primeval gladiatorial theatre. Love him or loathe him, there can be little argument that when it comes to playing it purely for laughs and turning total inhibition into a virtue, Sid Waddell is tops.

# Teddy Wakelam

When Captain Henry Blythe Thornhill Wakelam slumped back in his Twickenham seat for a half-time breather during the BBC's first ever running sports commentary, he was heard to say on air, "What about a beer?" Having been given barely a week to prepare himself for such a leap into the unknown, he was more than entitled to toast his achievement.

"Teddy" Wakelam's recruitment had been the result of a piece of whirlwind improvisation on the part of pioneering producer Lance Sieveking. In his autobiography, Wakelam recalled a telephone call on a January afternoon in 1927: "An unknown voice at the other end asked me if I was the same Wakelam who had played rugger for the Harlequins, and, upon my saying 'yes', went on to inform me that the owner of it was an official of the BBC, who would much like to see me at once on an urgent matter."

"Urgent" was something of an understatement. The date of the transmission was just a matter of days away and Wakelam was offered nothing more than a hasty audition at a schools match in Richmond Park. Having been selected ahead of his two rivals, he arrived at his "rickety-looking perch mounted on a scaffold platform at the end of the then single-decker West Stand" to find himself the subject of a press corps no doubt eager to assess whether this innovation would render their profession obsolete at a stroke.

The daunting challenge that faced Wakelam was made easier by Sieveking's inspired idea of enlisting a rugby enthusiast from the St Dunstan's hostel for the blind to sit directly in front of the commentary box window. By explaining the game directly to the sightless spectator, Wakelam managed to overcome his stage fright and deliver a commentary that burst with his natural enthusiasm for the game. "I was so wrapped up following the flight and fortunes of the ball, and so desperately keen to keep my man from St Dunstan's fully informed, that I raced away like a maniac," he recorded.

As the first practitioner of the new art, Wakelam felt himself obliged to compile a basic four-point guide - "a general rock-bottom upon which to build any further commentaries should the idea catch on". In fact, Wakelam had stumbled upon the ideal formula for commentating at his very first attempt and his efforts, as well as the concept, received favourable reviews. "That type of broadcasting has come to stay,"

## Teddy's Maxims

**Keep it simple**
Use ordinary everyday sentences and avoid journalese. Don't be too technical. Be natural.

**Maintain Continuity**
Keep going as well as you can, without padding up with too much uninteresting and dry material. Work in sympathy with your number two and thus avoid double-talking. Be clear.

**Be Fair**
Praise but don't criticise.

**Know your men**
Take the time to go and get to know the players. Be friendly.

**Lord's Pilgrimage**
At the home of cricket for
radio in 1935.

concluded *The Spectator*, while *The Times* lauded his description of play as "notably vivid and impressive". The only negative feedback came from the irate wife of a former Welsh international. In a letter she accused Wakelam of being a "plague and a menace" for inciting her excitable husband to smash up most of her living-room furniture.

In terms of technique, Wakelam's early experience of commentating on rugby taught him the importance of staying a fraction of a second ahead of the game. It helped him develop a fluency and composure in his work that drew the admiration of his audience. "How do you keep the enthusiasm within such chaste and dainty bounds?" enquired one of his listeners.

As 1927 progressed, Wakelam was able to cross off most of the major sporting occasions from his checklist of broadcasting firsts. Next in line was Wimbledon. Commentating on tennis came rather naturally to the former All England Club umpire, who revelled in the comparative luxury of being able to describe two easily identifiable players without the interference of the elements. In some other ways, however, it was much more of a challenge than commentating on football or rugby. The requirement for Wakelam and his co-commentator Colonel R H Brand to suffer the heat and oppressive atmosphere of the commentary box for a whole afternoon's play in the knowledge that they would be "going live" probably for only two or three short broadcasts demanded hefty endurance skills. The arbitrary nature of coverage could also be galling. At the climax of one particularly thrilling match, for example, Wakelam was told to halt his commentary for an announcement: "We are leaving here now and going over to the Girls' Friendly Society Concert at the Albert Hall."

Wakelam drew on his practical experience of the high-chair to develop a "glorified umpire-scorer" style. The easy pace of the rallies certainly helped. He and Brand calculated that the average time between one ping of the racket and the next was approximately one and two-fifths seconds, a gap that compared favourably to the half-second artillery shells of the modern era. Much of this valuable slack was taken up, however, if Mademoiselle Jedrzejowska happened to be playing Fräulein Krahwinkel as, in those days, commentators were obliged to use the polite form of players' names as much as possible.

Then came cricket. Though he said he had "worshipped a cricket bat" ever since he could stand, the experience wasn't a happy one. The plan had been to cover the afternoon sessions of the Surrey versus Middlesex match from The Oval and interrupt the regular programming for fifteen-minute periods of "descriptive narrative" once play was reaching a particularly exciting phase. Unfortunately, they had chosen the most insipid encounter in the history of local derbies. Maiden over followed maiden over and Wakelam and his co-commentator Alan Howlland were driven almost to distraction by the monotonous loop of dot balls. That afternoon put paid to live cricket commentary for several years, the format being eventually revived by Howard Marshall, who interspersed short bursts of ball-by-ball commentary among the more traditional eye-witness account approach.

Despite his belief that cricket was unsuitable for live broadcasting, Wakelam was at the microphone at Lord's in 1938 for the first television transmission. The coverage of the Ashes rubber was accorded the type of gushing reviews to which he had become accustomed; the magazine *Sphere* declaring that "watching a test match from the homely comfort of one's own armchair gives the thrill which comes with taking part in a miracle." It was only to be a brief cameo, however, as Tommy Woodroffe took over the following year for the final televised series before the outbreak of war.

Not all his debuts were quite so all-conquering. The first radio coverage of the FA Cup final in 1929 contained most of the elements of a West End farce. The BBC's only solution to the Football Association's ban on broadcasting from inside Wembley Stadium was to buy tickets for eight reporters, who would take it in turns to run back to a makeshift studio in a nearby flat, where they would give a report on a their allotted 15 minute segment of play. The first correspondent

**Making Hay**
On hand as rugby consultant for the Will Hay film "Boys Will Be Boys".

had the advantage of being an accomplished cross-country runner and was therefore unaffected by the sprint. Tommy Usher, who was a little more advanced in years, slightly "over-rated his powers of locomotion", as Wakelam put it, and arrived back at base "blowing badly". Momentary brain-fade was the logical consequence of his exertions and his opening gambit of "Chelsea have scored" caused no little amusement amongst the audience as Chelsea weren't even playing – the team in blue that day was Portsmouth.

Wakelam sympathised with his colleague's misfortune as he knew only too well the pressure of having to get it right. Some listeners would take portable radios into matches to try to catch him out, while those of a more pedantic bent would write him abusive letters on the most trivial points of detail. He received admonishment, for instance, for not realising that the friends of footballer Charles Buchan pronounced his name "Bew-can".

Wakelam may have been a hardened ex-army officer who had seen four years' active service in all the major theatres of the first world war, but he appeared to find commentating as stressful as the front line. In the hour or so after a commentary he reported a "ragged, distraught sense of things." Alcohol served no useful purpose, while an early cup of tea once caused him to "get up from the table and run like a hare".

His psychological discomfort was hardly surprising considering what the BBC expected of him. Just a few weeks into his broadcasting career his superiors invited him to perform a part of the Wales versus France rugby commentary in French. Typically unfazed, Wakelam put in another highly commended performance, raising his stock yet further as vicious words like *insaisissable* received perfect pronunciation as the ball skimmed its way along the three-quarter line.

Wakelam drifted away from commentating at the outbreak of the second world war, having taken up the post of propaganda officer in north Syria. He died on 10 July, 1963, aged 70.

It was a testament to Sieveking's judgement that the Cambridge blue he had plucked from obscurity would be regarded as the founder of the great dynasty of BBC sports commentators. Critics used to mutter that he was "making it up as he went along". A peerless visualiser of sport with perhaps the quickest mind in commentary, Teddy Wakelam could not have been paid a higher compliment.

# Murray Walker

What exactly accounts for Murray Walker's unique rapport with the British public? Why is this motor racing icon so incredibly popular? He brings neither a rapier wit nor a burgeoning expertise to the microphone, yet viewers everywhere adore him.

As a commentator, Walker's trump was an enthusiasm that found expression in those manic, yet wonderfully strident, nasal tones. He offered incessant, supercharged accompaniments that, like a Dalek suffering a panic attack, could cut through a cacophony far harsher than a mere grid of racing engines. Had Joshua and his seven trumpeting priests felt the need to commission a commemorative video of their assault on the walls of Jericho, they would have undoubtedly called for his services. "I have a voice that suits my sport," he says. "I am dealing with a harsh, aggressive, fast-moving sport and I have a harsh, aggressive, fast-moving voice."

Formula 1, the natural habitat for such exuberance, was just one in a series of "fast-moving" products to benefit from the Walker treatment. Realising he hadn't the ability to make a career out of racing motorcycles, he took his oratory talents to India to sell aspirin. As overseas manager for Aspro, he embarked on a six month soap-box tour of the subcontinent promoting the cure-all tablet with the accompaniment of eight bag-pipe playing Indians. Such verve curried favour with the blue-chip advertising agency McCann-Eriksson, which head-hunted him to manage its Esso account. Walker would remain an advertising executive for another 30 years, handling headline accounts such as Mars, Colgate, Vauxhall and Babycham.

Graeme Murray Walker was born in Birmingham on 10 October 1923 and brought up in Enfield, just north of London. The glamorous lifestyle of his father, Graham, who raced motorcycles successfully on the European Grand Prix circuit in the thirties, inspired him to seek out adventure and, as war approached, he yearned to become a fighter pilot. But, with his ambition stymied by short-sightedness, he took what he felt was the next most exciting option and joined the tank corps.

Walker's army career was stalked by controversy. Although he eventually achieved the rank of captain with the Royal Scots Greys, fighting his way across Holland and Germany in the vanguard of the British advance, he twice found himself on the cusp of a court-martial;

## Man and Motors

As well as two- and four-wheeled Formula 1, Walker lent his dulcet tones to powerboats, touring cars, rallycross and scrambling.

once for being drunk in the mess and again for traversing his turret in the direction of one too many overly liberated mademoiselles.

With the war ended, his brigade tried to demote him to corporal following his antics in setting up and running a motor cycle club for the men. He was, according to a report, "unreliable, unsuitable, untrustworthy and a bad example". On his demobilisation in 1947, Walker was relieved to make use of the safety net of his pre-war scholarship with Dunlop and joined its advertising department.

Walker's weekend commentating side-line was kick-started by accident in 1948. When attending a hill-climb event with his father, he was asked to stand in for the public address announcer, who had been summoned to provide commentary for the BBC. Seizing his chance, Walker throttled up over the PA, hoping to catch the ear of the producer. With what he described as a "non-stop barrage of facts, figures, hysteria and opinion" he managed to earn himself a station at Silverstone's Stowe corner as part of the team covering the 1949 British Grand Prix.

Walker specialised in the Isle of Man TT races in the fifties and took over as the BBC's number one motor cycle racing commentator on the death of his father in 1962. For a while, the BBC believed they had unearthed an all-round television presenter and proceeded to shoe-horn his reverberant style into events as motley as a Serpentine regatta, a weightlifting competition and a military tattoo. The reviews were

**Raymond Baxter** was for many years the BBC's voice of motor sport. Having piloted a Spitfire in World War Two, he had a first-hand appreciation of the workings of the high-performance piston engine. The BBC exploited this to the full, dispatching him to anywhere where the purpose of flanges, camshafts and other such widgetry required clarification. Born in 1922, Baxter had come to the BBC via the British Forces Broadcasting studios in Hamburg, where he had been station director. His insouciant fighter-boy attitude may have concerned his colleagues in terms of time-keeping, but it inspired some memorable pieces of commentary. He was, for instance, a serious competitor in the Monte Carlo rally and would manage to commentate while at the wheel. In sharp contrast to that of his successor Walker, Baxter's style was one of genteel sophistication. "I got just as excited," he explained, "but I tried to keep an outward aura of calm without being boring." The long-time host of television's *Tomorrow's World*, he introduced the first satellite pictures from Telstar in 1962 and commentated on Corcorde's maiden flight. He was made an OBE in 2003.

mixed, although he did receive a measure of sympathy from the *Evening Standard*'s Milton Schulman, who wrote, "Anyone who can, as he did, overcome the combined efforts of the United States Army and Air Force bands deserves a Purple Heart."

Walker reverted to the familiar territory of the bike track in the sixties, reporting on motorcycle meetings alternately for the BBC and ITV. ITV's popular weekend coverage of scrambling did much to raise the commentator's profile, but it was rallycross on the BBC's *Grandstand* that turned him into a household name. The hardy individuals who bounced and slid their Minis and Escorts across the lumpy morass that was Lydden Hill provided the mud-splattered canvas that ideally complemented Walker's crash-bang-wallop delivery.

The wanton contrariness of rallycross inspired the first of his legendary gaffes. Walker was, and would remain, the proverbial kiss of death. When fast-starting Piet Dam left his rivals trailing in his spray, Walker explained the advantage of his being in front: "...so with a clean windscreen he can see exactly where he's going." The very next instant Dam lost control and careered his BMW into a bank. *BBC Sports Personality of the Year*'s annual compilation of commentating howlers rapidly became the Murray Walker Foot-in-Mouth Show.

While Walker carried on with his mud pies, Raymond Baxter remained the cultivated voice of Formula 1. His calm and authoritative tones were crucial in disguising the crises of early intercontinental communication that habitually stretched the elasticity of the BBC's technical competence to the last fibre. For the few Grands Prix that the corporation chose to broadcast, Baxter would commentate from a studio in London, while a track-side Walker would relay the ever changing running order down an open line. Exposed to the elements and at the mercy of an unreliable black and white monitor, Walker needed to employ intuition and guesswork in equally generous measures to provide London with a half coherent story. Occasionally the line would go down altogether and the broadcast would dissolve into hapless farce.

Grand Prix racing was dropped by the BBC when the cars started to carry advertising and was resurrected only when James Hunt's victory in the 1976 world drivers' championship compelled the corporation to finally swallow its commercial scruples. The following year the *Grand Prix* programme was launched with Walker as commentator. The replacement of the urbane Baxter by the excitable Walker was not welcomed in the fustier circles of the motor racing establishment but his open, unaffected style quickly won over the critics.

> When you're bursting to tell people all about riveting that are happening, it is very difficult for anyone with a temperament like mine to dry up.

Walker would have accumulated enough air miles for a business-class return to Neptune over the course of a quarter of a century as the BBC's commentator for Formula 1. Yet for the first couple of years he ventured little farther than Shepherd's Bush, dubbing his commentary over 40 minutes of edited highlights. "Live" coverage did not commence until the 1980 season, by which time Walker had been joined in the commentary box by the recently retired Hunt.

Walker, who by his own admission was fixated by career security, regarded Hunt's arrival as a direct threat to his livelihood. The devil-may-care attitude of the former world champion immediately grated against Walker's earnest professionalism and led to a clash of personalities. Hunt exploited every opportunity to live up to his playboy reputation and his unreliability infuriated Walker, especially when he

# WALKER'S SLIPS

## (PART ONE)

"Alain Prost is in a commanding second place."

"We have had drivers going off right, left and centre."

"Well 'if' is a big word in Formula 1 - 'if' is Formula 1 spelt backwards."

"With half the race gone, there is still half the race to go."

"You can't see Alesi in the Ferrari because it isn't there."

"Do my eyes deceive me or is Senna's car sounding a bit rough?"

"He's obviously gone in for a wheel change. I say 'obviously' because I can't see it."

"This is lap 26 which, unless I'm very much mistaken, is halfway through this 58 lap race."

"The young Ralf Schumacher has been upstaged by the teenager, Jenson Button, who is twenty."

"Prost can see Mansell in his earphones."

"I've just stopped my start watch."

would often dawdle his way into his commentary position at the last possible second. While Hunt had been sampling *la dolce vita*, the ever assiduous Walker had not only trawled the pit-lane for useful scraps of technical information, but also walked the circuit in both directions. Once ensconced, Hunt the Shunt's attitude was no less diffident. During one particularly uneventful race, Walker prompted his colleague for a comment, only to find that a couple of bottles of lunchtime hospitality had sent the former McLaren driver to sleep.

Walker's fear that the charismatic Hunt was being groomed as his permanent replacement prompted him to try to side-line his rival by hogging as much air time as his lungs would allow. Hunt's inflated motor-racer's ego would have none of it and they ended up talking across each other so wilfully that the producer, Roger Moody, was forced to spike their one-upmanship by introducing a single, shared microphone.

Despite their contradictions, a chemistry developed that was to earn *Grand Prix* a three-line whip on millions of Sunday evening TV schedules. Walker relayed the drama with the awe-struck wonderment of a fan cast amongst his heroes while Hunt calmly, rationally and sometimes acerbically provided the driver's angle on technical and competitive aspects of the race. The double-act was spiced by Hunt's opinionated and often snootily disdainful manner. As the former champion, he felt he had the moral freedom to criticise drivers and eagerly singled out certain individuals for castigation. There was, for example, the hate-figure, Riccardo Patrese, whom he wrongly blamed for the collision that caused the death of Ronnie Peterson in 1978, and the laughing stock, Andrea de Cesaris, an Italian so slow he was dubbed the "mobile chicane". "The trouble with Jarier is that he's a French wally, always has been, always will be," was the type of comment that made Walker cringe. The viewers, conversely, loved it. When Hunt died suddenly from a heart attack in 1993, however, Walker lost not only a friend but his perfect foil.

As *Grand Prix* moved into the eighties, television viewers were finally able to put a face to the voice as Walker, now in his mid-sixties, offered the first of his wiggly-headed introductory pieces to camera: "and here we are in [insert name of circuit as appropriate] for what promises to be a *fantastic* race". The unfurling of banners at the British Grand Prix featuring the latest catchphrase suggested the cult of Murray Walker was starting to run.

*Grand Prix* fans could set their stopwatch by Walker's formation lap preamble. Without fail he would remind the viewer, for instance, that the cars were weaving to heat up their tyres and that the pole position driver was leading the parade slowly to minimise his time idling on the grid. It was part of the measured, tone-setting crescendo he would employ to tee the viewer up for the explosion of the start: "One light on, two, three, four, five...and it's...GO! GO! GO!"

Unlike virtually all other sports, the highlight of a Formula 1 race is the first few seconds when twenty-plus ego-maniacs attempt to funnel themselves into turn one, before it all tails off anti-climactically into a victory for a red Italian vehicle a couple of hundred miles later. But, having worked himself up to a frenzy for the pandemonium of the first corner, Walker barely let the pace of his cheer-leading drop for the full race distance. His tactics were to make a drama out of anything. Even if the cars were pootling around in splendid isolation, he would get viewers salivating at the news that Nigel Mansell had just sliced four tenths of a second off Keke Rosberg's half minute lead. He would even sensationalise the fact that hardly anybody was left in the race: "And just LOOK at the list of retirements so far - Prost OUT! Piquet OUT! Arnoux OUT! Warwick OUT! Cheever OUT!"

## DAMON HILL BECOMES FORMULA 1 WORLD CHAMPION, SUZUKA, 1996

"This is going to be a mighty emotional occasion for a lot of people, not least of whom is myself. And Damon Hill will be concentrating in the cockpit there, but when he comes out of it his arms will go up, the helmet will come off. That's his wife Georgie. She's seeing her husband become World Champion. Now she's seeing him win the Japanese Grand Prix because he's almost home...Damon Hill exits the chicane and wins the Japanese Grand Prix. I've got to stop....because I've got a lump in my throat."

## WALKER'S SLIPS

### (PART TWO)

"The atmosphere is so tense you could cut it with a cricket stump."

"I imagine the conditions in those cars is unimaginable."

"An Achilles heel for the McLaren team this year, and it literally is the heel because it's the gearbox."

"It's a sad ending albeit a happy one here at Montreal for today's Grand Prix."

"There's nothing wrong with the car, except that it's on fire."

"Now the boot is on the other Schumacher."

"There's only a second between them. One. That's how long a second is."

"Only a few laps to go and then the action will begin, unless this is the action, which it is."

"We're now on the 73rd lap and the next one will be the 74th."

"He [Damon Hill] doesn't know, but if anyone knows, he would."

"The beak of the Ayrton Senna chicken is pushing its way through the shell."

His commentaries gradually became more than complementary to the action, with increasing numbers of viewers tuning in to sample Walker's growing reputation for getting it wrong. Indeed it is this fallibility that is the other principal element of his appeal. The viewer appreciates the unpatronising companionship of a fellow enthusiast and willingly overlooks his foibles. Jonathan Palmer, Walker's first co-commentator after the death of James Hunt, summed up the challenges of processing so much information and relaying it logically and coherently: "To watch something, be thinking about it, analysing it and talking about it is a bit like a translator: you've got to be doing it all at once...there's no going back, there's no changing your words, you can't um and er and it's hard work." As the caller of the tune, Walker never had the luxury of hanging back and picking his moments like his summarisers.

Those who mock Walker fail to appreciate the restricted parameters in which a motorsport commentator is forced to operate. He doesn't have the luxury of a prime seat above the halfway line with the entire field of play set out conveniently in front of him. Instead he is crammed into a noisy shoebox packed with monitors feeding through coverage selected at the often parochial whim of the host broadcaster. To all those armchair critics who assume it's child's play, Walker issues this challenge: "Don't watch a race, but videotape it, replay it silently and do your own commentary, remembering that I have no control over the pictures arriving and departing the screen any more than you have - the local producer in whichever country we happen to be selects them. Then let me know how you get on."

For his producers, trying to staunch Walker in full flow was like calling to heel a Jack Russell with the whiff of bunny in its nostrils. The only way they could get him to shut up and take stock was by hollering questions in his earphones so that he would be forced to pause and listen. It seldom worked for long and he would soon be heedlessly haring blindly back down cul-de-sacs of logic. "Unless I'm very much mistaken, and I AM very much mistaken!" he famously exclaimed as the temptation not to give an incident more than half a second's contemplation became too much to bear.

Walker's jocular appraisal of his own short-comings ("I don't make mistakes, I make prophesies that immediately turn out to be wrong") is only half-right. When a commentator states "and now for some *spectacular* driving, watch THIS!" and the mud-caked Ford Escort in shot immediately engages in an extravagant flick-flack, it is not technically a mistake. However, when the viewer is told that the lump of twisted scarlet machinery in the tyre wall is Schumacher, when it is in fact his team mate Barrichello, it most definitely is.

But Walker was not just bluff and bluster, he was an immensely gifted broadcaster. When Ayrton Senna was killed at Imola in 1994, he switched tone instantly to relate respectfully and poignantly the death of not only possibly the greatest racing driver who ever lived but also a friend. Jonathan Palmer, like many others, believed it to be Walker's finest hour: "Murray was absolutely superb. Through his talents he was and is able to express the jubilation and devastation. The gravitas he puts into his voice is naturally felt but it is overlaid with a knowledge and responsibility to reflect the mood of what's going on". It is in those mercifully rare moments of tragedy, when sport is put into perspective, that truly great commentators are revealed.

At the end of the 1996 season, Walker signed off from the BBC in style, choking back the emotion as compatriot Damon Hill won in Japan to finally clinch the world championship. "I've got to stop now," he stumbled, "I've got a lump in my throat." These words would have made an ideal personal farewell for the 73-year-old commentator but ITV, the new holders of the rights to Formula 1, thought differently. Having paid £60 million to acquire the format that ritually vaporised their Sunday afternoon ratings, ITV desperately needed the voice of motorsport to lead its coverage.

Although the evergreen Walker adapted himself well to the different requirements of commercial television, one or two newspapers used Formula 1's drooping popularity as an opportunity to snipe at its unofficial talisman. In his autobiography, Walker recalled the comments of Mike Davidson of *The Daily Mail*: "Murray has become a trifle flat, a tad more repetitive. His cock-ups have begun to irritate rather than entertain…the unpalatable truth is that he finds himself fronting an inferior product bland enough to suit his fading talents."

The disagreeable odour of those words was engulfed by the tide of fragrant tributes paid to Walker during his farewell season of 2001. While the award of an OBE and a couple of honorary doctorates had already cited his "high intellectual and cultural distinction", he will be remembered more obviously as one of the few genuine personalities in sport – a broadcaster whose manners, modesty, warmth and skill caused him to be held in almost universal affection. Simon Taylor, a colleague on both BBC and ITV, summed up, without exaggeration, the scale of the popularity generated by this cult hero: "There are three great British figures the public have taken to their hearts, the Queen Mother, Elton John – and Murray Walker."

# Kent Walton

Kent Walton was British television's Mr Wrestling. For 33 years, his husky, mid-Atlantic voice presided over the antics of "pot-bellied men in leotards" as they grimaced their way into the hearts of the nation's lady pensioners. But it wasn't just the bingo-hall sisterhood that was whipped into a frenzy by the likes of Johnny Saint, Kid Chocolate and Kendo Nagasaki. The Queen, the Queen Mother and even Margaret Thatcher were also rumoured to be partial to a tea-time grapple.

Although pundits saw it as just a token effort in the network's early skirmishes with the BBC, wrestling rapidly built substantial Wednesday night audiences. After *World of Sport* was launched in autumn 1964, it went on to forge a seemingly unassailable slot in the Saturday afternoon schedule. Sandwiched in-between the tail-end of the ITV Seven and the 4.45 results service, it could trap, in an inescapable head-lock, twelve million viewers at its peak in the early seventies.

Born in Cairo on 22 August 1917, Kent Walton was the son of a finance minister in the British colonial government. He had fostered ambitions to become an actor, opting to try his luck at drama school rather than go to university. Unfortunately, he had only just started in repertory when the Wehrmacht's entrance stage right shunted him into the Royal Air Force, where he would serve as an air gunner and wireless operator in Bomber Command.

Having mixed with many Canadian fliers, Walton found his refined Charterhouse public school tones had deconstructed into a quasi-North-American drawl. The hip, lounge-lizard image he had accidentally cultivated nevertheless proved to be of great assistance in terms of his career development. On his return to the stage after the war, he changed his name (from Kenneth Walton Beckett) and branched out into radio, presenting *Honey Hit Parade* on Radio Luxembourg, and even made the odd appearance in feature films.[1]

When Independent Television started in 1955, the fledgling London broadcaster Associated-Rediffusion was quick to hire Walton, desperate as it was to scoop up anyone who had useful experience in the

[1] In 1953, he took his first leading role, co-starring with Donald Houston and cricketer Denis Compton in the eminently forgettable *Small Town Story*. In the seventies he would go on to associate himself further with the tattier end of the movie business when, together with *Crossroads* writer Hazel Adair, he produced such luminary cinematic works as *Virgin Witch* and the sex farce *Keep it Downstairs*.

entertainment media. He hosted the successful *Cool for Cats* and *Discs A-Go-Go* - shows that established the format for later pop-picking extravaganzas such as *Top of the Pops* - thereby cementing his reputation as the hippest dude on television.

It was as a sportscaster, though, that Walton was to really make his mark. He commentated on football, ice-hockey, skating and Wimbledon tennis (it is not generally appreciated that ITV had the television rights in the mid-fifties) and was a pivotal member of the team that produced the pioneering *Cavalcade of Sport*. One of his proudest moments came in 1964, when he anchored the ITV network's coverage of the Tokyo Olympics.

Wrestling, the sport with which Walton's name will always be synonymous, received its first airing on British television at 9pm on 9 November 1955, from West Ham Baths in East London. Having been given only a week to familiarise himself with a sport about which he knew nothing, Walton speed-read every reference book and manual he could lay his hands on. He even got into the ring with the great Mike Marino to learn the moves at first hand. "I ached for weeks after those sessions with Mike," he recalled. "But I would have never learned just how it felt without going into the ring and experiencing it myself." This enforced cramming shaped an informative commentary style that dutifully catalogued every half-nelson, forearm smash, body-slam or, indeed, nipple-tweak. He spent so much time watching the masters at work in practice bouts that he eventually became confident enough to start making up names for moves himself.

His style did, however, tip its cap to the show-biz element of the sport. Topping and tailing his broadcasts with banter lifted straight from his disc-jockeying phrase-finder - "greetings grapple fans" and "have a good week...till next week" - Walton developed probably the best-known signature routine in commentary.

Walton's traditional grounding led him to favour the "classical style" of wrestling practised by seasoned campaigners such as Jackie Pallo, George Kidd and Al "Rocky" Wall. "Too much of the gimmick stuff would not be beneficial to wrestling in the pure sense of the sport" he commented in the sixties. "Technical wrestling demands real ability, whereas some of the personality, popular stuff does not require much artistry."

At the turn of the seventies, Walton was nevertheless content to set aside his misgivings about the gradual dumbing down of wrestling. It was, after all, successfully shedding its "minority sport" tag and gaining fans from wholly unexpected quarters, and in the process making him

**REMEMBER THE GRAPPLING GREATS?**

The Borg Twins
Gomez Maximilliano
"Judo" Al Hayes
"Crybaby" Jim Breaks
Catweazle
Mal "King Kong" Kirk
Quasimodo
Kung Fu
Masambula
"Ironfist" Clive Myers
Billy Two Rivers
Mark "Rollerball" Rocco

a star. Frank Sinatra, apparently, once told Giant Haystacks that British wrestlers were the "best entertainers in the world", while Prince Philip, according to *The Daily Telegraph,* was "captivated by Johnny Kwango's head-butting technique".

Walton believed that wrestling's popularity was based on the fact it "portrayed men as they wanted to be and showed women the sort of men they wanted to meet." Whether real men truly aspired to the physique and ambiguous persona of Shirley "Big Daddy" Crabtree is questionable, but there's little doubting that female audiences found the thought of all that neat testosterone packed into a pair of skimpy trunks and knee-length boots an altogether more moving experience. "I've seen women having orgasms watching wrestlers," Walton insisted.

Critics dismissed television wrestling as little more than pantomime, sneering that every gibe, threat, not to mention most of the throws, had been choreographed days in advance with a precision worthy of Busby Berkeley. Walton, however, always vehemently championed its integrity, claiming that, while the animosity was mostly invented, the wrestlers fought to win every time. When it came to affiliating to a union to negotiate better fees, though, the wrestlers opted somewhat tellingly for the Variety Artists' Association.

The irony is that, as a ring-side commentator, Walton was in as much danger of injury as the wrestlers themselves. Participants tumbling through the ropes landed on him on at least three occasions; the first resulting in three stitches in a head wound, the second giving him a stiff neck for a week and the third jamming the microphone painfully in his mouth.

In the mid-eighties, the appearance of super-slick American WWF wrestling on Sky Television left its twee British cousin looking painfully dated. In 1988, the then head of ITV Sport, Greg Dyke (the man who gave the world Roland Rat) axed wrestling, bemoaning the image that irate hand-bag wielding grandmothers was sending to viewers and advertisers.

Wrestling's demise saddened Walton but he seemed to concede that, with every conceivable plot and storyline used up, the sport had had its day. "It's not the same. I don't really go now," he sighed in 1996. "It's mostly up North isn't it?"

Kent Walton died on 24 August 2003, aged 86.

# Eddie Waring

Eddie Waring's idiosyncratic Yorkshire warble made a unique and controversial contribution to the popularity of "rroogerby leeeague" and arguably an even greater one to the art of television mimicry. His unashamedly parochial tones were a gift for the top seventies impersonator Mike Yarwood who, wearing an undersized trilby at a jaunty 35 degree angle, turned "up and under" and "early bath" into the first catchphrases of commentary.

A rugby league man through-and-through, Waring spoke with the authority of a successful club manager. He made his name in the early forties when, having cleverly tapped into the pool of locally billeted international players, he transformed his home town team, Dewsbury, from local league whipping boys into the winners of the championship in 1942 and the Challenge Cup in 1943.

As a youngster Waring had shown no little talent as a sportsman. He shone as a sprinter and also as a footballer, being offered trials by Nottingham Forest and Burnley. He played both codes of rugby, but it was the thirteen-a-side version that tempted him to put pen to paper for the school magazine. Following a year in secretarial college, he joined his local newspaper and, in 1946, took a chance on developing his career by funding his own trip to Australia to cover the tour by Great Britain. The gamble paid off and he returned to pen regular columns for the *Sunday Pictorial* and the *Sunday Mirror*.

During a stop-over on the way back from the tour Waring sampled American television's raucous coverage of gridiron football and noted it as a model for its less upholstered British relative. In November 1951, he was given the chance to put his vision into practice when the BBC invited him to cover the first televised rugby league match, the second test between Great Britain and New Zealand from Swinton's now defunct Station Road ground. The home team's last gasp victory by 20 points to 19 was the perfect way for the sport to announce itself and in the following year league matches and the Challenge Cup final were broadcast for the first time.

The relationship between the Rugby Football League and the BBC was, however, far from harmonious. As ever, it was to do with exposure. The administrators' fears that the televising of matches would have dire repercussions at the turnstiles were borne out in November 1953, when the broadcasting of an international between England and France

> I don't know if that's the ball or his head. We'll know if he stands up.

halved attendances across the league. Unable to fill Wembley Stadium for its May show-piece final, the RFL found that the almost nominal rights fee on offer from the BBC was insufficient to cover the shortfall in gate revenue. The antagonism between the clubs and the broadcasters would simmer on for decades, reaching its peak in 1966 when Wigan locked the BBC's cameras out of their ground.

As the corporation's mouthpiece, Waring drew more than his fair share of the flak. Those for whom rugby league was the idealisation of gritty Northern machismo resented the light, knockabout touch of its most high profile ambassador. "While rugby union is treated with the importance of a state occasion," whined the actor, producer and professional Northerner Colin Welland, "Waring reduces it to mud wrestling." In 1976, the strength of feeling reached such a frenzy that the BBC was presented with a petition of a claimed 10,000 signatures demanding that Waring be removed from the gantry.

Had the corporation bowed to the clamour of the die-hards, the art of sports commentary would have been bereft of the first real entertainer. True, his chatterbox style and incessant "oooohs" and

GETTY IMAGES

"11-10 and all on this goal. And Don Fox to take it...Leeds 11, Wakefield Trinity 10. What a dramatic finish! Forty minutes gone and if he kicks to goal...whadda grandstand finish this is! He's missed it, he's missed it! He's on the ground, he's missed it! Well...and there goes the whistle for time. What a dramatic...everybody's got their head in their hands. And he's sure in tears, he's in tears. He's a poor lad."

"ahhhhs" may have grated, but Waring nevertheless proved amply that there was much more to his work than mere oscillation. He was probably the first television commentator, for instance, to employ the deliberately humorous aside. "They've got to keep their hands warm somehow," he would explain as sixteen stone forwards exchanged blows. He was also amusingly cavalier in his diagnosis of injuries. Remarks such as "He'll be alright. I saw his eyelids flutter" began to acquire him a cult following.

This talent for light comedy gave Waring a licence to roam and his enthusiastic custody of the "Fil Rouge" element of the ludicrously popular Friday night jamboree *It's A Knockout* brought him recognition *sans frontières*. To the further undoubted exasperation of his detractors in the rugby league fraternity, he won himself a role in Morecambe & Wise's version of "There's Nothing Like A Dame" and even made a shimmying appearance, clutching a golden egg, in *The Goodies and the Beanstalk*. His knack for self-promotion turned him into one of the most recognisable television personalities of the seventies.

While he may have lapped up the limelight, Waring remained a mystery to most of his colleagues. He kept his personal life so private that the BBC didn't even know where he lived - all correspondence was routed through the Queen's Hotel in Leeds, which he used as his office. Those who did know him well described him as a devout Christian with simple tastes, but with a weakness for luxury cars, expensive hotels and crooning.

By the time he retired from broadcasting in 1981, the world of rugby league finally owned up to Waring's achievement in extending the sport's popularity to a new audience. After the commentator died in October 1986, David Oxley, a former Chief Executive of the RFL, paid warm tribute: "He brought great feeling and a great depth of emotion to the game. He loved the players for their courage, character, humour and athleticism and he never, never held up the game to ridicule."

While arguments as to his value to the cause of rugby league will always simmer – and few could argue that there was ever a broadcaster who cut such a controversial figure within his own sport – Waring made a much more defined contribution to the evolution of commentary itself. He was the first "performer", the first commentator to fuel the popularity of a sport simply by virtue of the strength of his personality. By setting aside the starchy ambassadorial and educational duties that had long been essentials of the job, Eddie Waring gave commentators a licence to be themselves.

# Alan Weeks

Alan Weeks was the commentator with the Midas touch. His ownership of the second-string franchises of skating and swimming meant that, in terms of describing British Olympic gold medal-winning performances, he was a talisman like none other. David Wilkie, John Curry, Robin Cousins, Torvill & Dean, Duncan Goodhew and Adrian Moorehouse all reached their respective sporting zeniths propelled by a shrill Weeks soundtrack.

Water - whether in its liquid or solid state - was very much Weeks' element. It is with the ice-rink, though, that he became most closely associated. With flouncy shirts and bouquets one minute, flying sticks and body checks the next, it was an arena for a skilled commentator to parade his versatility and Weeks rose powerfully to the challenge.

His commentary career began when, after being demobilised from the navy as a lieutenant in 1946, he returned to his home town of Brighton and got a job as the publicity manager at the local sports stadium. At one of the many ice shows Weeks organised, his public address commentary was overheard by Peter Dimmock, who invited him to audition for the BBC. Dimmock had planned for him to commentate over a recording of an ice hockey match but, at the last minute, plans changed and his trial was broadcast live. So pleasingly assured and professional was his performance that, from 1951, the puck was to stop with Weeks for four-and-a-half decades.

In the post-war years, skating was the vogue entertainment: everything, it seemed, was "on ice". Its popularity bloomed to such an extent that Czech television estimated that each transmission of the Prague World Championships was watched by 100 million people. So, in response to Bryan Cowgill's appeal for new programming ideas, Weeks suggested launching a *Grandstand* competition to introduce the sport to the British viewing public. It wasn't long before exotic-sounding manoeuvres such as Lutz, Salchow and Axel (all named after their inventors) gained admittance to the nation's sporting lexicon.

After the thrills and frills of Curry and Cousins, who had toe-looped their way to the top of the Winter Olympic podium in 1976 and 1980 respectively, British skating reached its apogee in Sarajevo in 1984 with ice dancers Jayne Torvill and Christopher Dean's mesmeric interpretation of Ravel's "Balero". It was an emotional commentary for Weeks, who had observed the pair's progress from youngsters. "It's right

‘ Denis Law running beautifully! Denis Law there...and the ball is STILL there! It's free! Denis Law...and he's...scored! Brilliant! Absolutely brilliant! ’

BBC

## Get your skates on!

Weeks interviews Soviet ice dance champions Oleg Protopopov and Lyudmila Belousova. Note Protopopov's sporting of the newly developed low-drag bow tie.

across the board, that's it," he choked as the judges signalled artistic perfection, "what a marvellous, marvellous set of marks, eleven sixes!" A fortnight later he was broadcasting live at four o'clock in the morning when a power cut in Ottawa put back the couple's bid to take the world crown. Their paths crossed for the final time in Lillehammer in 1994, when 23.9 million viewers tuned in to hear him describe their narrow failure to repeat their Olympic triumph.

Over at the pool, Weeks' style was sometimes dismissed as trite and lacking in imagination. Blandishments such as "David Wilkie is absolutely superb!" drew characteristic scorn from *The Observer*'s Clive James, who jibed, "The brute fact so far has been that the swimming commentaries have added nothing to the pictures except file-card titbits about little Lodja Gdnsk of Poland being born Pfft and just missing out on a medal at the pan-European dry pool Games at Flart."

But what James didn't appreciate in Weeks' simplistic terminology was its ability to convey the genuine sense of wonder and amazement that sport can occasionally engender. When the little Soviet gymnast

Olga Korbut bewitched the Munich judges with an iconic floor exercise display, Weeks' rapturous reaction wrapped up the moment perfectly:

> "You really can't blame the audience for going for this girl. Apart from being very clever, she has such tremendous personality! Ha ha ha! That was TERRIFIC! How can you take it away from this girl? Isn't she marvellous? Olga Korbut has caused so many sensations this evening, it just isn't true...And she's done it! She's done it! 9.9! Olga Korbut wins the gold medal in the floor exercises. What a remarkable performance!"

He was also on excellent form when the USA caused the upset of the 1980 Winter Olympics by beating the Soviet Union in the semi-final of the ice hockey tournament:

> "Five seconds...and the United States have beaten the Soviet Union! I have never seen anything like it in my LIFE! An absolute SENSATION! The Americans are throwing their sticks into the air. They have beaten the mighty red machine, which is standing forlorn and dejected. The Russians stuttered against the Finns, they stuttered against the Canadians and now they've gone futt against the Americans!"

Weeks commentated regularly on football at World Cups and for *Match of the Day*, his style being very much of the "what a shot, what a goal" school. In his coverage of speedway he adopted a slightly more adventurous turn of phrase when, at the Internationale event at Wimbledon, he described Ove Fundin coming off the final bend "fighting his bucking machine." When questioned afterwards about his close shave, he replied, "As the words came out of my mouth, a great sweat broke upon my brow."

In 1970, Weeks became the first face of television snooker when he donned a bow tie of vampire moth dimensions to present the BBC2 showcase *Pot Black*. He retired as a commentator after the 1995 world figure skating championships in Canada.

Alan Weeks, who did justice to great Olympic moments with his exuberant and unpretentious style, died on 11 June 1996, aged 72. Arguably just a member of the BBC's commentating chorus line, he could always be relied upon to step forward to deliver a show-stopper. In the words of his *Times* obituary, he "instilled a rare state of pride in a nation of armchair sportsmen."

6 This might well be the night when Rodnina pulls everything out. 9

# Peter West

Peter West proved himself to be one of the most efficient and adaptable broadcasters ever to be employed by the BBC. Best known as a commanding and intrepid presenter of live television, he started out as a commentator on cricket, rugby and tennis. Over the years he lent his crisp and pleasant voice to a total of 33 sports, including diving, shooting, cycling, hockey and lacrosse. He also appeared regularly on BBC light entertainment programmes, hosting fifteen series of *Come Dancing*, six *Miss World*s and innumerable panel shows on both television and radio. In the course of a career that spanned almost fifty years, the broadcaster dubbed "The Great Inescapable" worked for every BBC department except drama.

Born in 1920, West was the son of a successful City trader. He was educated at Cranbrook School in Kent, where he excelled at cricket and rugby. He attended the Royal Military College at Sandhurst, but was invalided out of the army towards the end of the second world war with an arthritic back.

In 1947, with his chosen career in tatters, West was to benefit from a chance meeting with C B Fry at a cricket match at Taunton. So grateful was the venerable radio commentator that the young news agency reporter had volunteered to telephone his report into the *Sunday Graphic* that he recommended him to his producer at the BBC. West took a commentary test and was eventually invited by Rex Alston to cover South Africa's tour match against Warwickshire for television. "We're throwing you to the lions," warned Alston, but West, who had prepared by rehearsing silent commentaries to himself in unpopulated corners of stands, was able to prove he possessed the crucial ad-libber's knack. In 1952, he was promoted to join Brian Johnston and E W Swanton in the television commentary box for test matches. He remained there for another 34 years as commentator and then presenter, ultimately establishing himself as the face, if not the voice, of English cricket.

West started commentating on rugby union for television and radio in 1949 and became Dan Maskell's understudy at Wimbledon in 1956. Gradually West's burgeoning list of commitments prevented him from being able to do the necessary homework for rugby and in 1968, after a series of player mis-identifications, he was dropped in favour of the ever-fastidious Bill McLaren.

BBC

## Man from the Pru

Cricket benefited hugely from West's acumen in setting up sponsorship deals with companies such as The Prudential and Cornhill.

His association with Wimbledon continued until 1983. Having only ever played a little social tennis, this was a challenging new assignment. Covering play on Court One throughout the transmission, West didn't have the benefit of access to action replays and slow motion analysis for most of the early tournaments, and inevitably fatigue often became a factor. Nevertheless, West served up relatively few clangers. A fairly thin portfolio of howlers contained the observations that Betty Stove had "gone off the boil" and that Jan Kodes was "coming up fresh as a pansy" for the final set.

West commentated on five Olympic games, although it seemed the only time he got to describe a British success was when dubbing "live" commentary over recorded footage. Being responsible for many of the minority sports, West was party to much of the subterfuge that the BBC used to kid viewers into believing that commentators were

**Oval Office**

With E W Swanton (left) and Brian Johnston in 1953.

stationed at every vantage point at every event. Not many viewers would have guessed for example that when West followed up his commentary of an India-Pakistan hockey match with the words "and now over to David Coleman in the athletics stadium", they were in fact sitting next to each other.

His ability to produce coherent and believable commentaries at short notice on sports about which he knew nothing guaranteed that West would survive the Paul Fox commentator pogrom of the 1960s. Anthony Craxton, the television cricket producer, rated him as the "best he had", while radio's Peter Baxter was equally effusive: "Peter was a dream commentator, one of that generation who hid his skills behind an apparent amateurism. But those who worked with him knew what a pro he was."

The secret of his broadcasting longevity was his sheet-anchor dependability. His skill in taking a ten-second countdown for a fall of a wicket, whilst simultaneously pretending to look interested in the ramblings of Tom Graveney or Jack Bannister had his producers purring their gratitude, especially when rain stopped play. "We could chuck anything at Peter," said Nick Hunter, "he would be sitting there waiting and you would tee him up and away he would go." West's other attribute was his encyclopaedic knowledge of test cricketers. "He knew something about all of them, right off the top of his head," said Hunter.

Press critics, however, took a keen delight in rubbishing the man with the "patent leather parting and three inch grin". Yet he was far from the archetype of bland cosiness that many pretended. After the famous Headingley test of 1981, for example, West attempted to prize some words out of an England team that was by then at war with the fourth estate. "The media should never have written us off," huffed Ian Botham. "In that case," countered West, "why did the England team check out of their hotel this morning?"

Over the years, West fell out temporarily with sensitive types like Bob Willis and Jimmy Connors and even required personal protection at Harrogate after breaking a news story that led to the sacking of Yorkshireman Brian Close as England captain. The greatest vitriol, however, emanated from the audience of *Come Dancing*. "You conceited, sarcastic, biased English prig," railed one Scottish viewer, convinced of another Sassenach conspiracy. Yet in the very same post bag, a letter from Worcestershire caused the compere to dodge brickbats from the *other* side of Hadrian's Wall: "We are disgusted that a Scottish judge was chosen when a Scottish team was taking part. The whole show was obviously compered by Peter McWest."

It was a characteristic of West that he seemed to be held personally responsible for all manner of things out of his control. "We always know it's raining when we see your ugly mug on the box," wrote one frustrated cricket viewer, while another took him to task over some questionable lens work: "Can you please tell me if the camera crew take special delight in showing bowlers polishing the ball about their privates? We are keen enthusiasts but the female side of the family have to leave the viewing in disgust."

From 1971, West ran a hugely successful sports marketing company that brokered many lucrative sponsorship deals on behalf of both cricket and tennis. Described as the "epitome of the English gentleman", West retired from broadcasting in 1986 and died, aged 83, from cancer on 2 September 2003.

# Julian Wilson

Julian Wilson was a commentating Cinderella for whom the "ball" element of the story unhappily failed to materialise. In the era when television horse racing was at the peak of its popularity, the man with the distinctive radar ears and slick-back hair lay handily placed behind Peter O'Sullevan, waiting for his moment to take up the running. Alas, by the time O'Sullevan eventually cantered into retirement in 1992, the BBC's opinionated racing correspondent, having managed to alienate himself from his employers, was passed over in favour of the Australian Jim McGrath.

When a commentator waits vainly for his opportunity for a quarter of a century, resentment is an understandable emotion. In the early eighties, O'Sullevan had supposedly indicated to his understudy that he would step down from the microphone at the age of 65. In anticipation of the veteran duly calling it a day in 1983, Wilson turned down a tempting offer to become head commentator at ITV. O'Sullevan's subsequent clarification that he would carry on calling the horses until he "dried up" left Wilson hollering betrayal.

Whether the BBC would have been comfortable offering one of its highest profile roles to an individual as controversial as Wilson is questionable. The pixie-featured Old Harrovian had inherited the firebrand tendencies of his father, the respected but outspoken *Daily Mirror* sports scribe Peter Wilson, and was rarely less than robust in offering his side of the argument. He had also acquired himself a reputation as a minor-league hell-raiser. When not playing his fantasy role as the "debs-delight-wannabe", Wilson spent much of the swinging sixties boozing, gambling and canoodling. He even recalls with some pride getting his front teeth knocked out by a bottle-wielding prostitute.

Having joined the BBC in 1966 after answering an advertisement in *The Sporting Life*, Wilson unwisely set himself on a collision course with those BBC luminaries whom he deemed insufficiently qualified to pontificate on his specialist subject. When he sent a memo to the editor of *Sportsnight*, complaining that its presenter David Coleman had incorrectly and unfairly editorialised over Lester Piggott's riding of Nijinsky in the 1970 Prix de l'Arc de Triomphe, his boss Bryan Cowgill carpeted him with words of one syllable. It was only the first of a number of incidents at the BBC that left Wilson spitting bile. In 1982,

> **'** Warrshan, the 3.75 million dollar horse, proved itself to be a million dollars. **'**

he tendered his resignation, only to be persuaded otherwise, following the broadcast of a *Forty Minutes* documentary that he felt scandalously mis-represented racing's treatment of stable lads.

To be fair to Wilson, he was one of the country's leading authorities on horse racing and was therefore well-qualified to gripe. He was a skilled television racing correspondent, possessing the priceless knack of being able to sniff out a story. When it came to selecting a horse to profile prior to the 1973 Grand National, for instance, he had an inkling it had to be Red Rum.

Wilson's feel for the turf stemmed from the daily childhood ritual of picking winners from his grandfather's morning copy of *The Times*. By the eighties, he reckoned he was relieving the bookmakers of up to £30,000 a year. He also operated as a racing consultant, buying and managing thoroughbreds on behalf of enthusiasts such as Clement Freud. He was also a successful owner in his own right, with his horse Tumbledownwind winning the prestigious Gimcrack Stakes in 1977.

With frilly new presenters such as Sue Barker and Clare Balding making ground fast behind him, Wilson decided to retire from broadcasting in December 1996. "I can no longer be emotionally waylaid," he wrote on his departure from the corporation, "by the irritations of political correctness; incompetence in the commercial department; the bad manners and offensiveness of 'alternative' programmes; the lost concept of public service broadcasting; and the continual frustration of financial constraints."

Hell hath no fury like a commentator scorned.

# Kenneth Wolstenholme

To Kenneth Wolstenholme befell the honour of speaking the most celebrated piece of sports commentary in the history of broadcasting. When BBC Radio 4 conducted a survey to find the ultimate spoken-media phrase of the twentieth century, "Some people are on the pitch, they think it's all over - it is now" came fourth. Astoundingly, this inspired yet almost throwaway preamble to the pinnacle moment of English sporting achievement beat Churchill's "we shall fight them on the beaches". If the survey's respondents were to believed, Sir Winston had somewhat overstated his country's "finest hour".

Wolstenholme was born in Worsley, just outside Manchester, on 17 July 1920. At the age of four he was taken by his father to Burnden Park, the then home of Bolton Wanderers, to see his first football match. The experience was to spark a life-long love affair with football and his local team and he resolved to forge a career in sports journalism.

In 1938, Wolstenholme left Farnworth Grammar School (coincidentally the *alma mater* of 1966 World Cup hero Alan Ball) with moderately good qualifications and gained a trainee place on the *Manchester City News*. Before he had time to infiltrate the paper's sports department, however, Hitler's grey hordes had gobbled up Czechoslovakia and Wolstenholme, a member of the RAF Volunteer Reserve, was called up. Serving in the same squadron as cricket legend Denis Compton, Wolstenholme had a distinguished career as an RAF pilot, flying over 100 sorties over occupied Europe. In the early part of the war he defied appalling odds to fly daylight raids in the notoriously obsolete Blenheim light bomber before graduating to Lancasters and then the elite Mosquito Pathfinder force. He finished the war as an active squadron leader in the RAF's public relations department.

The war did nothing to dampen Wolstenholme's determination to make a career as a sports scribe. After being demobbed he managed to negotiate a press ticket for the 1946 FA Cup semi-final between Bolton and Charlton. There he met an acquaintance from his pilot training days who had become sports editor of the *Empire News*. His request for a short piece about league cricket in Lancashire prompted a series of commissions that eventually led to his being dispatched by the BBC in Manchester to cover the Scarborough Cricket Festival.

Wolstenholme made a less than auspicious start to his broadcasting career when, having been asked to fill in for half an hour while the

## Cup of Spoils

Wolstenholme received a fee of £60 for his 1966 World Cup final commentary.

players took lunch, he went into raptures about the colour of the tulips around the ground. His ramblings caught the ear of the gardening correspondent of the *Yorkshire Post*, who promptly wrote in to remind the BBC that tulips did not grow in September and demanded that the debutant be sacked. Despite the gaffe, Wolstenholme played the hardy perennial and soon found himself performing his first radio football commentary, a third division clash between York City and Stockport County.

With sport flickering onto the nation's television screens regularly for the first time, Wolstenholme had picked his moment perfectly. Persistence, timing and good fortune had combined to place him at the dawn of the age of television sport. And fate had offered him the national game.

Within half a dozen years he had followed Bolton to Wembley to commentate on the famous "Matthews" Cup Final. In that 1953 match, which Blackpool won 5-3, he spoke the first of several

## Spiritual Home

Up in the gods at the old Wembley Stadium. Most of the commentators who had the privilege believed it to be the best view in sport.

memorable sound-bites that were, in time, to etch themselves into the consciousness of all English football fans: "Now here's a man who's really fighting for his Cup medal. Can he score the winning goal now?" He had embarked on a BBC-TV commentating career that would take him all over the world, covering in total 23 FA Cup finals, sixteen European Cup finals and five World Cup finals. Not bad for someone who thought privately that television was a novelty and would never really catch on.

As the first regular television football commentator, Wolstenholme had no model to follow. He was the trend-setter. His crisp voice, which *The Daily Telegraph* described as "redolent of the comfortable armchair and a good pipe" made a successful transition to the screen and one of football's unfussiest commentary styles put its signature to the game.

Although he was an accomplished reader of football, Wolstenholme said what he saw and not a great deal else. As befits the minimalist, he undertook scant preparation - equipping himself with little more than the match programme and a pencil before taking up an uncovered vantage point close to the touchline. This early disdain for the stands came not from a desire to commune with his brethren supporters, but from a fear of heights.

A critic used the phrase "blunt instrument" to describe Wolstenholme's microphone manner, but the mechanics of commentating in the fifties made it impossible for sportscasters to indulge themselves stylistically. No co-commentators meant no "free-rides" and the absence of the action replay machine (not available until the 1966 World Cup) required them to memorise large chunks of play for instant recall and analysis in the event of a notable incident like a goal or a penalty. Flights of fancy and excursions into poetry were simply not appropriate to the age. He nevertheless did lack a certain natural subtlety and was often surprisingly candid in his appraisal of some players' abilities. It was a frankness that did not endear him to all.

He was not quite so forthright when obliged to say "post-watershed" surnames, though. Mike Treblicock (spoken as it is written), the unknown Cornishman who scored two goals for Everton in their FA Cup final win over Sheffield Wednesday in 1966, must have been mortified to learn after the match that he had been referred to throughout as "Treblico". *The Sunday Times* believed this to merit position number two in its list of the top ten of sporting "cop-outs".

Wolstenholme's recollections of the technical aspects of the early days of television football presentation are fascinating. The cameras, for one, were large, ungainly and hopelessly temperamental. For highlights games, two worked in tandem, one tracking the action while the other stood by to take over when the film ran out. They constantly jammed just at the wrong moment and Wolstenholme regularly found himself the target of an intensity of flak he had only ever experienced on bad nights over Bremerhaven. A typical example was the Home International between Wales and England at Cardiff when gremlins caused the cameras to miss the home side's comeback for a memorable 2-1 win. Irate Welsh fans bombarded Wolstenholme with spleen-venting 'phone calls and letters, convinced it was all another conspiracy on the part the "English Broadcasting Corporation".

On another occasion, Wolstenholme was on hand when a battle royal broke out at an Old Firm encounter between Rangers and Celtic. In a second half of much Glaswegian wailing and gnashing of teeth, there were multiple sendings-off and a pitch invasion in which fans fought with the players. Great television, had someone not forgotten to remove the camera's lens cap at half-time.

In the days before saturation coverage force-fed the armchair viewer with action from not only every match, but every dive, elbow and spittle ejection, producers had to take pot luck and hope that their chosen weekly match would live up to its billing. On one Saturday, Wolstenholme was lined up to commentate on Charlton against Huddersfield at The Valley. At the last minute the producer of *Sports Special*, Paul Fox, switched him to another "more interesting" fixture. As it turned out, they missed one of the most incredible games in the history of the Football League. With a player in hospital and down to

# 30 July, 1966

ten men, Charlton were 5-1 down with 23 minutes left to play. Johnny Summers then popped up to score five goals, helping Charlton claw their way back to win 7-6.

While the stodge of domestic football was his staple, Wolstenholme was in attendance for most of the major international and European matches of the monochrome era. The "Matthews" final and the visit of the Hungarians in 1953 were naturally highlights, but his favourite encounter was the 1960 European Cup final between Real Madrid and Eintracht Frankfurt: "A summer's evening, 138,000 fans, Puskas, Di Stefano and Gento. I could have watched them forever."

On 22 August 1964, a television institution made its debut when Wolstenholme went to Liverpool to introduce the new football magazine *Match of the Day*. The Football League was somewhat less sycophantic in its embrace of the concept of television coverage in those early black and white days and insisted snootily that matches - of which no prior advertisement was to be made - were only permitted to be broadcast on the new BBC2 channel at half-past six. The first match, a 3-2 victory for the home team over Arsenal, was only transmitted in the south of England and was watched by a far smaller audience than the 48,000 who had squeezed themselves onto the Anfield terraces. The basic format, however, was to remain a pillar of the BBC's Saturday night schedules into the next century.

The legend of "they think it's all over..." wasn't born until two months after the 1966 World Cup Final when BBC2 repeated for the first time the whole of England's 4-2 defeat of West Germany at Wembley. His casual description of Geoff Hurst's run in on the German goal before ramming home the decisive fourth captured the action so exquisitely that there were those who were convinced the commentary had been redubbed afterwards. In his autobiography, Wolstenholme told of a caller to a radio 'phone-in who insisted he had recorded proof of skulduggery. On playing back the tape, the evidence appeared to be damning: "Here's Hurst. Can he make it four? He has! He has!" The conspiracy theorist's intended incendiary turned into a damp squib on the revelation that he had, in fact, recorded the ITV commentary of Hugh Johns.

Wolstenholme caught the moment perfectly for Geoff Hurst's third goal. A modern commentator of loftier linguistic pretensions would never have uttered it, no doubt choosing to smother those few celestial seconds with gratuitous pre-packaged imagery. "He did it with plonking competence," wrote Simon Barnes in *The Times*, "but for five seconds he was a genius. And for that, he may never be forgotten."

The words have indeed been immortalised thanks to television programmes, commercials and even pop records. No doubt their resonance will only amplify with each passing year of English footballing under-achievement.

The World Cup of 1966 was the pinnacle of Wolstenholme's career but, as the decade drew to a close, it began to look as if his days of leading the line at the BBC were numbered. Every time he looked over his shoulder, there was the young pretender, David Coleman, performing ominous stretching exercises on the touchline. In the run-up to the 1970 World Cup Finals, Cowgill, by then the BBC's head of sport, told Wolstenholme that he would be covering West Germany's group in Leon as he had decided that Coleman needed "experience of commentating on England matches". Wolstenholme's contract stated the he was to commentate on all England internationals and he was understandably furious, believing a plot was being hatched to install Coleman in the commentary seat for the World Cup final, which contractually was also his preserve. Anger turned into rage when the next edition of the *Radio Times* invited viewers to "join David Coleman in the great bowl of the Aztec Stadium for football's greatest drama".

England's exit from the competition after a wretched 3-2 quarter-final defeat at the hands of West Germany gave Wolstenholme "a stay of execution". It was he, not heir apparent Coleman, who described the "sheer *delightful* football" with which the sumptuous Brazilians brushed aside Italy 4-1 in the final. The executives obviously felt that it would be easier to demote him after his contract expired the following year.

The plot thickened once more shortly before the end of the 1970/71 season when Cowgill informed Wolstenholme that Coleman would be commentating on the FA Cup final. This was again contrary to the terms of Wolstenholme's contract and the BBC were obliged to back down. Incensed that a new contract offer, although more lucrative, deprived him of all the headline matches, he resolved to leave the BBC rather than suffer the humiliation of being reduced to the ranks. "It wasn't that I wouldn't play second fiddle to Coleman," he wrote, "I wasn't willing to play second fiddle to anyone." Wolstenholme's final Wembley commentary match was the 1971 European Cup final between Ajax and Panathinaikos, which the Dutch side won 2-0. After leaving the BBC, Wolstenholme spent a season writing for *The Sun* (which ran a "Bring Back Wolstenholme" campaign) whilst working as a sales manager for British Caledonian Airways. In 1974, he wound down his commentating career with a cameo for Tyne Tees Television.

It was perhaps inevitable that the pace of football, which had accelerated frighteningly over the course of the 1960s, should leave exposed Wolstenholme's occasionally ponderous commentating style. The highly eventful 1967 Charity Shield between Tottenham and Manchester United brought both his frailties and strengths into sharp relief. When Spurs goalkeeper Pat Jennings punted clear a ball which bounced once over his opposite number, Alex Stepney, and then twice more into the unguarded net, the dumbstruck Wolstenholme could only offer a fragmented accompaniment: "Ooooh," he exclaimed as the ball leapt over the United goalie, "...it's...yes, a fan...tastic effort...eight minutes...gone...and Jennings...has scored...for...Tottenham!"

Yet when his guard was up, he communicated an exquisite United counter-attack, which was crowned by a trademark Bobby Charlton screamer, with gusto, lucidity and no little humour: "Now Law...oh a beautiful body-swerve to Kidd...John Aston in the middle...and here comes Charlton! Oh, a great goal! Oh that was a goal good enough to win the League, the Cup, the Charity Shield, the World Cup and even the Grand National!"

It was a pity that his 23 year relationship with the BBC should have had to disintegrate into acrimony. The arrival of colour coverage in 1969 coincided with the birth of the modern era of the game and Wolstenholme, with his Brylcreem and rather one-dimensional style, belonged to an age when dressing room floors were little more than

> His comments are now enshrined in history and are part of football's folklore. Not every commentator can claim to have such a special place in the affection of a nation, but he can.
>
> (ALAN BALL)

mosaics of discarded Craven "A" cigarette butts. Yet, never one to decry his own abilities, he refused to concede that his approach had become dated. He bemoaned, for one thing, his successors' apparent fixation with statistics and waffle, "They all state the obvious. 'That's gone for a throw-in', they'll say when the viewers can see it for themselves." Motson and co. may point to Wolstenholme's persistent fraternisation with the phrase "it's a goal" before taking too much criticism to heart.

Wolstenholme retired from commentating in the mid-seventies but returned to television in 1992 to provide voice-overs for Channel Four's twice-weekly coverage of the Italian first division. His distinctive tones and unique standing lent credibility to *Gazetta Football Italia* and the instant success of the weekly round-up of news and action from Serie A helped to forge the channel's reputation as an innovator in sports presentation. It also helped to establish an enduring state of robustness to the Wolstenholme current account; the stake he took in Chrysalis, *Gazetta*'s production company, feathered his retirement nest very prettily. He did less well, though, from his re-recording of his famous line for the BBC's "quiz" *They Think it's All Over*. To his annoyance, he received not a penny in royalties.

Among the less well known facts about Wolstenholme is that he was sued successfully for libel by Clement Freud, who was upset by an article alleging that the comfortably-girthed politician had claimed he could emulate the four minute mile recently achieved by his friend Roger Bannister. He was also involved with the Liberal Party, for whom he was almost selected as the parliamentary candidate for Rochdale. When not talking politics he turned a penny as one of the first football agents, representing several players including John Charles. He was also blessed with more than just physical bravery, courageously continuing to present *Sports Special* while only he knew that his teenage daughter was dying of leukaemia. A true professional.

On 25 March 2002, weeks after making his last television appearance on a celebrity edition of the quiz show *The Weakest Link*, Wolstenholme succumbed to the heart condition that 36 years earlier had almost prevented him from taking his seat at Wembley for his defining moment.

His legacy was outstanding. He was one of only twelve recipients of the Baird Medal for Services to Television and he was awarded a silver medal for services to international sport by the Brazilian Sports Confederation. Add to this his wartime decorations of the Distinguished Flying Cross and Bar and it is easy to appreciate the remarkable life of Kenneth Wolstenholme.